LIBRARY ADMINISTRATION AND STAFF TRAINING

LIBRARY ADMINISTRATION AND STAFF TRAINING

By

Deepak Kumar

BLISc, MLISc
Librarian
Sardar Patel Subharti Institute of Law
&
Subharti Institute of
Fine Art & Fashion Design
Subharti University, Meerut (U.P.)
(India)

DPH

DISCOVERY PUBLISHING HOUSE PVT. LTD.
NEW DELHI-110 002

Published by:
Tilak Wasan
DISCOVERY PUBLISHING HOUSE PVT. LTD.
4383/4B, Ansari Road, Darya Ganj
New Delhi-110 002 (India)
Phone : +91-11-23279245, 43596064-65
Fax : +91-11-23253475
E-mail : discoverypublishinghouse@gmail.com
sales@discoverypublishinggroup.com
parul.wasan@gmail.com
web : www.discoverypublishinggroup.com

***First Edition:* 2014**

ISBN: 978-93-5056-424-0

Library Administration and Staff Training

Printed at:
Dynamic Printers
Delhi

Preface

The human resources department is located administratively within library administration. The library human resources department is responsible for recruiting and coordinating academic searches, civil service and student hiring, maintaining personnel records for library employees, coordinating staff training, and administering supervisory training. Library Administration and Staff Training, many books have been written on this topic. This modest effort is another pearl in the sequence. This book has been designed in mind the mentality of the general reader's language which is easy to understand. The aim of this book is to provide students and lecturers with a clear concise and comprehensive introduction to the Library Administration and Staff Training. We hope that the discussion made in this book will help the readers to understand and learnt about the different aspects of "Library Administration and Staff Training" in a most comprehensive way.

—Editor

Contents

1

Introduction

WHAT IS LEARNING AND DEVELOPMENT? WHY IS IT SO IMPORTANT?

UNDERSTANDING LEARNING AND DEVELOPMENT

It's amazing how so many of us go through so many years of schooling, but have such little understanding of learning and development. Before reading about the many aspects of learning and development in this topic in the Library, including learning and development programmes and practitioners, it's best to start with a basic understanding of what learning and development is and how to best benefit from it. Also, it's useful to understand the common terms and the sometimes subtle differences between them.

If you will be doing training and development with yourself (and almost every adult will be at some time in their lives) or with others, you should know the differences between training children and teens versus training adults. Adults have very different nature and needs in training. Also, there are some common beliefs about training that just aren't true. Understand those misconceptions so you don't build your training around those illusions.

BENEFITS OF LEARNING AND DEVELOPMENT

We often think that the biggest benefit of learning is that we get a diploma or credential. As we get wiser, we realize there are so many more benefits than that. Knowing the benefits will help motivate you to design your own training plans and programmes, and to motivate others to participate as well. Perhaps one of the biggest benefits is the appreciation that you can be learning all the time, even if you are not in a formal training programme.

RELATIONSHIP OF LEARNING AND DEVELOPMENT TO PERFORMANCE

We tend to assume that training leads to learning, which leads to doing better in our lives and work — it leads to increased performance. However, you will very likely get more out of your trainings and be more successful in promoting trainings to others if you understand more about the relationship between training and performance. That understanding is especially useful when designing training to increase performance or to redesign training programmes that don't seem to be as successful as you wish.

DIFFERENT TYPES OF TRAINING AND ACTIVITIES

INFORMAL VERSUS FORMAL TRAINING, SELF-DIRECTED VERSUS OTHER-DIRECTED TRAINING

There are different major forms of learning and development. We're most familiar with formal and other-directed forms of learning and development, that include the strong attention to the systematic structure and evaluation of the learning and development, especially as used in schooling. That is somewhat ironic, because the most common forms of learning and development are informal and self-directed — they occur without strong attention to a systematic design and evaluation and without many experts guiding us through those experiences.

TYPES OF ACTIVITIES FOR LEARNING AND EVELOPMENT

There are many approaches to learning and development and many types of activities that can be undertaken to learn. We're most used to thinking of the formal, other-directed activities, such as attending courses or lectures. However, most of the types of learning are informal and unstructured. An awareness of these other types will broaden your possibilities for intentional learning and for designing training for yourself and others.

MOVEMENTS IN ORGANIZATIONAL TRAINING AND DEVELOPMENT

The field (or many would argue, the profession) of training and development has undergone dramatic improvements, especially with the inclusion of computer- and Web-based technologies. We're also expanding the concept of learning beyond the learning of individuals — we're thinking that groups and organizations can learn, too. (Although the topics of the learning organization and knowledge management are fairly recent and still popular, many people would disagree that they're actually learning and development programmes — those people might assert that they're actually forms of organizational performance management. However, the two topics still seem to be so broad and changing, that they're referred to here as movements.)

PREPARATION FOR DEVELOPING TRAINING AND DEVELOPMENT PROGRAMMES

EXAMPLES OF PROGRAMMES IN THE WORKPLACE

Before this Library topic goes on to explaining how to design and develop training programmes, it's useful to get a quick impression of various types of training programmes. A training programme is an intentionally designed, (hopefully) highly integrated set of activities that are aligned to accomplish a certain set of results among learners. Many of us might not be used to thinking of the following as programmes in the workplace.

HOW TO ENSURE TRANSFER OF TRAINING — TRAINING THAT STICKS

One of the biggest concerns of trainers — and those paying for training — is whether the learners will indeed understand and apply the new information and materials from the learning and development activities, that is, whether the new information and materials will transfer to the learners.

DEVELOPING SYSTEMATIC TRAINING AND DEVELOPMENT PROGRAMMES

INSTRUCTIONAL SYSTEM DESIGN (ISD) AND THE ADDIE MODEL

Formal approaches to learning and development often have the highest likelihood of transfer of training. A formal approach to learning and development usually follows a systematic and consistent framework. Systematic means that the framework is designed to guide learners to achieve an overall set of goals — goals to address a need or situation, then associates objectives and activities to achieve those overall goals, and evaluates the activities and results to be sure the goals were achieved. Instructional system design (ISD) is the activities to ensure that the design of training is very successful in achieving the goals of the training. One of the most common ISD models is ADDIE, which is an acronym for assessment, design, development, implementation and evaluation — you can discern from the acronym that ADDIES is a systematic design of training.

- **ADDIE Phase 1 — Assessing Your Training Needs:** Needs Assessment to Training Goals: What overall results or outcomes should be accomplished by learners? Those outcomes usually are identified from the results of assessments, or measurements, of what a person or workplace needs to accomplish in order to achieve some desired level of performance. An outcome might be the ability to perform a complex job.
- **ADDIE Phase 2 — Designing Training Plans and Learning Objectives:** What learning objectives must be accomplished by learners in order to achieve the overall outcomes, and what activities must be undertaken by trainers and learners to accomplish those objectives? The integration of the overall

outcomes, objectives and activities and also how they will be evaluated comprise the design of the learning and development programme. Learning objectives often are described in terms of new learning — new knowledge, skills and competencies.

- **ADDIE Phase 3 — Developing Training Activities and Materials:** Now it's important to get even more clear on what resources must be obtained and developed in order to undertake the activities to achieve the objectives. Resource might include certain expertise, facilities and technologies. Development might include several trainers and learners reviewing the design of the training to ensure it meets their nature and needs.
- **ADDIE Phase 4 — Implementing Your Training Programme:** Now you're ready to have trainers and learners participate in the programme, to undertake the activities and evaluations of learning. Implementation often results in refining the original design of the training programme.
- **ADDIE Phase 5 — Evaluating Your Training Programme:** As trainers and learners participate in the programme, evaluation should occur of the quality of the activities and the extent of achievement of the objectives. After the programme, evaluation should occur to assess the extent of achievement of the overall goals of the programme. Evaluation might focus on short-term, intermediate and long-term outcomes.

HOW DO MANAGERS MANAGE?

The studies by researchers showed that from street gang leaders to the President of the United States, managers do not spend their time planning, organizing, coordinating, and controlling as the French industrialist, Henri Fayol said they did in 1916 and as most writers on management have continued to repeat ever since. They are not like the orchestra leader who directs the component parts of his organization with ease and precision. Instead, they spend their time reacting to crises, seizing special opportunities, attending meetings, negotiating, talking on the telephone, cultivating interpersonal and political relationships, gathering and disseminating information, and fulfilling a variety of ceremonial functions. Researcher says:

- I was struck during my study by the fact that the executives I was observing—all very competent by any standard—are fundamentally indistinguishable from their counterparts of a hundred years ago (or a thousand years ago. for that matter). The information they need differs, but they seek it in the same way—by word of mouth. Their decisions concern modem technology, but the procedures they use to make them are the same as the procedures of the 19th Century manager. Even the computer, so important for the specialized work of the organization, has apparently had no influence on the work procedures of general managers. In fact, the manager is in a kind of loop, with increasingly heavy work pressures but no aid forthcoming from management science.

The Mintzberg view is by no means unique. There is a growing number of management scholars who are questioning the conventional view of management and what managers do. In a critical review of *On Management*, a book of articles selected from 25 years of the *Harvard Business Review*, Albert Shapero, a management professor at the University of Texas, strikes a similar note:

- The term "management" conjures up images of control, rationality, systematics; but studies of what managers actually do depict behaviours and situations that are chaotic, unplanned, and charged with improvisation. The Managerial life at every level is reflexive—responding to calls, memos, personnel problems, fire drills, budget meetings, and personnel reviews. Occasionally, however, we find at managerial levels individuals who go 24 hours without being interrupted by meetings or phone calls. They are the longrange planners, the people in O.R., E.D.P., financial or market planning, or market research. Management is really for them. The bulk of the articles in *On Management* are concerned with ideas from the world of the staff functionary.

ARE MANAGEMENT SYSTEMS REALLY USED?

What about the claims of widespread use of new scientific management systems and techniques? Is it really true that managers in business, government, and other institutions are using them extensively while we library administrators are lagging far behind? Let's first look at what a few of the management experts say about the use of these systems in general, and then we will look at their use in libraries. William R, Dill, dean of the Graduate School of Business Administration at New York University, makes this sober assessment:

- For all the progress we have made in developing good approaches to planning, forecasting, budgeting, and control, and for all the enthusiasm we in schools of management have helped to build for these approaches, their use has been fitful and sporadic, even in the most analytically sophisticated and goal-oriented institutions. In corporations that are pointed out as models for what can be accomplished. the outputs of planning, budgeting, and modeling staffs are often quietly ignored by operating people when times are good: these outputs often seem irrelevant in times of sudden challenge or change. Analysis and planning are still far from foolproof ways to anticipate change and potential crises.

Aaron Wildavsky, dean of the Graduate School of Public Policy at the University of California, Berkeley, has written a number of articles in which he argues convincingly, citing evidence and authorities, that the major modern information systems like PERT, MBO, PPBS, Social Indicators, and Zero Based Budgeting have not worked and cannot work. About PERT (Programme Evaluation Review Technique), he says that: "the few studies that exist suggest that outside of construction, where one activity tends to follow another, PERT is rarely successful."

On MBO (Management by Objectives), he says: "The trouble with MBO is that the attempt to formalize procedures for choosing objectives without considering organizational dynamics leads to the opposite of what was intended—had management, irrational choice, and ineffective decision-making." "The main product of MBO, as experience in the United States federal government suggests, is, literally, a series of objectives. Aside from the unnecessary paper work, such exercises are self defeating because they become mechanisms for avoiding rather than making choices. Long lists of objectives are useless because rarely do resources remain beyond the first few."

On PPBS, Wildavsky is equally harsh. He says that "Programme budgeting does not work anywhere in the world it has been tried," and that "no one knows how to do programme budgeting." His assessments of Social Indicators and Zero Based Budgeting are in a similar vein.

These realistic assessments that we are getting from authorities like Mintzberg, Shapero, Dill. Wildavsky, and others should serve to remind us to maintain a healthy skepticism whenever we read about the effectiveness and widespread use of new management systems and techniques. We librarians should guard against the tendency we have to look for panaceas and to accept uncritically the claims and promises made on behalf of each new management theory or system that appears.

Consider the minimal impact on libraries as compared with the initial promise, for example, of PPBS, Operations Research, MBO, and even Participative Management. To the best of my knowledge, PPBS has not been successfully implemented in a single library and I doubt that it ever will be. Interest in it is rapidly waning.

The practical application of Operations Research in libraries has been extremely limited to date. One of the earliest and best known economic analyses of library decision making was done in the MIT Libraries in 1969. The report of that study came to this sobering conclusion: "Although helpful, an economic analysis of a university (or public) library is insufficient because libraries operate as political systems and thus improving libraries requires political analysis." In an excellent article on library decision making, Jeffrey Raffel, an economist and co-author of the MIT study begins by saying that "in general, the more important the decision, the less beneficial a cost-benefit analysis is to library decision makers," and concludes by saying that "it is time that we all recognized the politics of libraries and acted accordingly."

In a classic paper on Management by Objectives in academic libraries, James Michalko, after a thorough, critical review of the literature, recommends against the use of MBO in libraries on the grounds that it is a limited approach which is costly and difficult to implement and which yields uncertain results.

Participative management is another "new" management technique that has been particularly oversold in the last decade. In fact, it is considered by many librarians to be the perfect management system. Good management has always included consultation and participation, it is just the name, the faddishness, and some of the formal structures that are new. When used properly and honestly, participative management is a useful process at all levels, and not just by top managers on major decisions as is sometimes assumed. It is essential that there be appropriate consultation and participation of interested and competent staff members on important decisions affecting them. But participative management will not bring on the management millennium in libraries.

Participative management is not decision making by committee or by staff plebiscite. Good management requires that when all the facts have been gathered and analyzed and all the advice is in, the appropriate administrator has to make the decision and take responsibility for it. Knowing when and how to seek and take advantage of consultative advice and prior approval of decisions where appropriate is one of the most important managerial skills. Decisions should be made at the lowest competent level. The library's critical strategy decisions involve a world outside the library and must usually be made by the director and his chief associates. Staff committees can give good advice on such matters, but they simply do not have the information, the knowledge, or the perspective required to make those decisions—and they cannot take responsibility for the results.

One extreme form of participative management, the collegial or faculty system of governance, was developed for academic departments: it works badly there and worse or not at all in libraries. Where it appears to work, it is because those involved have tacitly made concessions to traditional hierarchical systems and the demands of the environment while preserving the collegial form. A library is not an academic department, it is a service organization and should be so administered. A librarian by any other name is still a librarian and it is time for mature acceptance of that fact.

Perhaps the reason that participative management has been embraced so enthusiastically and uncritically by librarians in recent years is not because of its management benefits, but because it appears to be the model that best justifies faculty status.

It is assumed that because faculty members participate in a collegial academic decision-making process, that model is the appropriate one to use in libraries—if librarians are to achieve faculty status. Much of the library-based management literature since 1970 is self-serving and reflects a direct or indirect preoccupation with matters of staff status and benefits frequently hidden behind arguments for participative management. It is time that we recognized this natural bias and took steps to overcome it by giving more attention and weight to the more objective management literature from outside the library field.

Two recent articles on participative management in libraries, one by James Govan and the other by Dennis Dickenson, give encouraging evidence that the library profession is beginning to take a more realistic and balanced view of the advantages and limitations of participative management and collegial governance. Govan reminds us that:

> Librarians cannot afford to degrade services nor alienate their users in an effort, however enlightened or well-in-mentioned to make their jobs more challenging and satisfying. Participation and consultation cost time and money and often, like faculty deliberations, produce rather conservative results. In this connection, it is useful to remember Maslow's belief that Theory Y is possible only in periods of affluence. It is also healthy to recall Drucker's statement that service institutions do not operate for the people who work in them.

In his perceptive article, Dickenson tries to provide "an antidote for some of the more extreme and sometimes naive interpretations of participative management that appear from time to time in library literature."

Peter Drucker summed up an important truth about management when he said in response to an interviewer's question about the efficacy of new management techniques: "The young people today expect to see business run by theory, knowledge, concepts, and planning. But then they find it is run like the rest of the world—by experience and expediency, by who you know, and by the hydrostatic pressure in your bladder."

This is not just the way business is run, it is the way libraries are run as well. And it is the way they will continue to be run despite the current rhetoric about the managerial revolution that is being ushered in by the use of new quantitative and psychological management systems and theories. Why? Because a library operates in a political environment and nearly all the really important decisions that are made at the highest levels have an overriding political component. They are rarely the product of cost benefit analysis or Operations Research where the various factors are weighed and compared and the "best" or most cost-effective course is chosen. These management techniques can be useful sometimes to implement a programme or a project in the most effective manner after the political decision to proceed has been made. They can also be useful in providing a rationale to support some essentially political decision that is being proposed or advocated, or to impress higher authorities or constituents with the competence of the managers and the rationality of their decision making process. Management systems, particularly PPBS, ZBB, and PERT are used in government and military bureaucracies largely because they are mandated by law or regulation.

In the library world, as in education, business, and government, few major programme decisions are made solely or even largely on the basis of careful studies of needs and costs. Consider, for example, decisions to build a new library building, to open a new departmental or branch library, to achieve excellence in some special subject discipline, or to embark on a major automation programme. These programme decisions are usually the result of an initiative or vision by an imaginative and powerful person, perhaps a library director a dean, a president, a mayor, or other official. They are political, emotional, or even personal decisions—justified, rationalized, and perhaps implemented with the assistance of various kinds of analyses and studies, but seldom derived from them.

It is important that librarians understand how and why these really critical decisions are made so that they will not be disillusioned or discouraged when they discover that the "best." the most efficient, or the least expensive solution frequently loses out to the one that is the most politically expedient or attractive.

THE QUANTITATIVE APPROACH

Scholars think it is important to make a distinction between the claims made on behalf of complex quantitative management systems such as Operations Research and Cost-Benefit Analysis, and the collection and analysis of quantitative data in libraries to assist in rational decision making. Scholar is questioning the validity and usefulness of these complex systems, but scholar is not questioning the need for and use of quantitative studies for measuring and evaluating library services. Quite the contrary, we need to know more about libraries, their resources, and how they are actually used. We have relied historically upon input data, e.g., the number of books acquired, the number of serials subscribed to, the number of books circulated, the dollars spent, etc. The qualitative characteristics of these data are dubious; we desperately need reliable measures of library effectiveness.

Following the pioneering work by Fremont Rider in 1940 on the growth of research libraries, there has been an increasing number of extremely valuable quantitative studies such as those by Fussier, Lancaster, Buckland. and other works of solid quality. The findings of such studies provide the theoretical foundations and practical knowledge that working library managers need to draw on to help them think clearly and creatively about library management and to make sound decisions based on valid data. This is especially true in this time of transition when the conventional wisdom of our profession will not suffice to see us through.

As one of the library managers for whose benefit and use such studies are presumably made, researcher thanks the authors and urge them on to greater productivity and precision. Researcher also urge them to try to keep their studies as simple as possible and to summarize their findings in readable English.

Unfortunately, a good deal of the quantitative research that is done in the library field is unintelligible, irrelevant, or too complicated and theoretical for any practical use in libraries. Much of it is written in the language of higher mathematics which is incomprehensible to most managers. This is particularly true of studies that are made by academics outside the library field such as statisticians, economists, psychologists. Operations Research people, etc. Their goal is not necessarily to do studies that are useful, but to demonstrate their mathematical prowess, to test theories and methodologies, to get published, and to award doctoral degrees to deserving graduate students. They select the library as their laboratory because it is convenient and because they think it is virgin territory ready for easy exploitation. They are more interested in the process than in the results.

The most useful library research is done by librarians or others with a serious long-term interest and involvement in libraries who work with librarians in a spirit of genuine collaboration. They are trying to make an impact. It is the difference between a class assignment and the real thing, between war games and war.

A notable exception to this criticism of academics is the landmark work by William J. Baumol and Matityahu Marcus, Economics of Academic Libraries. These two economists went to unusual lengths to explain their statistical methods and to summarize their conclusions with refreshing brevity and clarity.

As a consequence, their work is widely read and frequently cited.

Management scientists and other quantitatively oriented researchers frequently wonder why the results of quantitative research studies are not used more by practicing library managers in the decision making process. One reason is that the mathematics and the methodologies required are far too complex and difficult for operating managers to learn and apply in their busy work environments. Few senior library administrators have the kind of staff support needed to successfully carry out complex analyses. Another and equally important reason is that the quantitative approach does not and cannot take into sufficient account the complex of political, organizational, and psychological factors that characterize the real work where people are more potent than numbers or logic.

The quality of many decisions could be significantly improved if we had more and better data, but many of the more important decisions have a relatively small quantitative component. As a library director, I seldom have a critical need for more quantitative data than are available from regularly kept statistics or by having someone make a special and usually simple survey and analysis of the problem. When the data are simply not available or too difficult to assemble, researcher can usually find a satisfactory way to manage without them. My real problem has nearly always been to correctly assess the political rather than the economic or quantitative factors. It is fairly easy to determine the most cost-effective course of action with or without detailed data. It is much harder to map out and implement a successful strategy for achieving it, to assess how the various persons and groups affected will perceive the manager's intentions, and how they will react to the decision. Someone said that quantification is not synonymous with management. Finding the best or most cost-effective course of action is not the same as getting it accepted. Sometimes the quality of a decision is critical, other times, it is acceptance.

Effective decision-making processes in large academic and public libraries involve complex sets of policies, procedures, and problems which require a variety of different kinds of information and approaches. Some decisions will be authoritarian, some will be collegial, some will be made by committees, and some will be made by combinations of the above. Library directors are not all-knowing, nor are the collective judgments of library faculties and committees infallible. Different situations call for different approaches. There are no simple formulas and no easy answers.

The new management systems that we have been discussing in this article divide into two general categories. There are quantitative systems such as Operations Research, PPBS, and ZBB, and psychological or behavioral systems such as Theory Y (and its variants) and MBO. In each system, there are a number of concepts, ideas, tools, and techniques that have validity and can be used to advantage by library managers, but as comprehensive systems they are all far too theoretical, complex, and simplistic to be applied successfully by ordinary managers in the day-to-day work environment. Few managers have the time or the specialized knowledge and skills required to make these systems work, and those that do are probably astute enough to manage as well or better without them. In the hands of amateurs—and this is most of us— the quantitative systems frequently produce misleading and wrong solutions, while the psychological or behavioural systems can lead to the manipulation and misuse of people. The real danger with both kinds of management systems is that they offer mechanistic formulas for dealing with complex realities and keep us from thinking about and solving our management problems in practical, realistic, and common sense ways.

Despite the many claims to the contrary, management is not yet a science. It is still an art, but is very much an art that can and should be mastered and practiced by librarians.

TRAINING AND SUPPORT TO USERS

The importance of the library as a resource centre and the endeavor of the management to exploit the resources gathered over the years with a lot of investment, need not be over emphasized. However, it has been the experience of many a library, especially those attached to organisations, the use of their resources appear to be little compared to the efforts put in building up the resources. As such there appears to be a constant need to initiate outreach programmes in order to enhance the usage of the library to the maximum extent. Library is looked upon as a centre for learning. The Library has to strive to repackage the material that is received in the library in the form of Alerts, reviews, digests, abstracts and databases to enhance library utilization and improve readership. Also, in view of the rapid developments in Information and Communication Technologies, the role of a librarian is not like what it used to be a few decades ago. Added to IT, satellite communication systems, networking, Internet and intellectual property rights, have all made the library environment more complex. Further, the budgetary constraints, inadequate infrastructure, falling standards in human resources are all compelling the librarian to change his attitude from a mere custodian of information to that of a facilitator. As the library is a service institution there should be close interaction between the information providers, processors and users to enhance the effectivity of any resource centre Keeping in view the above factors, National Institute of Rural Development (NIRD) conducted a learning programme on. This programme provided a forum for the users of information and the library personnel to come together, to understand each others way of dealing with information and how the information barriers can be overcome and what best practices are to be adopted to increase the utilization of the resources of the Library through various training programmes.

LIBRARY UTILIZATION AND READERSHIP ENHANCEMENT (LURE)

When CORD conducted the one-day programme LURE I in 1991, had a modest goal to find out the ways and means to increase the library utilization by adopting innovative methods tolure the readers. This was based on a feeling that we have been investing in the library huge amounts of money year after year, trying to equip the library with more relevant reading material and also recruit trained personnel to make the resources more useful. While we are trying to build up a tempo, we had a feeling somewhere along the line that the readers or users are still not coming along with us. This feeling lead us to an introspection which gave rise to the impetus for conducting a programme for the first time on LURE in 1991. As stated earlier, the learning programme provided an opportunity for interaction between the library professionals and our own users in understanding the lacunae in promoting exploitation of library resources. In the first workshop on LURE in 1991 several issues were thrown up such as the following:

ISSUES FOR CONSIDERATION

As the reader is reluctant to come to library, it may be necessary that the library has to go to the reader. Naturally, that situation will determine the kind of services that are planned or envisaged to enhance the usage of the library. The issues that influence the usage hinge upon how the information needs are gauged and the methods that are adopted to identify those needs. Some of the other major issues identified are:

- Focus of the parent organisation
- Information collection

- Information processing
- Information search in the Internet era
- Information dissemination
- Information barriers

The workshop offered a set of simple but effective steps to increase the library use with suggestions like involvement of users in procurement of literature, client based services etc., The other major recommendations include:

- The book selection and acquisition are both important and modalities like participatory practices have to be followed;
- User education and user services have to be frequently conducted by the library to improve the interaction between users and the library personnel;
- A brochure on the library highlighting the library collection, cataloging and classification system followed and the services offered would be more useful;
- immediate computerization of all activities of library;
- creation of new services like abstracting, alerting service, reference and making digests on specific topics etc.,
- augmentation of facilities for document supply and other physical facilities like proper sign boards, stools to reach higher shelves, etc., and
- strengthening of the resource sharing at the local level.

These recommendations were taken seriously as they were particularly important in the over all development of the library utilization. Fortunately, most of the suggestions would be implemented with a telling effect on the positive response of the readers.

LURE – II

After a gap of nearly two years, CORD thought of again reviewing the library utilization with the completion of library automation. Accordingly, in 1993 a second programme on LURE was conducted. This time with a difference. The impetus came from the management of parent organization. There was a constant refrain from the management that with automation is there any improvement in the utilization of library resources? How many faculty are visiting the library? What is the ratio between faculty and participants of various training programmes that visit the library? What special arrangements were made to familiarize the participants with the new automation etc.,

These were a few of the questions that were bothering the management. Also, with computerization of library procedures, a new barrier is likely to be perceived by the users. Such 'Automation anxiety' may have to be taken into consideration in designing training programmes on library initiation.

Accordingly, the participants were chosen from not only the users of the library but also the participants of the then running courses, besides other librarians of neighbouring institutions. The programme was conducted in 3 sessions. In these sessions several papers based on cases illustrating the circulation facility, visitors register, pattern of usage of library on different dates and use of various information products of CORD were presented. These studies provided a picture of the pattern of library usage after the automation which appeared to be promising and provided the guidance as to how to increase awareness and access to information. Several suggestions emerged based on the discussions and some of which are as follows:—

- **Information Products:**
  - The coverage of indexing and abstracting services done through CORD Index and CORD Abstracts is found to be satisfactory. However, emphasis may have to be given to the immediate interest of the faculty members depending on their research and training programmes.
  - The journals that are covered in CORD Alerts may have to be displayed at a designed place for their immediate location and identification of articles given in the service.

- **Maintenance:**
  - Upkeep and maintenance of various sections will provide the necessary incentive for the users to browse.
  - Library staff should be trained and motivated to assist the readers.
- **User Studies:**
  - Though the faculty members are patronising the library, there is a scope for improvement.
  - Visitors to the Library are not always recording their visits in the prescribed register and so it did not reflect the total visits made by the academic staff in comparison with non-academic staff. A strict vigil on the visitors register may have to be maintained to satisfy the management.

The other major recommendations include:

- Promotion of library with a professional image is essential;
- Library staff should be trained in inter-personnel communication skills;
- There is a need to display current journals in more attractive and useful manner like displaying latest issues at a prominent place, rearranging of primary journals in alphabetical sequence, etc.,
- NIRD publications should be displayed prominently for outside visitors.
- A marketing approach to its library and information products is essential. For this purpose Library counters and surrounding areas should be used for display of not only for acquired publications but also NIRD publications.
- There are about 3000 participants in a year coming to NIRD to participate in the training programmes, who should be given orientation tour to the library for better appreciation of the resources. Also, a session on information resources, and information management relevant to the theme of any course wherever possible should be arranged apart from display of the publications pertaining to the training programme.

- A faculty directory, user manual, training of staff on information technology etc., are other suggestions that emerged from the programme.

After LURE-II in 1993 there was marked improvement in the appreciation of library services, the physical facilities and the environment in the library. Non-book material like CD-ROMS, videos, electronic journal have slowly started to show their presence. In the mid 90s internet opened gates to the Information sources world wide, and made possible access to information from a remote location. As a result it has become more important to look into the problems of transforming a traditional library into an information clearing house.

LURE – III

Against this backdrop a 3rd LURE programme was conducted in the year 1998 after a gap of 5 years. This learning programme was made into a National Workshop inviting papers from all over India on various themes such as library utilisation; techniques of readership enhancement; evaluation of library services; internet and changing role of the librarian etc. Participants from several parts of the country made their presentations based on their own back-home experience in user education and identification of user needs. This workshop revealed various kinds of experiments that are on-going in several parts of the country by innovative librarians and demystifying the Internet for the librarian and the user. Information search in the Internet era has totally changed the way the readers look for information. Searching Internet should become a matter of routine in any special library, to make the expression "Internet is Librarianship" truly applicable. Some of the other major recommendations of the workshop were:

- Continuous study of user needs.
- Development of communication skills of the library personnel.
- Role of parent organization in recognising the contribution of their libraries and supporting their activity.
- Design and update of user manual in the fast changing information technology environment.

- Change of attitude of librarians to the market driven economy and interact with the users more closely and make users appreciate the library services.
- A thematic approach to all the library services have to be i.e., the information products of the library like CORD INDEX, CORD ABSTRACTS should follow the themes identified for the research and training of the institute.
- The Selective Dissemination of Information (SDI) service can perhaps be concentrated on a faculty or a discipline at a time. Once a faculty is studied for a period of 6 months or so as a focussed group the impact on the group and its activities perhaps be quantitatively measured.

CORD is giving continuous training to the Library staff in the above areas in order to serve the clientele for effective use of Library Resources. They are also deputing the staff to other training programmes to get trained in these as well as new emerging areas. Simultaneously providing training and support to the users for better utiliztion of the resources without any barriers. Thus a new era emergd where information driven activities gained importance which will hopefully energize the users as well as information specialists to come together and work for the better uilization of information following the best practices in information dissemination through regular training programmes.

INTERNET TRAINING FOR ACADEMIC LIBRARY STAFF

Educational institutions are being encouraged by the Government and other organizations to upgrade their resources for research and education. Consequently the academic libraries of the higher education institutions are also being upgraded. Internet has proved to be boon in this endeavor. Internet has helped these libraries to be interconnected and share their resources and also to access resources in remote locations. Internet connections have been growing in the recent years with good connectivity and access.

But are these libraries fully geared up especially in terms of their employees' skills to be able to fully utilize the Internet for the benefit of the academic community? It has already been widely discussed that training is essential for the staffs to work in a network and automated environment. The Library Association Working Party on Training cites in its Policy Statement that training "is of fundamental importance to all levels of staffs working in all types of library", contributing to "greater efficiency and continuity, with real cost benefits". Since technology keeps on changing it becomes even more necessary for the staff to be trained in Internet.

OBJECTIVES

The present study aims to understand the status of Internet training for the academic library staff within greater Guwahati. Since the importance of Internet is growing in today's academic environment therefore the issue of training the academic library staff in handling Internet is becoming important. So this study will investigate the various training methods used in the academic libraries, the content of such training, problems encountered and whether any evaluation is undertaken for such training. The investigation will also try to reveal the attitudes of the library managers with regard to training their staff on Internet. In order to understand the status of Internet training for the staffs of the academic libraries a sample of six academic libraries was taken. A questionnaire-based survey of the sample was conducted. The questionnaire contained both close-ended questions and open-ended questions.

The questionnaire was prepared based on some existing studies already done on understanding the Internet training of academic library staff. Comprehending the importance of the study the author personally went to the respective libraries to collect the data.

INTERNET AND ITS USE IN ACADEMIC LIBRARIES

Many of us by now are familiar with Internet especially those working in the academic libraries. This is because the academic libraries have been the pioneer in the field of automation and Internet. Internet has become essential for today's education and research in the academic institutions. Library being a hub of research and academic activities are therefore being provided with Internet connections. The Internet is a unique information resource, bringing a wide range of material from around the world to a local machine. One of the earliest usages of the Internet was to access the OPAC i.e. the Online Public Access Catalogues of different libraries or within a campus. The union catalogues which lists the holdings of several libraries was another important tool accessible through net.

Another area of growing importance for academic libraries is that of electronic journals. Big publishing houses like Elsevier, Springer, ACM etc. are providing packages of their journals to libraries in electronic form via Internet. So at nominal subscription the libraries can access to these costly journals, which are becoming increasingly popular with the users.

Thus grew consortia based subscription in India. INDEST, INFONET and CSIR Consortium are the examples of library consortia for sharing journals and bibliographic information. These consortia based journal subscription are available through the Internet. The Indian National Digital Library in Engineering Science & Technology i.e. INDEST was set up by the Ministry of Human resource Development (MHRD) for subscription to electronic resources for 38 institutions including IISc, IITs, NITs, IIMs, etc. Over 6000 e-journals are accessible through this consortium, which has its headquarters in IIT Delhi. Infonet Contortia is set up by UGC and operated through its INFLIBNET Centre, Ahmedabad. Over 100 Universities are its members. It covers disciplines like Arts, Sciences, Mathematics and statistics etc. About 4000 full text electronic journals from 25 publishers are currently accessible. CSIR e-journal Consortia provides access to 3300+ e-journals from 11 publishers to all CSIR S&T staff of different CSIR institutions located around India.

These consortia not only provide full text access but they also give access to bibliographic databases like COMPENDEX,

INSPEC SciFinder Scholar, and Web of Science etc. Many open access materials important for education and research are available on the Internet. They are very useful in the context that they are not fee based and also don't have restricted access and are thus becoming very popular with students and researchers. Communicating with users is very important in academic libraries.

Widespread access to the Internet has also created new means of communicating with users. In some cases, Internet technologies (e.g. email and publishing on Web pages) are used to reproduce an existing service in another medium, such as online "suggestion boxes". However, there is "added value" to such a service as users can mail in their suggestions from terminals on or off campus at a time convenient to them. Email enquiry or reference services also represent an extension of mainstream library activity - although some academic librarians initially had concerns about being able to meet the demand of such a service. Reference and enquiry services in academic libraries in the main seek to teach their users how to search for information themselves, rather than answering the enquiries themselves, as is more likely to be the case in a special library.

A significant number of British academic libraries have adopted electronic mail enquiry or information services - at the University of Hull the "email help line" is treated as an extension of the Enquiry Desk service. Anecdotal evidence suggests that electronic enquiry services are not overwhelmed, and most users do stay within the parameters of the service. The most successful email enquiry services have developed their procedures and boundaries prior to the service going live.

As many enquiries fall into the category of Frequently Asked Questions, these can thus be answered by existing position statements. Electronic mail also has great potential to cut down on the mountain of paperwork involved in sending out recall notices, notifying readers that items can be collected etc. Some library systems allow students to renew loans (provided no other reader is waiting for the book) directly via the OPAC or to request a renewal via email.

Similarly, weblogs or simply blogs are now becoming very popular on the Internet as a communication medium. A library weblog can be used to:

- Providing news information for users
- Providing links to recommend internet sources
- Book reviews, information about new books
- Providing entertainment or amusement for users
- Providing news or information for librarians
- Book discussions
- Provide news or information for the trustees
- Provide research tips
- Communication among the librarians (in a library system).

The library can make good use of the electronic mail system of Internet i.e. Email to communicate reservation alert, current awareness services like SDI, new arrivals of books and journals, receiving interlibrary loan request and sending overdue notices to the users. In addition to these specialist services academic librarians also make use of the Internet information that is available to all users. Much bibliographical and price information can be found from online bookstores and Web sites for professional organizations and publishers. A wide range of factual information from government and NGO sources is available too.

Although librarians have more skepticism about the well-publicized Web search tools than most users, such services can be valuable, particularly for easily defined topics (such as names or abbreviations) and the sheer range of material indexed, subjects covered and the speed with which they search can make them useful when a clear starting point is not obvious. They may not always retrieve a full answer, but may give helpful clues.

Internet resources are just another information medium academic librarians are extending their skills to encompass it. So they may offer a current awareness service to teaching and research staff to inform them of new Web sites and discussion lists; they will apply established criteria to assessing the content of information sources or the effectiveness of secondary services like search tools.

The hypertext nature of the Web makes it easy to make additional explanation or instruction for a resource as an optional choice. This concept of instruction at the point and time of use is harder to achieve in the physical library.

WHY INTERNET TRAINING IS NECESSARY

In the Internet age there is acute need of Internet specialists. These specialists will be armed with the necessary skills and training to help the users to locate their information pin pointedly and efficiently on the net. Libraries specially the academic libraries would have a great demand for these specialists.

Internet connectivity in the academic libraries is growing day by day. So, the present administration of the academic institutions should take necessary steps to equip the library staff with the required skills and training on Internet. Training can help to understand many essential aspects of the Internet such as follows:

- Are we using the right type of Internet connection for our needs? Are we getting a good deal?
- How quickly can we find what we looking for on the Internet? We should be able to find useful information about virtually any topic in less than a minute. If you're taking longer, you're doing something wrong.
- How do we know if we are safe? Most people who contract viruses or other nastiest thought they were protected.
- Are we using email correctly? Or are we really annoying we our colleagues and they are too polite to tell us? We might be unpleasantly surprised to learn the truth.
- How do we avoid those terrible pop-up windows?
- How do we know if information is real or a hoax?
- How can we make surfing faster?
- How can we get the maximum satisfaction without spending more time on net?

As noted by Paula L. Matthews while employing Internet in academic libraries one of the important issues for the administrator is the implementation library staff training. "A lack of training can result in:

- Poor staff performance;
- Lack of motivation;
- High staff turnover;
- Resistance to change;
- Costly errors or accidents;
- Unfulfilled objectives;
- Undesirable low standards of service.

Academic librarians may well draw on training materials available on the Internet for the higher education community. Recently the issue of whether librarians should learn HTML (Hyper-Text Markup Language) was debated on a North American discussion list. The conclusion was that knowledge of basic HTML was necessary in order to prepare presentations and information guides, which are an integral part of the librarian's professional role. As an increasing number of academic libraries experience some measure of "convergence" with other academic support services, library staff has many opportunities to augment their IT skills and collaborate with colleagues in other services. The combination of technical knowledge and the ability to evaluate information sources is a powerful argument for the continued need for LIS professionals in higher education.

The users of the Academic libraries including some faculty member do not have net skills. In such cases the academic library staff has to come forward to help them. For readiness the staff should have some kind of net skills. The transition of traditional library resources to technology based library resources has put a lot of pressure on the academic library staff. Unless the staff is kept up to date on Internet skills he will face more pressure to work in such conditions. So training of staff has become a necessity in today's context

RESEARCHING AND BENCHMARKING BEST PRACTICE IN LIBRARY STAFF DEVELOPMENT

Most university libraries throughout the world are engaged in some level of staff development. Benchmarking of staff development activities however is not widespread and little useful data exists to enable meaningful comparisons between university libraries within national borders, let alone provide meaningful international perspectives. Three studies in the first half of this decade examined staff development policy and practice in the university library sector in Australia and the United Kingdom. Significantly, the studies enabled limited international comparisons where none had been previously possible. In January 2008, two university library organisations – CAVAL in Australia and EMALINK in the United Kingdom - commenced a joint project to further develop this process of comparison by benchmarking staff development practices within their member libraries. Although located in different hemispheres and literally half a world away from each other, CAVAL and EMALINK were assessed as good candidates for a benchmarking study. Both organisations are roughly similar in terms of their size, composition and orientation. Prior to 2008, they had also already shared expertise relating to staff development and key personnel had worked together as members of IFLA's Continuing Professional Development and Workplace Learning Section. A collaborative project thus appeared to offer CAVAL and EMALINK a unique opportunity to provide value to their member libraries in two key ways:

- By identifying, comparing and generally sharing knowledge about current staff development practices and processes; and,
- By establishing common measurement points, indicators and best practice benchmarks to assist with planning improvements in future staff development practices and processes.

On the ground, the project aimed to obtain data and test various assumptions that would enable the development of a practical tool to facilitate ongoing benchmarking between CAVAL and EMALINK member libraries. Longer term, the project hoped to inform the development of a marketable "dashboard" of indicators for benchmarking staff development activities in other libraries at national and international levels.

CAVAL also planned to establish a database of indicators in order to build up a longitudinal data set to facilitate trend analysis. In tandem with these aims, the project also sought to demonstrate how recent developments in information and communications technology (ICT), particularly social networking technology, have helped to facilitate international collaborative library research projects. Originally projected for completion in late 2008, the project encountered logistical challenges on the Australian side within several months of commencement. Rather than delay or compromise the entire project, CAVAL withdrew temporarily, thereby allowing EMALINK to push ahead with a pilot survey of its members in the United Kingdom. In this way, EMALINK was able to complete base level data collection already undertaken by CAVAL in 2006.

This chapter constitutes a progress report and case study of the CAVAL – EMALINK library staff development benchmarking project to July 2008. The chapter outlines the drivers for benchmarking in library staff development and discusses why applied research of this kind is of potentially such great value to university and other libraries in the context of current issues impacting staff development: for example, recruitment and retention of staff. Details are provided of the research methodology agreed by CAVAL and EMALINK, and the benchmarking dimensions investigated by the project. With preliminary data from EMALINK available in early July 2008, the paper reports on initial findings and considers important practical lessons in international collaboration learned to date.

UNDERSTANDING THE VALUE OF BENCHMARKING

In the context of libraries, benchmarking may be defined as an ongoing structured process by which we evaluate the functions, work processes and services of other organisations (not always libraries) recognised for their leadership and innovation. This process of evaluation is undertaken for the purpose of organisational comparison and improvement. The concept of *competitive benchmarking*, later 'benchmarking', was first popularised by the Xerox Corporation in the late 1970s as an innovative response – at that time – to strong competition in a market segment that it had hitherto dominated. Xerox refined the concept of benchmarking through the 1980s and eventually promulgated a ten-step benchmarking process. Despite there now being many competing process models for benchmarking, most can trace their origins back twenty years to the original Xerox process, and early variations. Other influences cited as significant in the development of the concept of benchmarking include the quality assurance movement and just-in-time manufacturing methods.

Indeed, Deming's classic four step quality improvement process still forms the basis of many benchmarking exercises. Benchmarking is essentially concerned with understanding how processes work – through observing and studying work methods and practices – and then identifying good or best practice. Benchmarking seeks to learn from the observation of such good and best practice, and to make improvements necessary to reach identified standards of good and best practice. Assessment of improvement is based on review and comparison with other like organisations; hence the significance of a good match between CAVAL and EMALINK. Drawing on Deming's four step process, Ford and Longbottom each propose useful models for benchmarking; Ford specifically in the context of benchmarking human resource development (HRD). It is Longbottom's 'PAIR' approach however that resonates through the methodology applied in the CAVAL-EMALINK project:

- **Planning** - investigation, measurement and examination of the strengths and weaknesses of current processes;
- **Analysis** – identifying potential benchmarking partners and then exchanging information, and observing and comparing processes;
- **Implementation** – adaptation and modification of processes based on learning from the analysis stage;
- **Review** – ongoing review and refinement with the intention of achieving continuous improvements.

Within the higher education sector, libraries have frequently been early and enthusiastic adopters of benchmarking techniques. University libraries in Australia, New Zealand and the United Kingdom, for example, have all been at the forefront in adopting and applying benchmarking processes to various aspects of their operations. In the case of Australia, the work of scholars has been important in outlining suitable frameworks and encouraging the adoption of benchmarking methods in university libraries. Noting the need to identify benchmarks which would assess efficient use of resources and the quality of the contributions which university libraries make to the realisation of university objectives, McKinnon *et al* proposed a range of criterion reference benchmarks with the intention firstly of identifying attributes of good practice and then using those attributes as benchmarks for further evaluation. The *Council of Australian University Librarians* has encouraged benchmarking between its members and has facilitated a range of studies in various operational areas including client satisfaction with library services, performance and effectiveness of document delivery services, availability of sought materials, cataloguing, and the re-shelving of library materials.

Several trans-national benchmarking projects have also been undertaken with Australian libraries as a key partner, for example between libraries in Australia and New Zealand and Australia and the United Kingdom.

STAFF DEVELOPMENT RESEARCH IN AUSTRALIA AND THE UNITED KINGDOM

Attempts to examine and benchmark staff development practice in Australian university libraries can be traced back more than twenty years; with more recent work in Australia and the United Kingdom attempting to update and expand that work. Both early Australian surveys by Trask and Gray revealed a paucity of human resource development in the university library sector, albeit balanced by an emerging recognition at that time of the importance of developing people. In 2001 and then again in 2005, Smith explored the extent of commitment to staff development, linkages to strategic organisational priorities, and the focus of staff development activity. The overall picture presented by these 2001 and 2005 surveys was of a strong commitment to investment in human resource development – a picture very different to that found in the earlier 1983 and 1986 analyses. Smith concluded that the major influences on the focus of staff development programmes in Australian university libraries included:

- Increasing scope and volume of electronic publishing, with consequent changes in required staff skills and knowledge;
- Increasing involvement of university library staff in teaching information literacy (with needs for skill development on the part of those staff doing such teaching);
- Changing organisational demographics (in particular ageing workforces), and actual or impending retirements of staff (particularly senior staff) – this resulting in the need for succession planning and development of new leadership and management capability; and,
- The imperative for regionally isolated libraries to grow and develop skills and capability within their existing workforce.

For the first time, the 2005 survey explored budget allocations for staff development. This was interesting as a measure in its own right of the level of commitment to staff development activity. It also enabled benchmarking against a comparable survey undertaken in the United Kingdom, and several other available benchmarks including those of the *American Society for Training and Development* and *UNESCO*. In 2004, motivated partly by the 2001 Australian study, Yeoh investigated staff development in a cross section of university libraries in England, Scotland and Ireland. That survey found, inter alia:

- A strong commitment to staff development as part of institutional strategic organisational management;
- Formal written statements of commitment to staff development in just over half of the organisations surveyed;

- A planned and structured approach to staff development in most organisations; and,
- A structured appraisal and review of these activities in two thirds of organisations.

It was also keen to develop common staff development indicators and a database to enable longitudinal studies. In retrospect, the survey instrument developed by the project team was arguably too broad, encompassing 97 questions over 46 pages, and too complex; partly a outcome of trying to align the survey with international studies.

As a result of the CAVAL survey's complexity, details of staff development practice within member libraries were largely obscured by other issues relating to recruitment and retention and succession planning. Although providing a highly detailed and ultimately fascinating snapshot of human resources in CAVAL member libraries in late 2006, the project stalled after presentation of the preliminary findings in March 2007. "The research project generated an immense amount of data that is of varying degrees of completeness and indeed of value."

The research instrument itself was complex, which potentially added further complications to the ability to undertake an effective comparative analysis and interpretation of the responses." Interestingly, researcher comments echo those of Ford, writing on benchmarking HRD: "choosing the wrong set of metrics is one of the surest ways to doom a benchmarking study." For CAVAL, the over-riding challenge of the 2006 *Benchmarking of Staff Development Practice in CAVAL Member Libraries* project was how to go about "extracting the desired key measurement points needed if benchmark levels of practice and processes are to be established within the membership of the consortium."

With resources allocated to the CAVAL project exhausted by early 2007 and other projects moving to the fore, further progress on benchmarking staff development seemed unlikely in the short term. As one door closes, however, sometimes another opens. Enter at this point EMALINK, the East Midlands Library Information Network, representing the 10 university and higher education libraries comprising the United Kingdom's East Midland University Association (EMUA).

WHY BENCHMARK BEST PRACTICE IN LIBRARY STAFF DEVELOPMENT?

Before reporting on the methodology and early findings of the 2008 CAVAL-EMALINK study, it is important to understand the significance of benchmarking best practice in staff development to libraries in general. Libraries, it was long argued, were simply the sum of their collections – print and later electronic. A big library was ipso facto a good library. The majority of contemporary library measures still reflect this preoccupation with the physical item, even where electronic resources have taken precedence. The rise of the internet and increasing demands from customers have however progressively turned the focus of library managers to their people – arguably always their best information 'assets'. People and the environments in which they live and work are not static though, and the parallel processes of personal and professional development must be ongoing. Thus libraries, particularly university libraries, have come to realise the significance of better understanding staff development through benchmarking. Many are returning to the origins of benchmarking as an organisational improvement tool, and Spendolini's simple elevator definition of benchmarking as "learning from others". Researcher that "changes in the academic library workplace mirror those of other workplaces in the new millennium." Expanding on this theme, researcher observes:

> Following the nature of the work, the organisation of the institution is constantly shifting, requiring staff in all areas to perform a greater variety of tasks. The operations daily become more automated and more technical. The workforce becomes more diverse. The pace quickens. The budget tightens. And the tensions mount.

For libraries, particularly university libraries, there are also specific challenges to address. The last two decades have seen greatly increased emphases on access to information and knowledge management. Changes and developments in the ways and means of organising and accessing recorded knowledge have been both rapid and profound; with increasingly sophisticated information systems evolving as a result. As IFLA acknowledges, libraries and those who work in them have an increasingly important role to play in such an environment:

> The quality of service provided to the public by library and information science institutions depends on the expertise of their staff. Constant flux in the needs of societies, changing technologies, and growth in professional knowledge demand that information workers must expand their understanding and update their skills on an ongoing basis.

As a consequence of this transformation, human resource professionals in libraries are observing a range of issues impacting on and influencing staff development.

Focusing on university libraries, the issues are as follows:

- The need for library staff to keep current with continuous changes in information technology and with information itself;
- A related need to coordinate technical training for library staff, and find the expertise and resources to provide it;
- A strengthening of libraries' traditional customer service orientation in order to compete with Internet search engines and online booksellers;
- Further development of libraries' orientation towards teamwork, made necessary by shrinking budgets, decreases in staff numbers, and the rise of multifunctional teams;
- Additional support required for both new and experienced managers;
- Growth of the teaching and training role of university library staff, particularly but not exclusively those in professional positions; and finally,
- The need to provide meaningful staff development as a means of recruiting and retaining staff.

The imperative to maintain and upgrade the skills, knowledge, and abilities of library and information staff has been recognised, and is reflected, in the significant priority allocated to human resource development (HRD) activity in many libraries. As a strategic organisational priority it is important that HRD is assessed and, where necessary, improved and that this be a continuing cyclical activity. Benchmarking has clear potential to achieve that end. Indeed, benchmarking has particular applicability for HRD because the activity naturally lends itself to cooperative and collaborative working between institutions. Ford proposes a series of metrics which may be usefully applied to benchmarking staff development. Some are relatively straightforward to measure and calculate, while others are more challenging. In broadly escalating degrees of difficulty in measurement these metrics include:

- Expenditure on staff development activities expressed as a percentage of payroll;
- Average hours spent on staff development per employee per annum;
- Average staff development cost per participant per hour;
- Percentage of employees undertaking staff development activity per annum;
- Average percentage of positive ratings of staff development activities by participants;
- Average percentage of gains in learning reported by participants in staff development activities;
- Average percentage of improvement in on-the-job performance as a result of participation in staff development activities;
- Cost savings and efficiency gains as a result of participation in staff development activities.

The eventual goal is to take raw data and convert it to ratios or percentages that can be monitored easily over time – in effect, a staff development 'dashboard'. Although nowhere near this level of sophistication, IFLA's *Continuing Professional Development and Workplace Learning Quality Guidelines Project* has published useful best practice indicators for staff development. IFLA requires that there be:

- Regular learning needs assessment.
- Broad range of learning opportunities, both formal and informal; formal offerings in a choice of formats, designed to meet identified needs, in modules structured to cover topics from introductory through advanced.
- Organizational commitment and leadership from staff development and continuing education administrators with expertise in adult continuing education.
- Widely disseminated information about continuing education and resources, accurately described.
- C[ontinuing] E[education] activities design that includes learning objectives aligned with identified needs; follows principles of instructional design and learning theory; selects course instructors on the basis of both subject knowledge and teaching ability; attends to transfer of training and feedback.
- Consistent documentation of individuals' participation in learning and recognition of continuing learning in hiring and promotion decisions.
- A minimum of 0.5 to 1.0 % of institutional budget earmarked for staff development, as stated in *The public library service: IFLA/UNESCO guidelines for developmen.*
- About 10% of work hours provided for attendance at workshops, conferences, in-service training, and other educational activities, and for informal learning projects.
- Evaluation of continuing education and staff development offerings and programmes.
- Research that assesses the state of CPD and examines the efficacy and outcomes of continuing education and staff development programmes.

CAVAL-EMALINK STUDY METHODOLOGY

In October 2007, Ian Smith and Graham Walton proposed that CAVAL in Australia and EMALINK in the United

Kingdom undertake a joint study to identify best practice in staff development in member libraries. They highlighted a number of benefits to individual member libraries, including:

- Acquisition of staff development data to inform and guide ongoing change processes;
- Opportunity to undertake national and international level comparisons; and,
- Opportunity for international partnering and skills exchange.

Within the context of developing and delivering the project, the proposal acknowledged that university libraries are busy organisations and that no funds had been budgeted for the project by CAVAL or EMALINK in 2008. It was considered crucial therefore that the work should not be time or resource intensive, particularly in relation to project management and data collection.

A relatively brief web based questionnaire was suggested to minimise the time and effort required for survey development, administration and analysis. Smith and Walton proposed that the project should be jointly overseen by a small team of nominated representatives from the CAVAL Human Resources Group and EMALINK.

This working group would take responsibility for jointly developing and administering the survey questionnaire, analysing the data obtained, and producing a summary report for dissemination to individual member libraries.

The proposed study methodology called for data collection to take place through a web based questionnaire, with questions taking no more than 20 minutes in total to complete.

In scoping the 2006 staff development benchmarking study involving CAVAL member libraries, Smith originally proposed eight benchmarking dimensions:

- Budget allocation for staff development expressed as a percentage of total payroll costs. Further, what elements are covered by that budget and what budget model is applied for staff development (e.g., centralised or distributed)?

- Approval criteria and processes – how are staff development applications assessed and approved?
- Links between staff development priorities and strategic planning;
- Organisational approaches to the development, documentation and evaluation of staff development plans;
- Common themes and priorities in staff development plans;
- Application of *Rodski* results in setting staff development objectives - have staff development investments in turn improved *Rodski* ratings?
- Coordination of staff development in CAVAL member libraries – how and by whom?
- Evaluation of staff development programmes by the organisation and measurement of the return on investment (ROI).

By mid-July 2008, EMALINK had received an encouraging seven responses from a total membership of ten university libraries. In 2006, CAVAL received responses from all eleven members.

2

Leadership

INTRODUCTION

During the early nineteenth century, Wellington's and Napoleon's observations made sense. With the onset of battle, communications became muddled, artillery was immobilised, and a commander's ability to control his forces was limited. Consequently, the leadership of a single general could prove decisive in battle by maintaining clarity of command and control. We are now at a totally different stage of warfare. This not to say that the fog of war has completely lifted, but visibility and synchronised actions, and the speed, precision, and lethality of response is beyond comparison to anything that has preceded it.

The battlefield success of the doctrine and technology of Network Centric Warfare was not based upon a single brilliant plan, or a single individual or group, but rather was a property of the network, both technologically and organisationally. As Operation Iraqi Freedom so vividly illustrated, battle plans can now be changed very rapidly, affecting all aspects of operations—strategy, tactics, logistics and PSYOPs, operations, kinetics, and all types of forces.

The competencies that make NCW a success are network properties; they are no longer solely the province of charismatic leaders or chance, but the result of diverse competencies and a new understanding of the role and growth of network leadership, and how it is learned and rewarded.

EARLY LEADERSHIP

Leadership among Greek warriors was based upon "a first among equals" principle. Such leadership was a product of a culture of equality and mutual accountability. In a very tangible sense, cultures are networks of social relationships. Military cultures, especially in battlefield situations, have highly articulated roles and codes of conduct and mutual accountability.

Although an individual may gain prominence and status apart from a group, it is often not the result of individual achievement, but how the individual exemplifies certain traits that represent the best traits of that group, such as sacrifice, decisiveness, courage, initiative, and prowess. In fact, to attribute successes to the individual that derive from the group undermines a core principle of true leadership: the group comes before the individual.

In the following stanzas taken from Alfred Lord Tennyson's ode to Wellington, many of the qualities that continue to make leaders great are captured:

* ...Mourn for the man of amplest influence, Yet clearest of ambitious crime, *our greatest yet with least pretence,* Great in council and great in war, Foremost captain of his time, *rich in saving common-sence* And, as the greatest only are, In his *simp licity sublime...*
* *... Who never sold the truth to serve the hour,* Nor palter'd with Eternal God for power; Who let the turbid streams of rumor flow Thro' either babbling world of high and low; Whose life was work, whose language rife *with rugged maximus hewn from life;* Who never spoke against a foe; Whose eighty winters freeze with one rebuke All great self-seekers trampling on the right. *Truth-teller was our England's Alfred named;* Truth-lover was our English Duke; Whatever record leap to light He never shall be shamed...

By embodying the best qualities of a group, a military leader does not try to elevate himself above his peers, but brings Honour and distinction to them, be they his company, brigade, division, or service. These qualities of "simplicity sublime" and "truth-teller" are parts of the best of military culture. They are hard to transfer from the field of battle into bureaucratic and administrative assignments, where often different kinds of codes of conduct are rewarded. As noted earlier, small networks of 150-200 individuals can still be coordinated by face-to-face relationships and personal codes of Honour and accountability.

At such a scale, combat relationships are more transparent and accountable, and hence, not so easily "gamed" and "politicised" as in hierarchical, formal organisations. It is not surprising that many who succeed on the battlefield fail to adjust to the rules of a bureaucratic organisation, whose codes of success are often at variance with those of the battlefield group.

In bureaucratic organisations, successful leadership can entail the subordination of the interests of the group to the promotion of the individual, as visibility to outside parties is associated with an individual leader who is *personally* credited with a certain policy or success. Under such circumstances, the leader in bureaucratic groups becomes a marker, a kind of shorthand, for the success or failure of an issue, policy, or campaign—not the exemplar of the group.

This kind of leadership can entail taking much of the credit and little of the blame, thereby undermining the very principles of transparency and accountability upon which effective peer networks depend. The systemic failure of corporate leadership and governance in the United States over the last 10 years can be partly attributed to a bureaucratic culture wherein a company's success was almost totally attributed to the skills of the CEO and senior management.

This was reflected in senior executive compensation packages that ballooned to 301 times the average worker's pay package. Yet when the downturn came, and even widespread fraudulent practices were revealed, very few corporate leaders were held accountable, and shareholders and employees assumed the bulk of the losses. These failures were neither personality - nor individually-based, but were systemic in terms of how leaders were selected, cultivated, rewarded, and held accountable. The systemic subversion of governance leadership roles needed to achieve independence, truth telling, and transparency has been its own kind of perverse "network effect." This chapter's treatment of leadership is not founded upon any "great man" leadership model.

This is not to say that individual qualities are not important, but rather that sustainable and replicable qualities of leadership are treated here as a network property, made possible by the combination of the character of the social network and the individuals themselves. Moreover, it will be argued that there are several different types of leadership roles and the relative importance and combination of these roles depends upon the circumstances and structure of the organisational networks involved.

THE CORE OF LEADERSHIP

Leadership is the art of engaging the hearts and minds of ordinary people to achieve extraordinary results. This Isn't the Company I Joined, I've been interviewing gifted leaders from a wide range of industries. Each has his or her unique corporate responsibilities to carry out. Each has to deal with widely different competitive pressures, customer demands, marketing strategies, stockholder expectations, and Workforce requirements.

Each represents an organisation that is affected in specific ways by the new global economy, the IT revolution, the disappearance of stable currency values worldwide, and the collapse of the old Industrial business paradigm as an organising model for their companies. But all share one thing in common: an apparently innate set of emotional and intellectual qualities that make up what I call the Core of Leadership.

The components of that core are:

* Vision.
* Integrity.
* Trust.
* Values.
* Vulnerability.
* Motivation.

Together they produce what we all instantly recognise as leaders. How they do it is easier to note in practice than it is to define in principle. Because we aren't just talking about special skills or strategies these people exercise, we're talking about individual character. Like the force of gravity or the lump of uranium in a nuclear generator, the leadership core works invisibly. And like any living system, it sometimes works intuitively and mysteriously. But its positive effects upon others can be readily observed, and those observations, in turn, can be put to immediate use by anyone charged with leading fellow employees at any level of an organisation.

LEADERSHIP AS VISION

In contrast to control-minded authority of the past, today's leaders must exercise power through a shared purpose and vision. An organisational vision is not the same as long-range or even strategic planning. Planning is a linear process; progression Towards a goal. Vision is more holistic — a sense of direction that combines a good business strategy with a comprehensive organisational purpose that declares its own importance.

A vision describes a business as it could become over the long term and outlines a feasible way of achieving this goal. To transform an organisation, leaders must adopt and communicate a vision of the future that impels people beyond the boundaries and limits of the past. Leaders who articulate such visions aren't mystics, but broad-based thinkers who are willing to take risks. Visionary leaders don't have to be brilliant, highly innovative, or incredibly charismatic. But they do have to be intently focused on what it is they are trying to achieve. Fred Smith, ounder and Chief Executive Officer of Federal Express, put it in these very practical terms: "If there is any indication that the leader is not totally committed to achieving the vision, then all the sweet talk in the world will not get people to support it."

LEADERSHIP AS INTEGRITY

A leader must be seen to stand for something, must act from deep-seated principles, and must rely on strong personal beliefs. Leading with integrity implies a willingness to embody the attitudes and Behaviours you want to see in employees. Steve Wikstrom is the Co-Chief Executive Officer of Reell Precision Manufacturing Corporation, a $35 million company that produces wrap spring clutches and constant torque hinges for foreign and domestic customers. "In our company we try to create relationships that allows us to 'call' one another on Behaviour that doesn't represent our values.

A recent example occurred during the development of our latest strategic plan. Every year we get the top dozen leaders together once a week, for six to eight weeks. At the end of each of the weekly sessions, we have 'homework' assignments to prepare for the next meeting. At the beginning of one session, a participant told us that at the last meeting he had offered to send us information that we had agreed to review and return with our comments. He went on to say that of the twelve messages he sent out, only three responses had been received. He then asked all of us what we were going to do about this issue of 'irresponsibility.' The meeting stopped and we discussed how to better Honour our commitments. Right at the top of the organisation's leadership, we are aware of the need to mirror whatever Behaviour we expect to receive in kind."

LEADERSHIP AS TRUST

Until recently, managers' primary function has been supervision — telling employees what to do and measuring how well they did it. But the new breed of knowledge workers increasingly don't want or need to be micro-managed. They need to be set free in the sphere of their own authority. They need to be trusted. Trust is an attitude of confidence in another person, a positive set of expectations about that person's competencies and character. The powerful influence of one person's expectation on another's Behaviour is known as the "Pygmalion Effect." Eliza Doolittle explains it in George Bernard Shaw's play Pygmalion: "You see, really and truly, apart from the things anyone can pick up, the difference between a lady and a flower girl is not how she behaves but how she's treated. I shall always be a flower girl to Professor Higgins because he always treats me as a flower girl and always will; but I know I can be a lady to you because you always treat me as a lady and always will." The difference between leaders who complain about the lack of responsibility in today's employees and those who speak with pride of the creative contribution and dedication of their staff may lie in the realm of management's expectation.

LEADERSHIP AS VULNERABILITY

Recognition of the potential of the Workforce for contributing solutions to organisational problems has increased while the infallibility of leaders and the certainty of management tasks have declined. The unquestioned authority of leaders in the corporation of the past has been replaced by the need to acknowledge the expertise of those below, and to enlist employees as true partners. Moving from a model in which leadership made all the decisions and knew all the answers to an organisational environment of openness, candor, and empowerment takes a willingness by leaders to become and remain highly vulnerable.

There has never been a time in which our organisations have experienced more uncertainty and chaos. It may sound ironic, but the corporate leader who can say to his or her employees, "Sure, I'm scared too," will have done more for company morale with that single admission than a dozen phony pep talks ever could. Why? Because, as Sue Swenson, president of Leap Wireless, observes: "When leaders are perceived as human and vulnerable, employees identify with those attributes and begin to see the potential for success and leadership in themselves."

LEADERSHIP AS VALUES

Webster defines value as "a principle, standard or quality considered inherently worthwhile or desirable." The root is the Latin valor, which means strength. Values are a source of strength for an enterprise or an individual. As leadership strategy moves from coercion to cooperation, the key to bonding people to the goals of the organisation automatically becomes the intangibles — relationships, commitments and shared values.

Founding President and Chief Operating Officer of Ritz-Carlton Hotels, "Values are the heart and soul of our organisation. It is not enough for people just to fill functions. They have to know what we are all about." Leaders must stay focused on values and keep them energised — which is the hardest part.

For that, you need to find processes that renew and revitalise values. One process that Ritz-Carlton uses is called the "Line Up." Fifteen minutes before shift begins every day, the leader of the line up goes through the basics of that day. Employees of R-C all over the world are reminded of the same "value of the day," as prepared by the corporate office. Added to that is a "teaching" — an issue brought to our awareness, based on customer-service input, and then some comments about the daily value that are customised to the individual hotel.

LEADERSHIP AS MOTIVATION

The secret to being a great motivator is realising that motivation isn't something that can be forced or ordered. Motivation is an intrinsic capacity of human beings that can be tapped, nurtured, and developed — but never coerced. In essence, all motivation is self-motivation.

It manifests when leaders hold a compelling vision of the future, have a strong personal desire to realise the vision, and possess the ability to engage people's individual motivation in the common cause of that vision so that a true interconnection emerges. Motivational leaders inspire exceptional levels of commitment and performance. Prior to forming his own public relations firm, Bob Dilenschneider served as president and CEO of Hill and Knowlton.

He talked with me about his most memorable boss: "Barney Clarke, the CEO of Columbia Gas Systems, was brilliant — a genius who thought way outside the box.

Although I suspect he had the answers all the time, he spent hours talking with us, involving us and making us feel as if we were an integral part of a huge change — as if we were making history.

And he got so much out of all of us. We'd work 'round the clock. Working with Barney was exciting, exhausting, incredibly intense, and absolutely thrilling!"

THE RELATIONSHIP BETWEEN LEADERSHIP AND INFLUENCE

What is the relationship between leadership and influence? Is leadership always influence and is influence always leadership? To say that leadership always entails influence is like saying that all snow is white. It's true but the inference doesn't work the other way. That is, not all white things are snow. Similarly, although all leadership is influence, there are lots of types of influence that don't count as leadership.

Here are a few examples:

* Intimidating or forcing someone to do something.
* Bribing someone to do your bidding.
* Paying for things you want someone to do for you.
* Teaching a student to behave better in a classroom.
* Encouraging your children to eat their vegetables.

The last two examples are not leadership because they have nothing to do with a group striving to achieve a goal. Teaching students and encouraging children to eat vegetables is for their own interest, not for the good of a larger group. Similarly, salespeople may be very influential but their influence is self-interested. The salesperson and the customer do not constitute a group.

FORMAL AUTHORITY AND LEADERSHIP INFLUENCE

Suppose you are the boss and you decide to ramp up production by 50 per cent, requiring everyone to work faster and longer hours without overtime. Is this leadership? No, it may be influence but it is not leadership because the employees had no choice.

To say that leadership is informal influence means that followers have a free choice to follow or not. What are some prime examples of true leadership influence? One of the most familiar is Martin Luther King's demonstrations against segregation on buses which led the U.S., Supreme Court to outlaw this practice. King had no formal authority or other power to move the U.S., government.

This is the real meaning of leadership. Another example of genuine leadership influence was the Sony employee who influenced management to adopt his idea for PlayStation despite their feeling that Sony wasn't into making toys. Whenever you convince your colleagues or your boss to adopt a new idea, you have shown them leadership. Or, you might simply set a good example for others and, if they follow, you have shown leadership. Market leading businesses influence their competitors to change course, another example of real leadership. When executives make decisions that take their teams in new directions, they are taking managerial actions, NOT showing leadership because employees have no choice. To count as leadership, influence must be informal and followers must get on board completely of their own free will. Leadership is also a group phenomenon and is aimed at serving some unselfish purpose, something to improve the group's effectiveness. For this reason, even if your children willingly follow your plea to eat their vegetables, you haven't shown leadership because you and your kids are not a group working Towards a common goal.

INFORMAL LEADERSHIP AND INFLUENCE

We often distinguish between formal and informal leadership. The only difference between these concepts is that the informal leader takes charge informally. The formal leader has been given formal authority to govern the group while the informal leader is granted this role by the group itself. The informal leader has personal power - charisma, knowledge or some form of expertise that the group values. It is vital to recognise that the conventional concept of informal leadership is not the same thing as saying that all leadership influence is informal. The conventional concept, formal or informal, is all about being in charge of the group. The claim made here is that real leadership is independent of position, as it was in the case of Martin Luther King. He was not an informal leader in the conventional sense - the Supreme Court didn't recognise him as their informal leader.

As another example, a technical geek might influence his peers to adopt a new piece of software. He has influenced them informally. However, this geek might be so disinclined to manage the group that they might never view him as their informal leader - someone who they would turn to for help in organising their day to day work, who they would look to for advice and the resolution of conflict. The geek's informal leadership is a one-off act, not an ongoing role. His influence is informal but he is not what we normally call an informal leader because he has no interest or ability to take charge of the group in a managerial sense. So what? By reformulating the meaning of leadership, I am saying that the old distinction between formal and informal leadership is outdated. There is really only formal and informal management because all leadership is informal where this term refers to willingly following someone's lead NOT to informally taking charge of the group.

THEORIES

Students of leadership have produced theories involving traits, situational interaction, function, Behaviour, power, vision and values, charisma, and intelligence among others.

EARLY HISTORY

The search for the characteristics or traits of leaders has been ongoing for centuries. History's greatest philosophical writings from Plato's Republic to Plutarch's Lives have explored the question of "What qualities distinguish an individual as a leader?" Underlying this search was the early recognition of the importance of leadership and the assumption that leadership is rooted in the characteristics that certain individuals possess.

This idea that leadership is based on individual attributes is known as the "trait theory of leadership."

This view of leadership, the trait theory, was explored at length in a number of works in the previous century. Most notable are the writings of Thomas Carlyle and Francis Galton, whose works have prompted decades of research. In Heroes and Hero Worship, Carlyle identified the talents, skills, and physical characteristics of men who rose to power. In Galton's Hereditary Genius, he examined leadership qualities in the families of powerful men. After showing that the numbers of eminent relatives dropped off when moving from first degree to second degree relatives, Galton concluded that leadership was inherited.

In other words, leaders were born, not developed. Both of these notable works lent great initial support for the notion that leadership is rooted in characteristics of the leader. For decades, this trait-based perspective dominated empirical and theoretical work in leadership.

Using early research techniques, researchers conducted over a hundred studies proposing a number of characteristics that distinguished leaders from non-leaders: intelligence, dominance, adaptability, persistence, integrity, socioeconomic status, and self-confidence just to name a few.

RISE OF ALTERNATIVE THEORIES

In the late 1940s and early 1950s, however, a series of qualitative reviews of these studies prompted researchers to take a drastically different view of the driving forces behind leadership. In reviewing the extant literature, Stogdill and Mann found that while some traits were common across a number of studies, the overall evidence suggested that persons who are leaders in one situation may not necessarily be leaders in other situations. Subsequently, leadership was no longer characterised as an enduring individual trait, as situational approaches posited that individuals can be effective in certain situations, but not others. This approach dominated much of the leadership theory and research for the next few decades.

REEMERGENCE OF TRAIT THEORY

New methods and measurements were developed after these influential reviews that would ultimately reestablish the trait theory as a viable approach to the study of leadership. For example, improvements in researchers' use of the round robin research design methodology allowed researchers to see that individuals can and do emerge as leaders across a variety of situations and tasks. Additionally, during the 1980s statistical advances allowed researchers to conduct meta-analyses, in which they could quantitatively analyse and summarise the findings from a wide array of studies. This advent allowed trait theorists to create a comprehensive and parsimonious picture of previous leadership research rather than rely on the qualitative reviews of the past.

Equipped with new methods, leadership researchers revealed the following:

* Individuals can and do emerge as leaders across a variety of situations and tasks.
* Significant relationships exist between leadership and such individual traits as:
  - Intelligence.
  - Adjustment.
  - Extraversion.
  - Conscientiousness.
  - Openness to experience.
  - General self-efficacy.

While the trait theory of leadership has certainly regained popularity, its reemergence has not been accompanied by a corresponding increase in sophisticated conceptual frameworks. Specifically, scholars noted that trait theories still:

* Focus on a small set of individual attributes such as Big Five personality traits, to the neglect of cognitive abilities, motives, values, social skills, expertise, and problem-solving skills.
* Fail to consider patterns or integrations of multiple attributes.

* Do not distinguish between those leader attributes that are generally not malleable over time and those that are shaped by, and bound to, situational influences.
* Do not consider how stable leader attributes account for the Behavioural diversity necessary for effective leadership.

ATTRIBUTE PATTERN APPROACH

Considering the criticisms of the trait theory, several researchers have begun to adopt a different perspective of leader individual differences - the leader attribute pattern approach. In contrast to the traditional approach, the leader attribute pattern approach is based on theorists' arguments that the influence of individual characteristics on outcomes is best understood by considering the person as an integrated totality rather than a summation of individual variables. In other words, the leader attribute pattern approach argues that integrated constellations or combinations of individual differences may explain substantial variance in both leader emergence and leader effectiveness beyond that explained by single attributes, or by additive combinations of multiple attributes.

BEHAVIOURAL AND STYLE THEORIES

In response to the early criticisms of the trait approach, theorists began to research leadership as a set of Behaviours, evaluating the Behaviour of 'successful' leaders, determining a Behaviour taxonomy and identifying broad leadership styles. David McClelland, for example, Leadership takes a strong personality with a well developed positive ego. Not so much as a pattern of motives, but a set of traits is crucial. To lead; self-confidence and a high self-esteem is useful, perhaps even essential. Kurt Lewin, Ronald Lipitt, and Ralph White developed in 1939 the seminal work on the influence of leadership styles and performance. The researchers evaluated the performance of groups of eleven-year-old boys under different types of work climate.

In each, the leader exercised his influence regarding the type of group decision making, praise and criticism and the management of the group tasks according to three styles:

* Authoritarian,
* Democratic and
* Laissez-faire.

Authoritarian climates were characterised by leaders who make decisions alone, demand strict compliance to his orders, and dictate each step taken; future steps were uncertain to a large degree. The leader is not necessarily hostile but is aloof from participation in work and commonly offers personal praise and criticism for the work done. Democratic climates were characterised by collective decision processes, assisted by the leader. Before accomplishing tasks, perspectives are gained from group discussion and technical advice from a leader.

Members are given choices and collectively decide the division of Labour. Praise and criticism in such an environment are objective, fact minded and given by a group member without necessarily having participated extensively in the actual work. *Laissez faire* climates gave freedom to the group for policy determination without any participation from the leader. The leader remains uninvolved in work decisions unless asked, does not participate in the division of Labour, and very infrequently gives praise.

The results seemed to confirm that the democratic climate was preferred. The managerial grid model is also based on a Behavioural theory. The model was developed by Robert Blake and Jane Mouton in 1964 and suggests five different leadership styles, based on the leaders' concern for people and their concern for goal achievement. B.F. Skinner is the father of Behaviour Modification and developed the concept of positive reinforcement. Positive reinforcement occurs when a positive stimulus is presented in response to a Behaviour, increasing the likelihood of that Behaviour in the future. The following is an example of how positive reinforcement can be used in a business setting. Assume praise is a positive reinforcer for a particular employee. This employee does not show up to work on time every day.

The manager of this employee decides to praise the employee for showing up on time every day the employee actually shows up to work on time. As a result, the employee comes to work on time more often because the employee likes to be praised. In this example, praise is a positive reinforcer for this employee because the employee arrives to work on time more frequently after being praised for showing up to work on time. The use of positive reinforcement is a successful and growing technique used by leaders to motivate and attain desired Behaviours from subordinates. Organisations such as Frito-Lay, 3M, Goodrich, Michigan Bell, and Emery Air Freight have all used reinforcement to increase productivity. Empirical research covering the last 20 years suggests that reinforcement theory has a 17 per cent increase in performance. Additionally, many reinforcement techniques such as the use of praise are inexpensive, providing higher performance for lower costs.

SITUATIONAL AND CONTINGENCY THEORIES

Situational theory also appeared as a reaction to the trait theory of leadership. Social scientists argued that history was more than the result of intervention of great men as Carlyle suggested. Herbert Spencer said that the times produce the person and not the other way around. This theory assumes that different situations call for different characteristics; according to this group of theories, no single optimal psychographic profile of a leader exists. The theory, "what an individual actually does when acting as a leader is in large part dependent upon characteristics of the situation in which he functions." Some theorists started to synthesise the trait and situational approaches. Building upon the research of scholars academics began to normatise the descriptive models of leadership climates, defining three leadership styles and identifying which situations each style works better in. The authoritarian leadership style, for example, is approved in periods of crisis but fails to win the "hearts and minds" of their followers in the day-to-day management; the democratic leadership style is more adequate in situations that require consensus building; finally, the laissez faire leadership style is appreciated by the degree of freedom it provides, but as the leader does not "take charge", he can be perceived as a failure in protracted or thorny organisational problems. Thus, theorists defined the style of leadership as contingent to the situation, which is sometimes classified as contingency theory. Four contingency leadership theories appear more prominently in the recent years: Fiedler contingency model, Vroom-Yetton decision model, the path-goal theory, and the Hersey-Blanchard situational theory.

The Fiedler contingency model bases the leader's effectiveness on what Fred Fiedler called situational contingency. This results from the interaction of leadership style and situational favourableness. The theory defined two types of leader: those who tend to accomplish the task by developing good-relationships with the group and those who have as their prime concern carrying out the task itself. There is no ideal leader. Both task-oriented and relationship-oriented leaders can be effective if their leadership orientation fits the situation. When there is a good leader-member relation, a highly structured task, and high leader position power, the situation is considered a "favourable situation".

Fiedler found that task-oriented leaders are more effective in extremely favourable or unfavourable situations, whereas relationship-oriented leaders perform best in situations with intermediate favourability. Victor Vroom, in collaboration with Phillip Yetton and later with Arthur Jago, developed a taxonomy for describing leadership situations, taxonomy that was used in a normative decision model where leadership styles were connected to situational variables, defining which approach was more suitable to which situation. This approach was novel because it supported the idea that the same manager could rely on different group decision making approaches depending on the attributes of each situation. This model was later referred as situational contingency theory. The path-goal theory of leadership was developed by Robert House and was based on the expectancy theory of Victor Vroom. The essence of the theory is "the meta proposition that leaders, to be effective, engage in Behaviours that complement subordinates' environments and abilities in a manner that compensates for deficiencies and is instrumental to subordinate satisfaction and individual and work unit performance.

The theory identifies four leader Behaviours, achievement-oriented, directive, participative, and supportive, that are contingent to the environment factors and follower characteristics. In contrast to the Fiedler contingency model, the path-goal model states that the four leadership Behaviours are fluid, and that leaders can adopt any of the four depending on what the situation demands. The path-goal model can be classified both as a contingency theory, as it depends on the circumstances, but also as a transactional leadership theory, as the theory emphasises the reciprocity Behaviour between the leader and the followers. The situational leadership model proposed by Hersey and Blanchard suggests four leadership-styles and four levels of follower-development. For effectiveness, the model posits that the leadership-style must match the appropriate level of followership-development. In this model, leadership behaviour becomes a function not only of the characteristics of the leader, but of the characteristics of followers as well.

FUNCTIONAL THEORY

Functional leadership theory is a particularly useful theory for addressing specific leader behaviours expected to contribute to organisational or unit effectiveness. This theory argues that the leader's main job is to see that whatever is necessary to group needs is taken care of; thus, a leader can be said to have done their job well when they have contributed to group effectiveness and cohesion. While functional leadership theory has most often been applied to team leadership, it has also been effectively applied to broader organisational leadership as well.

In summarising literature on functional leadership These functions include:

* Environmental monitoring,
* Organising subordinate activities,
* Teaching and coaching subordinates,

* Motivating others, and
* Intervening actively in the group's work.

A variety of leadership behaviours are expected to facilitate these functions. In initial work identifying leader behaviour, Fleishman observed that subordinates perceived their supervisors' behaviour in terms of two broad categories referred to as consideration and initiating structure. Consideration includes behaviour involved in fostering effective relationships. Examples of such behaviour would include showing concern for a subordinate or acting in a supportive manner towards others. Initiating structure involves the actions of the leader focused specifically on task accomplishment. This could include role clarification, setting performance standards, and holding subordinates accountable to those standards.

TRANSACTIONAL AND TRANSFORMATIONAL THEORIES

Eric Berne first analysed the relations between a group and its leadership in terms of Transactional Analysis. The transactional leader is given power to perform certain tasks and reward or punish for the team's performance. It gives the opportunity to the manager to lead the group and the group agrees to follow his lead to accomplish a predetermined goal in exchange for something else. Power is given to the leader to evaluate, correct and train subordinates when productivity is not up to the desired level and reward effectiveness when expected outcome is reached. The transformational leader motivates its team to be effective and efficient. Communication is the base for goal achievement focusing the group on the final desired outcome or goal attainment. This leader is highly visible and uses chain of command to get the job done. Transformational leaders focus on the big picture, needing to be surrounded by people who take care of the details. The leader is always looking for ideas that move the organisation to reach the company's vision.

EMOTIONS

Leadership can be perceived as a particularly emotion-laden process, with emotions entwined with the social influence process. In an organisation, the leader's mood has some effects on his/her group.

These effects can be described in 3 levels:

* The mood of individual group members. Group members with leaders in a positive mood experience more positive mood than do group members with leaders in a negative mood. The leaders transmit their moods to other group members through the mechanism of emotional contagion. Mood contagion may be one of the psychological mechanisms by which charismatic leaders influence followers.
* The affective tone of the group. Group affective tone represents the consistent or homogeneous affective reactions within a group. Group affective tone is an aggregate of the moods of the individual members of the group and refers to mood at the group level of analysis. Groups with leaders in a positive mood have a more positive affective tone than do groups with leaders in a negative mood.
* Group processes like coordination, effort expenditure, and task strategy. Public expressions of mood impact how group members think and act. When people experience and express mood, they send signals to others. Leaders signal their goals, intentions, and attitudes through their expressions of moods. For example, expressions of positive moods by leaders signal that leaders deem progress Towards goals to be good.The group members respond to those signals cognitively and Behaviourally in ways that are reflected in the group processes.

In research about client service, it was found that expressions of positive mood by the leader improve the performance of the group, although in other sectors there were other findings. Beyond the leader's mood, her/his behaviour is a source for employee positive and negative emotions at work. The leader creates situations and events that lead to emotional response. Certain leader behaviours displayed during interactions with their employees are the sources of these affective events. Leaders shape workplace affective events. Examples – feedback giving, allocating tasks, resource distribution. Since, employee Behaviour and productivity are directly affected by their emotional states, it is imperative to consider employee emotional responses to organisational leaders. Emotional intelligence, the ability to understand and manage moods and emotions in the self and others, contributes to effective leadership in organisations. Leadership is about being responsible.

NEO-EMERGENT THEORY

The Neo-emergent leadership theory espouses that leadership is created through the emergence of information by the leader or other stakeholders, not through the true actions of the leader himself. In other words, the reproduction of information or stories form the basis of the perception of leadership by the majority. It is well known that the great naval hero Lord Nelson often wrote his own versions of battles he was involved in, so that when he arrived home in England he would receive a true hero's welcome. In modern society, the press, blogs and other sources report their own views of a leader, which may be based on reality, but may also be based on a political command, a payment, or an inherent interest of the author, media or leader. Therefore, it can be contended that the perception of all leaders is created and in fact does not reflect their true leadership qualities at all.

ENVIRONMENTAL LEADERSHIP THEORY

The environmental leadership model describes leadership from a group dynamics perspective incorporating group psychology and self awareness to nurture "Environments" that promote self-sustaining group leadership based on personal emotional gratification from the activities of the group. The Environmental Leader creates the psychological structure by which employees can find and attain this gratification through work or activity.

It stems from the idea that each individual has various environments that bring out different facets from their own

Identity, and each facet is driven by emotionally charged perceptions within each environment... The Environmental Leader creates a platform through education and awareness where individuals fill each others emotional needs and become more conscious of when, and how they affect personal and team emotional gratifications. This is accomplished by knowing why people "react" to their environment instead of act intelligently. "Environmental Leadership is not about changing the mindset of the group or individual, but in the cultivation of an environment that brings out the best and inspires the individuals in that group.

It is not the ability to influence others to do something they are not committed to, but rather to nurture a culture that motivates and even excites individuals to do what is required for the benefit of all.

It is not carrying others to the end result, but setting the surrounding for developing qualities in them to so they may carry each other. The role of an Environmental Leader is to instill passion and direction to a group and the dynamics of that group. This leader implements a psychological support system within a group that fills the emotional and developmental needs of the group.

STYLES OF LEADERSHIP

In the past several decades, management experts have undergone a revolution in how they define leadership and what their attitudes are towards it. They have gone from a very classical autocratic approach to a very creative, participative approach. Somewhere along the line, it was determined that not everything old was bad and not everything new was good. Rather, different styles were needed for different situations and each leader needed to know when to exhibit a particular approach.

Four of the most basic leadership styles are:

* Autocratic.
* Bureaucratic.
* Laissez-faire.
* Democratic.

Autocratic Leadership Style

This is often considered the classical approach. It is one in which the manager retains as much power and decision-making authority as possible. The manager does not consult employees, nor are they allowed to give any input. Employees are expected to obey orders without receiving any explanations. The motivation environment is produced by creating a structured set of rewards and punishments. This leadership style has been greatly criticised during the past 30 years. Some studies say that organisations with many autocratic leaders have higher turnover and absenteeism than other organisations. Certainly Gen X employees have proven to be highly resistant to this management style.

These studies say that autocratic leaders:

* Rely on threats and punishment to influence employees.
* Do not trust employees.
* Do not allow for employee input.

Yet, autocratic leadership is not all bad. Sometimes it is the most effective style to use.

These situations can include:

* New, untrained employees who do not know which tasks to perform or which procedures to follow.
* Effective supervision can be provided only through detailed orders and instructions.
* Employees do not respond to any other leadership style.
* There are high-volume production needs on a daily basis.
* There is limited time in which to make a decision.
* A manager's power is challenged by an employee.
* The area was poorly managed.
* Work needs to be coordinated with another department or organisation.

The autocratic leadership style should not be used when:

* Employees become tense, fearful, or resentful.
* Employees expect to have their opinions heard.
* Employees begin depending on their manager to make all their decisions.

* There is low employee morale, high turnover and absenteeism and work stoppage.

Bureaucratic Leadership Style

Bureaucratic leadership is where the manager manages "by the book" Everything must be done according to procedure or policy. This manager is really more of a police officer than a leader. He or she enforces the rules.

This style can be effective when:

* Employees are performing routine tasks over and over.
* Employees need to understand certain standards or procedures.
* Employees are working with dangerous or delicate equipment that requires a definite set of procedures to operate.
* Safety or security training.
* Is being conducted.
* Employees are performing tasks that require handling cash.

This style is ineffective when:

* Work habits form that are hard to break, especially if they are no longer useful.
* Employees lose their interest in their jobs and in their fellow workers.
* Employees do only what is expected of them and no more.

Democratic Leadership Style

The democratic leadership style is also called the participative style as it encourages employees to be a part of the decision making. The democratic manager keeps his or her employees informed about everything that affects their work and shares decision making and problem solving responsibilities. This style requires the leader to be a coach who has the final say, but gathers information from staff members before making a decision. Democratic leadership can produce high quality and high quantity work for long periods of time.

Many employees like the trust they receive and respond with cooperation, team spirit, and high morale.

Typically the democratic leader:

* Develops plans to help employees evaluate their own performance.
* Allows employees to establish goals.
* Encourages employees to grow on the job and be promoted.
* Recognises and encourages achievement.

Like the other styles, the democratic style is not always appropriate. It is most successful when used with highly skilled or experienced employees or when implementing operational changes or resolving individual or group problems.

The democratic leadership style is most effective when:

* The leader wants to keep employees informed about matters that affect them.
* The leader wants employees to share in decision-making and problem-solving duties.
* The leader wants to provide opportunities for employees to develop a high sense of personal growth and job satisfaction.
* There is a large or complex problem that requires lots of input to solve.
* Changes must be made or problems solved that affect employees or groups of employees.
* You want to encourage team building and participation.

Democratic leadership should not be used when:

* There is not enough time to get everyone's input.
* It's easier and more cost-effective for the manager to make the decision.
* The business can't afford mistakes.
* The manager feels threatened by this type of leadership.
* Employee safety is a critical concern.

Laissez-Faire Leadership Style

The laissez-faire leadership style is also known as the "hands-off" style. It is one in which the manager provides little or no direction and gives employees as much freedom as possible. All authority or power is given to the employees and they must determine goals, make decisions, and resolve problems on their own.

This is an effective style to use when:

* Employees are highly skilled, experienced, and educated.
* Employees have pride in their work and the drive to do it successfully on their own.
* Outside experts, such as staff specialists or consultants are being used and,
* Employees are trustworthy and experienced.

This style should not be used when:

* It makes employees feel insecure at the unavailability of a manager.
* The manager cannot provide regular feedback to let employees know how well they are doing.
* Managers are unable to thank employees for their good work.
* The manager doesn't understand his or her responsibilities and is hoping the employees can cover for him or her.

VARYING LEADERSHIP STYLE

While the proper leadership style depends on the situation, there are three other factors.

That also influence which leadership style to use:

* The manager's personal background. What personality, knowledge, values, ethics, and experiences does the manager have. What does he or she think will work?
* The employees being supervised. Employees are individuals with different personalities and backgrounds. The leadership style managers use will vary depending upon the individual employee and what he or she will respond best to.
* The company. The traditions, values, philosophy, and concerns of the company will influence how a manager acts.

LEADERSHIP DEVELOPMENT

Leadership development refers to any activity that enhances the quality of leadership within an individual or organisation. These activities have ranged from MBA style Programmes offered at university business schools to action learning, high-ropes courses and executive retreats.

DEVELOPING INDIVIDUAL LEADERS

Traditionally, leadership development has focused on developing the leadership abilities and attitudes of individuals. Just like people aren't all born with the ability to, say, play football like Zinedine Zidane or sing like Luciano Pavarotti, people aren't all born with the ability to lead. Different personal characteristics can help or hinder a person's leadership effectiveness and require formalised programmes for developing leadership competencies. Yet, everyone can develop their leadership effectiveness. Achieving such development takes focus, practice and persistence more akin to learning a musical instrument than reading a book. Classroom-style training and associated reading is effective in helping leaders to know more about what is involved in leading well.

However, knowing what to do and doing what you know are two very different outcomes; management expert Henry Mintzberg is one person to highlight this dilemma. It is estimated that as little as 15 per cent of learning from traditional classroom style training results in sustained Behavioural change within the workplace.

The success of leadership development efforts has been linked to three variables:

* Individual learner characteristics.
* The quality and nature of the leadership development Programme.
* Genuine support for behavioural change from the leader's supervisor.

Military officer training academies, such as the Royal Military Academy Sandhurst, go to great lengths to only accept candidates who show the highest potential to lead well. Personal characteristics that associated with successful leadership development include leader motivation to learn, a high achievement drive and personality traits such as openness to experience, an internal focus of control, and self-monitoring.

Development is also more likely to occur when the design of the development programme:

* Integrates a range of developmental experiences over a set period of time. These experiences may include 360 degree feedback, experiential classroom style Programmes, business school style coursework, executive coaching, reflective journaling, mentoring and more.
* Involve goal setting, following an assessment of key developmental needs and then evaluate the achievement of goals after a given time period.

DEVELOPING LEADERSHIP AT A COLLECTIVE LEVEL

More recently, organisations have come to understand that leadership can also be developed by strengthening the connection between, and alignment of, the efforts of individual leaders and the systems through which they influence organisational operations. This has led to a differentiation between leader development and leadership development. Leader development focuses on the development of the leader, such as the personal attributes desired in a leader, desired ways of behaving, ways of thinking or feeling. In contrast, leadership development focuses on the development of leadership as a process.

This will include the interpersonal relationships, social influence process, and the team dynamics between the leader and his/her team at the dyad level, the contextual factors surrounding the team such as the perception of the organisational climate and the social network linkages between the team and other groups in the organisation. One practical example of developing leadership specifically so as to influence an organisation's safety culture is described by Burman and Evans. Both forms of development may mutually influence each other, as exemplified in the concept of "Deep Change" in Robert E. Quinn 's 1996 book of the same title.

Leadership development can build on the development of individuals to become leaders. In addition, it also needs to focus on the interpersonal linkages between the individuals in the team. In the belief that the most important resource that an organisation possesses is the people that comprise the organisation, some organisations address the development of these resources. In contrast, the concept of "Employeeship" recognises that what it takes to be a good leader is not too dissimilar to what it takes to be a good employee. Therefore, bringing the notional leader together with the team to explore these similarities brings positive results. This approach has been particularly successful in Sweden where the power distance between manager and team is small.

SUCCESSION PLANNING

The development of "high potentials" to effectively take over the current leadership when their time comes to exit their positions is known. This type of leadership development usually requires the extensive transfer of an individual between departments. In many multinationals, it usually requires international transfer and experience to build a future leader. Succession planning requires a sharp focus on organisation's future and vision, in order to align leadership development with the future the firm aspires to create. Thus successive leadership development is based not only on knowledge and history but also on a dream. For such a plan to be successful, a screening of future leadership should be based not only on "what we know and have" but also on "what we aspire to become". Persons involved in succession planning should be current leadership representing the vision and HR executives having to translate it all into a Programme.

Meir Jacob and Amit Cohen three critical dimensions should be considered:

1. Skills and knowledge.
2. Role perception and degree of acceptance of leading role.
3. Self-efficacy.

These three dimensions should be a basis of any leadership succession programme.

TYPES OF NETWORK LEADERSHIP ROLES

There are at least eight different kinds of leadership roles in a networked organisation. Each of these can be associated with specific network *signatures* consisting of patterns of links and nodes and the social rules governing their interactions. For example, some network leaders, such as visionaries, primarily generate new information and typically do not directly request others to perform tasks for them.

They generally work in conjunction with connector and facilitator leaders who help them get their information out. Connectors, unlike visionaries, may have many symmetric dyadic interactions and act as gateways for a variety of sub-networks, whereas truth-teller leaders may only interact weakly with other members, having strong ties with a relatively small number of peers. Many of these roles can coexist in the same person.

However, as networks grow in scale and complexity, these roles often become highly differentiated and expressed as Searle's *institutional* facts.

The Exemplar or "Alpha Member"

Most peer networks, whether they are military, technological, recreational, adolescent, criminal, terrorist, artistic, professional, or athletic, are founded by individuals who exemplify the standards and qualities that characterise the best competencies of the peer network. These are the role models that others imitate. Sometimes their role can be simply symbolic, even ceremonial, but they are nonetheless important in setting the tone and culture of the organisation. Successful and charismatic founders of new organisations, from Bill Gates, Steve Jobs, and Sam Walton to Osama Bin Laden and Aum Shinrikyo, all embody values and personalities that become the values of their organisation. These leaders also exemplify the assessment criteria and set the standards for becoming a member of a network. In the military, each Service has its own types of exemplars: pilots and Seals for the Navy; Green Berets, and Rangers for the Army; and fighter pilots for the Air Force. These exemplars embody what is considered the most difficult and admired professional qualities that set that Service apart.

The Gatekeeper

For every network there are membership rules—criteria for being included, retained, elevated, and excluded. The gatekeeper decides who is in and who is out. In Congressional politics, the party leadership plays this role by deciding who gets what committee assignments and whose bills take precedence in a legislative agenda. This is a role that President Johnson as the former majority leader of the Senate understood brilliantly, while President Carter—an outsider, visionary, truth-teller, and moralist—never fully appreciated. In many military organisations, the drill sergeant often plays multiple leadership roles, acting as exemplars, enforcers, and gatekeepers. He weeds out recruits whom he believes fail to meet the standards of his unit. The gatekeeper role is especially important for elite units that seek to achieve a high degree of exclusivity based upon exceptional standards of excellence. Like the doorman to exclusive clubs, the gatekeeper role is a combination of truth-teller, applying the standard for admittance, and enforcer, denying admittance to those parties that fail the test.

The Visionary

The role of the visionary leader is to imagine futures, determine what is limiting about the present, and show what is possible in the future. Visionary leaders such as Steve Jobs, Winston Churchill, Walt Disney, Craig Venter, Billy Mitchell, and Thomas Edison are a constant fount of new ideas and are "at war with the present." Many high technology startups have been founded by visionaries, but eventually end up being run by operatives or fixers.

The visionary leader imagines new possibilities, creating new institutional facts and realities, and therefore plays a critical role in moving networked organisations in new directions. This is an absolutely critical role in the start-up or crisis phase of an organisation. However, it can also be disruptive in circumstances where continuity and execution are critical to success.

Visionaries play a vital and sometimes contentious role within the military. They are often the first to see weaknesses in prevalent military doctrine, to espouse new technologies and doctrines, and therefore, to challenge current leadership and entrenched interests. Consequently, unless they are able to prove themselves within wartime, their ideas can languish for decades.

Rare are the individuals such as Lord Nelson or Napoleon, who were both visionaries and the senior commanders. In the case of Billy Mitchell, Col. John Boyd, or even Winston Churchill, it was only later in their careers that their innovations were appreciated. However, as the nature of warfare today is in constant transition with respect both to doctrine and new technologies, the visionary will have increased influence. The visionary role is best coevolved with that of the truth-teller.

The Truth-Teller

In every network organisation, someone has to keep the network honest. This entails the very challenging task of identifying free riders and cheaters. In knowledge-based organisations, it is also about ferreting out half-truths, spin, blunders, and lies. Such a leadership role can become easily compromised.

Like the accounting function in a corporation or the judicial function in the legal system, truth-tellers can lose their independence, and Hence, effectiveness. Since, these are often the first roles to go in times of stress, successful leadership is exemplified here by independence, transparency, accuracy, and candor in the face of enormous pressure. As Tennyson's ode to Wellington eloquently and astutely expresses, truth telling and resistance to the lure of fame go hand in hand and are a critical and enduring signature of effective leadership.

One of the arguments for modesty in leadership is that the lure of celebrity and its attendant rewards can compromise independence and hence, credibility. Therefore, if a leader is to be an effective truthteller, he or she must also be credible, and even the hint of self-dealing can undermine his effectiveness. The challenges are especially acute and consequential within military organisations. If credibility breaks down, trust soon becomes the next casualty, and then the overall effectiveness of the chain of command.

The admonition "Don't shoot the messenger" is taken from military experience and reflects the high potential cost of reporting unwanted information. In response to such pressures, the military developed the doctrine of "ground truth" after the Vietnam War. The truth telling goal is to provide authenticated and accurate reporting of the outcomes of missions.

It can take enormous courage to resist the inevitable pressures of peers and superiors to report what they want to be known, rather then the truth of the matter. Being a truth-teller can be highly unpopular and a long road to advancement.

Even highly established and previously unchallenged military institutions can come under enormous pressure for truth telling. The armed forces newspaper, *stars and stripes* , undertook its own "ground truth investigation" into morale in Iraq in 2003 and was widely censured by some members of Congress and threatened with a reduced budget for its reporting. Similarly, the success and credibility of the enquiry into the alleged tortures within Abu Ghraib and elsewhere within Iraq and Afghanistan will depend upon individuals assuming very strong truth-teller leadership roles.

The Fixer

This is an individual who knows how to get things done and measures him or herself not just by how many people they might know, but rather how they can get things done that others cannot. Such individuals are results oriented. They "know where the bodies are buried" and what "makes people tick." In politics, they are the operatives, the Mr. Fix-its. They are all about opening and closing loops—getting tasks done. In Tennyson's words, they abide by the "rugged maxims hewn from life."

They are without illusions and are inherently pragmatic. They may interact with a range of other network leaders—visionaries, truth-tellers, and connectors—but always with a concrete outcome in mind. Within the military there is the archetype of the "scrounger," an individual who is highly skilled at finding and assembling "found" materials, people, and resources to solve a variety of human and mission needs, from chocolate and silk stockings during WWII, to scrap iron as armor platting for Humvees in Iraq. Fixers are gifted improvisers, what the French call "bricolagers," who take common available materials and repurpose them into something useful.

In contrast to those who work through formal channels and depend upon approved procedures, fixers typically are "rule benders" and work through informal networks. Within the British Army during the late Victorian period, the Quartermaster was famous for the orderly but creative acquisition of supplies under the most trying and unpredictable of circumstances.

The Connector

These network leaders participate in multiple social networks, connecting not only with a large number of members, but a highly diverse number of members as well. They are known for having numerous friends, connections, and contacts—for being consummate networkers. Like the visionary leaders, they can introduce variety and options into a network through the diversity of people with whom they interact.

They are critical for identifying and accessing new resources and helping to get a message out. By building links across network boundaries, they can help a networked organisation break out of the "lock ins" of scale-free networks and introduce greater diversity, and Hence, robustness. During WWII, General Eisenhower as the Supreme Allied Commander developed a reputation as a highly accomplished connector leader by virtue of his ability to relate to the different interests and cultural styles of the allied commanders.

He was able to make and sustain connections among contending parties in order to keep the alliance together and on course. He was also able to exercise significant control over those whose primary allegiances were to different military organisations.

The Enforcer

In smaller networks, this role is often combined with that of the gatekeeper and even the truth-teller. However, in larger networks it is an independent role. Enforcement can mean physical coercion, but more often entails psychological or peer pressure.

Like the truth-teller function, independence and transparency are critical for overall network effectiveness. Clearly, force and military means are the enforcement methods of last resort, but are necessary in order to buttress other forms of enforcement, which can vary from guilt and shame to legal redress. Most networks have their own forms of redress and enforcement that entail exclusion.

The power of ostracism in Greek city-states, for example, was extremely effective because it not only removed an individual's right of protection but destroyed their social identity as well. An exceptional example of a senior commander acting to enforce discipline across all levels of command was the Duke of Wellington's order during the Peninsular Campaign in 1807. Wellington issued an order that any breach in military discipline towards the treatment of the Spanish civilians and military would result in an immediate flogging and hanging. Paul Kennedy, this order was enforced with impartiality and force and was instrumental to Wellington's success.

The Facilitator

In order for a network to grow and evolve, it must be able to add new members and reach across network boundaries in order to do so. The facilitator role is pivotal in creating communities or sub-networks that provide the greatest form of network value. By assuming a leadership role in helping others, facilitators create value that benefits an entire network or community, whereas a connector, while playing a similar value creation role, appropriates value to himself and only indirectly benefits the overall group.

The role of facilitator in many respects resembles that of the "community coordinator" in the development of communities of practice, a method developed for helping to create and leverage knowledge. Within the military, this role is filled primarily as a staff function to a commander, and therefore may not appear to have the caché of the connector or visionary leadership roles. However, in networked organisational structures where decisionmaking is be more distributed and less hierarchical, this leadership role is vital to coordinating and enabling other actors and decisionmakers.

In the case of networked organisation, the facilitator role and the associated skills of enabling cooperation and self-organisation will play a more critical role than within current hierarchical organisations. When self-synchronisation depends upon peer-based cooperation, the facilitator role is a prerequisite for effective operations.

NETWORK STRUCTURES AND LEADERSHIP ROLES

Social networks self-organise to acquire and allocate resources such as information, goods, favours, access, privileges, and protection. As discussed earlier, the specialisation of roles in social networks has been demonstrated to have strong long-term survival value, and therefore has been biologically encoded through evolutionary forces as innate psychological or personality traits.

These traits are reflected in how people read social cues, detect cheaters, create and share ideas, and form affinities with strangers. In addition to having innate social exchange competencies, some alpha or exemplar individuals are especially proficient at a skill or exhibit a prised trait that warrants widespread emulation and imitation. Typically, alpha individuals have a special physical prowess, physical attraction, intelligence, social proficiency, or some combination of these traits. When one considers Cosmides and Tooby's findings on innate social exchange algorithms and Damasio's analysis of the neuro-physiology of social emotions combined with Dunbar's studies on the role of grooming and language in social groups, a compelling argument can be made that these different roles are an evolutionary stable strategy that makes possible the efficient functioning of any self-organising social network.

Few of these network roles have any intrinsic individual value. However, when combined with other roles, they enable the organisation and functioning of complex networks of exchange relationships. Leadership in this context can be regarded as a proficiency in any one or combination of these network roles.

In this sense, some individuals may have greater innate talents than others, but the effectiveness of these gifts is dependent upon the overall qualities of the network and the roles of other members of the network. Network leadership roles assume different levels of importance depending upon the phase of evolution of a networked organisation. This fact is often not fully appreciated in the business leadership literature where visionary leaders are periodically revered and reviled depending upon the ebb and flow of their company's earnings.

The value of such leadership roles might be more fruitfully understood by attempting to determine the conditions under which a visionary role is adaptive and when it is not, thereby recognising that it is one of many combinations of leadership roles that is required. Likewise, the absence of certain critical leadership roles, such as truth telling, can contribute to the failure of corporate governance or the excesses of overly zealous visionaries.

A further example of the importance of different kinds of network leadership roles can be found in the failure of large organisations to manage relationships across functional and organisational boundaries. Here the high "agency costs" of coordinating across organisational or functional boundaries is largely due to the absence of leaders who are connectors and who know how to interact and affiliate with third parties to build trust. These are what Burton identifies as the *tertiaries*, the brokers between organisational networks. In each of these examples, there are leadership roles whose value and appropriateness depend upon the state of the network.

The effective governance of a networked organisation should therefore involve knowing the status of the organisational network, being able to assess the strengths and weaknesses of different roles, and then allocating the appropriate leadership assets to improve the overall performance of the network.

This is something that Louis Gerstner understood when he first took the job of CEO at IBM. Initially, he was criticised for being insufficiently visionary, to which he responded that the company had become too enamored of its own vision and detached from reality. What was needed, he contended, was a good dose of truth telling, an operational overhaul, and then a new vision. These were different leadership roles that he seemed to switch in and out of comfortably and effectively.

JOINT LEADERSHIP AND META-LEADERSHIP

Just as there are different leadership roles *within* social networks, there are also metaleadership roles that cut *across* networked organisations. When it comes to leading across different organisations, such as coalition partners, partnerships, alliances, joint command, or multi-agency missions, a new set of meta-leadership roles comes into play. These roles are different from those in a hierarchical organisation where subordinates are required to execute orders or follow management directives and are held accountable for doing so.

In joint command efforts, on the other hand, collaboration is peer-based, consensual, and mutual. There are no prior histories for building reciprocity, trust, or transparency. Therefore these have to be created anew over time.

Moreover, as the leadership role is more one of governance than of command, the issue becomes how to cooperatively develop metrics and protocols that respect the integrity of each of the respective organisations. That being said, creating new meta-networks is much the same as creating any peer networked organisation, except that the units are significantly larger and each has its own distinctive culture.

Certain leadership roles have to be established for all participants—specifically, what Behaviours or traits best exemplify the qualities and standard being sought of the meta-network. Since, leadership in joint efforts typically rotates over time, exemplar leadership roles should be filled by those who have qualities that are not closely identified with any one particular organisation or Service. Rather, an effort should be made to give this networked organisation its own independent identity.

An early visionary can act as the exemplar member and personify the desired qualities, thereby setting a precedent for others to follow. However, there should be an effort to identify other network leadership roles and the associated metrics and protocols that the different representatives of the joint organisations would undertake.

This networked approach to joint leadership differs significantly from the traditional, hierarchical Napoleonic staff codes wherein a small number of fixed staff personnel with limited specialisation perform most of the joint leadership support functions. The networked approach more closely resembles former Marine General Anthony Zinni's proposal for a Modular Commander Center, which stresses specialisation and flexibility. As a former CENTCOM commander, General Zinni recognised that commanders had variable missions requiring combinations of different functions, resources, and partners.

In effect, the command structure had to be agile enough to adapt to the different circumstances of the mission from unilateral humanitarian missions to coalition-based major combat. The combinations of skills for each differed significantly and therefore would entail specialised social network protocols and combinations of different network leadership roles and skills. Under such conditions where it is difficult for one coalition partner to exert authority over another, as many of the organisations are sovereign and independent, the only form of effective control is the selective exclusion of partners or the minimisation of their role.

The qualities of the connector and the facilitator network leadership roles are especially important at this senior level and have their own specialised "social protocols" and skills for setting and coordinating joint missions.

LEADERSHIP AND SCOPE OF CONTROL

In hierarchical and bureaucratic organisations, leadership is often confused with scope of control and authority—power. In such organisations, leaders are given the latitude, even the expectation, to exercise significant control at all levels of the organisation. This is often expressed in budgetary terms: the willingness and the ability to control, cut, or redirect a subordinate's budget.

The power of a superior is virtually absolute in such organisations as they have the authority to project control all the way down the organisation. There are no autonomous layers, and in this sense, decision rights are not protected but revocable and alienable. Usurping local control and autonomy through topdown budgetary restrictions can undermine the efficacy and self-organising capabilities of an organisation and thereby prevent it from effectively learning and adapting.

The integrity of local rules and allocation protocols have to be maintained, and while there can be a decrement in the gross resources available to a subordinate or sub-network, these resources should not be explicitly earmarked or constrained, as such interventions will prevent the network from being self-organising.

This is the same type of issue as the requirement for tactical autonomy in a command system, where the supra-ordinate strategic layer determines the objectives and the assets to be allocated, but the subordinate commander has the authority and the responsibility to make the tactical decisions.

In a networked organisational model where there are also independent layers of selforganisation and different types of protocols for interaction, the transecting of layers by a supra-ordinate to a subordinate, in effect, micromanaging and second-guessing, is dangerous for the well-being of the network.

It transforms a collective, networked asset into an episodic individualised asset, thereby undermining trust and accountability. This may happen out of frustration by a senior manager wanting to get things done and going outside official channels.

However, in every case it undermines the collective capability of a networked organisation to self-organise. For this reason, it is very important to move away from the individualised model of leadership and authority and to develop governance mechanisms that build up the overall ongoing assets of the networked organisation. Network leadership roles that are held accountable to the interests of the whole will yield far more efficient, effective, and accountable organisational structures than those that are governed through sporadic and episodic interventions that undermine local authority.

SOCIAL CURRENCIES AND SENIOR LEADERSHIP

One of the innate social exchange algorithms that all people seem to have is the ability to trade favours in order to build social relationships and systems of mutual obligation. In the traditional societies long-studied by anthropologists, this is manifested in gift exchange systems where social obligations are created and repaid through the exchange of gifts. Even without a physical accounting of who owes what to whom, people are very proficient at keeping score, not only in terms of knowing how much is owed, but what is owed—favours, goods, payments, or special privileges.

The exchange of gossip is a very powerful "social glue" and plays a vital role in keeping a group together and informed of the status of its members. Different social groups have different systems of exchange, different kinds of tokens—what we call *social currencies* – for creating affinities, building relationships of mutual advantage, and enabling the valuing and trading of different kinds of skills, privileges, and goods. In other words, people in social and work networks create their own markets around their particular skills and resources and use these transactions to build social cohesion and trust within and across social networks.

Social currencies are typically denominated in the types of skills and resources that define a social network. For example, in some *professional* networks, the prevalent social currencies are knowledge, expertise, and access to important events and people; in other *soical* networks, social status and privilege of membership can be the principle inducement.

In many cases, the social currencies that fuel the many informal networks that make up businesses and formal organisations are often more powerful than other more traditional forms of inducement, such as financial incentives. Indeed, most large organisations are made up of peer networks of constituencies who, by virtue of shared skills and mutual interests, act more on the behalf of their network than for benefit of the overall organisation. Members within these networks realise that their peer relationships have more influence over their future success than the formal organisation or enterprise.

Successful senior leaders, for example, know what the currencies are for such peer networks and they know when and how to cash in their chips to advance their interests and those of their peer networks.

This kind of behaviour is often dismissed as politics, and when undertaken in an opaque, self-serving, and episodic manner, can completely undermine the trust and efficacy of an organisation. Nonetheless, it is through such shrewd negotiations that truly effective and credible senior leaders arise, and it is as natural as breathing for most accomplished senior leaders.

These senior leaders, however, tend to combine for a variety of leadership roles, with particular emphasis on connector leadership skills. They tend not to be visionaries or truth-tellers, who by bent of personality can be so committed to their vision and truth telling that they fail to build the requisite social capital with their peers to advance to more senior levels. Examples in the military are Billy Mitchell, George Patton, and John A. Boyd. The leadership roles that emerge under these circumstances are the connector, fixer, and facilitator.

Such leadership roles seem better adapted to reading and responding to complex social signals and building the requisite social capital to assume senior leadership roles. In this camp, one would find Dwight Eisenhower, Omar Bradley, and George Marshall. Only under the rarest of circumstances do you find military leaders who combine visionary roles and skills with those of the connector, exemplar, and fixer: Lord Nelson, the Duke of Wellington, Carl Phillip von Clausewitz, Otto von Bismarck, and George Marshall.

The challenge is not to eradicate such Behaviour, but to harness it by making the coining, exchange, accrual, and cashing in of social currencies wholly transparent and driven by criteria that support the mission and capabilities of the entire organisation. One of the most ubiquitous and natural of social currencies is reputation.

It is not surprising that it is the driving force behind so many different Open Source and peer production networks. Individuals can have multiple reputations and a reputation in one field may not be easily transferable into another, because reputation is highly contextspecific and subject to the conditions of local rules.

Nonetheless, just as trust can be transitive—*e.g.*, I trust whom you trust—especially if it is predicated on strong ties established over long periods of time, so can reputation be transitive even when circumstances may not warrant it. For example, someone who is a great hockey player may not be a great businessperson, but because of the desire of one group to affiliate with another, reputation points or social currencies garnered in one area are often convertible into another.

Careers can often be built by leveraging a highly visible success in one area of endeavor to a succession of successes in other areas of endeavor such as athletics, business, academia, politics, and public service. The challenge is to trade up and to increase the cumulative value of a personal currency.

Great "cross network players" include George Washington, Benjamin Franklin, Henry Kissinger, Ronald Reagan, Arnold Schwarzenegger, and Rupert Murdock. A remarkable fact is the extent to which high reputation ratings are transferable across domains, especially in the case of "world class" ratings where Nobel Laureates, NBA athletes, film stars, and media commentators can form a common peer group, irrespective of glaringly different competencies.

It would seem that extremely high competency creates a peer network of celebrity and achievement. In terms of building robust social networks that offer the right combination of leadership roles to achieve a larger organisational purpose, what might be good for the individual may not be good for the organisation. Visionaries, for instance, may provide needed innovation and achieve significant personal and organisational success through their visions. Yet if such visions are not challenged by truth-teller leaders and held accountable by enforcers, they may result in "false" successes and inappropriate learnings at the cost of the organisation's success.

Visionary leaders, on the other hand, would have moved on to other organisations and social networks based upon their proclaimed "success". Similarly, an excess of truth telling and enforcement leadership can stifle both innovation and risk taking, just as an excess of connector leadership within private firms can result in acquisitions that are neither strategic nor synergistic.

Associate Dean of the Yale School of Management and head of the CEO Institute, companies tend to go through a succession of CEO leadership roles without a coherent understanding of how they relate to either one another or to the interest of the corporation and its shareholders.

A NETWORK DEFINITION OF LEADERSHIP

One of the great unknowns in the business and organisational development literature is what accounts for great leadership. It is one of the softest areas of the social sciences, having defied rigorous analysis for decades. Yet, leadership is considered one of the key ingredients for the success of any organisation. The position taken here is that leadership is both born and nurtured. The evidence for the biological and evolutionary basis underlying the personality associated with leadership is compelling and growing. Individuals have innately different leadership capacities in the same way that they have different mental and physical capacities.

These personality traits are some of the genetic variables that evolution periodically and randomly shuffles. But what makes a personality trait—such as the ability to interpret emotional cues, to connect with other people, to detect cheaters, to gossip and trade favours—a property of the social network are the rules that govern how individual members interact and cooperate.

In this sense, leadership is a network effect that can result in highly responsive and effective leaders, or contrarily, degradation into kleptocracy or demagoguery.

On the other hand, if networked organisations can be designed that select for certain leadership roles and competencies that can be measured, evaluated, and improved upon, then leadership ceases to be an ineffable quality, but becomes a tangible asset that can be learned, improved upon, and replicated.

Table 2.1 summarises some of the potential metrics of network leadership that are associated with the eight different leadership roles. These lists are not meant to be definitive, but rather illustrative of how explicit network metrics might be related to both the definition network roles and the self-management of those rules through the appropriate metrics and feedback.

Table. 2.1 Network Properties of Leadership.

Network Roles	Signature Pattern	Types of Links	Performance Metrics	Social Currencies
Exemplar	star, asymmetric	inform, challenge, assert	independence, trust, reach, completion	expertise, reputation reputation, rate, trust,
	access transparency gateway, hub, weak links, power law	Gatekeeper uninvite	asymmetric, independence, completion, reputation	invite, offer, access, information, reputation
Visionary	star, sparse asymmetric, strong ties, weak links	inform, question, challenge, assert	social capital , reputation, initiation, reach, trust	expertise, information, reputation
Truth-Teller	dense, sub-networks, strong ties,	question, request, inform, assess, challenge	independence, reputation, transparency, trust	reputation, trust
Fixer	strong ties, weak links, hub, power law	request, offer, question, assess, directive	completion rate reputation, reach reputation Connector	access, goods, services, income,
	symmetric, gateway, weak links, small world	inform, access, invite, offer, request	density, diversity, redundancy, reach, trust	access, favours, reputation
Enforcer	strong ties, subnetwork, power law	directives, compliance, request, question	completion rate reputation, transparency, trust	access, favours, reputation
Facilitator	gateway, sparse, GFN	invite, request, offer	completion rate diversity, initiation, reputation	reputation, access, favours

SIGNATURE PATTERN

Much of the research on social networks stresses the fact that an individual's role in a social network is dependent upon their structural position in the network. Individuals who act as go-betweens or connectors are typically seen as having a network signature measured in terms of how many other members are linked to them and the directionality of these links.

The field of social network analysis is still in its early phases of development, and there are many different types of network measures: density, power laws, hub-and-spoke, small world effects, reach, strong ties, weak ties, stars, subnetworks, clusters, clumpiness, constraints, redundancy, effective sise, etc., These measures for the most part ignore the type of links and try to derive a description of a network principally from its topology. As Barabasi observed in noting the limitations of his own analysis of scale-free networks and as Watts noted in his critique of small world effects, the types of links are very important, as are the rules governing the addition and removal of links. Hence, a description in terms of structure alone is insufficient.

TYPES OF LINKS: TAGGED

The fact that two parties are only removed by three to six links is no guarantee that one party can access another. It all depends upon the nature of the links. Not everyone can or ever will have access to one another. There are social, cultural, and economic rules that preclude certain forms of interaction. More importantly, for the purposes for understanding network leadership roles, the tagging of the links is associated with the nature of the leadership role. Visionaries' characteristically originate informational links, and, unlike fixers, are not in the business of asking people to commit to completing tasks, whereas gatekeepers are periodically inviting and uninviting people to join a group. The notion of tagged links as discussed here is very similar to Searle's notion of "speech acts," forms of dialogue that people use to get other people to do things. This is a fertile and highly developed field of linguistics—discourse analysis and pragmatics—that offers significant promise for identifying the grammars of interactions among members of a social network. There are rules or social protocols for the addition and removal of combinations of such links, thereby making most complex social networks not scalefree.

PERFORMANCE METRICS

Given the visibility that being a member of a network provides and the opportunity to track and measure interactions, it then becomes possible to provide relatively simple, straightforward, empirically based measures related to the quality of leadership. For example, a leader should not lose track of people, resources, or projects, but have a high completion rate for the number of commitments or "loops" that he has initiated. Measures can tell how many loops remain open, how fast they are being closed, and who is the bottleneck. In a world of such visibility, there can be real accountability. Perhaps the initial metrics are not correct and do not reflect true performance. They then could be modified over time through feedback, and adjusted to drive the desired Behaviours.

As was noted in the earlier analysis of peer-to-peer networks, reputation is a widely shared performance metric and a profound driver of Behaviour. There are more sophisticated measures such as reciprocity and social capital measures, but every performance measure would have to be adjusted for the particular needs and circumstances of the networked organisation. This can be an important measure because each network and leadership role evolves its own social currency, and these currencies are relational measures indicating the status of an individual's relationships with others in the network. The ability to amass significant amounts of social currencies can translate into effective leadership. The ability to convert from one social currency account into another can greatly facilitate a leadership role, such as a connector or a fixer. This is an important dimension of network interactions and needs to be understood in order to direct overall network Behaviours.

DEVELOPING NETWORK LEADERS

VISIBILITY AND DIGITISATION

As more and more interactions become digitised and observable, opportunities abound for using the naturally occurring data about the volume and the nature of the interactions among members of network organisations. Collaborative technologies, as simple and ubiquitous as e-mail, make it possible to make visible the millions of social interactions among the participants in networked organisations and thereby gain insight and eventual control over how members manage their work relationships. Not only is it possible to capture data about who is interacting with whom, but it is also possible through analytics to identify some of the emergent network leadership roles. Simple modifications to existing collaborative platforms make it possible to identify the network signatures of different types of leadership roles.

By making different members' Behaviours visible to one another, and by developing metrics for rating leadership performance, many of the techniques that are used in peer production systems—Open Source, eBay, and even MMORPGs—can be applied to the self-synchronised management of networked organisation. For example when setting up multifunctional or cross-organisational teams through e-mail, it was possible for all the members to see who communicated with whom about what topics and how frequently. A new kind of self-enforcing accountability could be introduced.

Furthermore, by providing metrics of responsiveness, connectedness, loop closing, and peer ratings, not only would shared awareness be increased but new forms of self-synchronisation would emerge. As more data on the interactions of social networks becomes available, it should not be too long before network leadership roles are identified in much the same way that different roles are identified in online games and peer production systems. It is just a matter of time before network leadership roles become digital, and by virtue of their becoming digital become measurable, teachable, and systematically deployed to maximise network performance.

IDENTIFY PERFORMANCE METRICS FOR NETWORK LEADERS

Social network analysis has identified some of the preliminary network structures associated with different kinds of leadership roles, such as the importance of connectors and hubs in network organisations, or how small world effects can be achieved. With the advent of social software to manage social interactions, form *ad hoc* groups, close decision loops, and enable self-synchronisation Behaviours, leadership qualities that had been unmanageable intangibles for so long can be measured, improved, and taught in a way that was never before possible. With the wide-scale adoption of RFID and mote technologies for tracking physical assets in real time, and the enormous strides in information sharing, improved awareness, collaboration, and self-synchronisation demonstrated by the war in Iraq, the time is not so distant when leadership roles will be measured and tracked digitally and become an integral part in how networked organisations are managed. These cumulative innovations will significantly reduce agency costs and improve the flexibility and productivity of large-scale organisations by orders of magnitude. New metrics will make it possible to measure the degree of trust, reciprocity, successes, failures, social capital, diversity, network value, etc., within an edge organisation. By making all assets—physical, human, content, and interactions— observable and providing for the selective disclosure of information and the dynamic allocation and revocation of security access, it will be possible to have much more secure and robust networked organisations.

CAREER PATHS

In order for new models of network leadership to be adopted and become an integral part of networked organisations, there have to be clear career paths that reward the skills of network leadership as a recognised part of career development. In military organisations where the alpha leadership role is still wedded to certain traditional combat roles, identifying new alpha roles that exemplify important and valued competencies outside those of the traditional military culture could prove challenging. In forms of warfare that are increasingly informational, analytic, sensemaking, and collaborative, communication and interaction skills are becoming increasing important.

New kinds of competencies will be selected and need to be rapidly incorporated into the training of all recruits. By having explicit, real-time measures not only of important leadership traits but also the demand for different types of leadership roles, human resource departments will have an easier time not only in developing credible and practical work performance criteria, but also in anticipating the demand for current and new types of leaders and skills. As suggested earlier, through the real-time content analysis and tagging of messages, primarily e-mail and instant messaging, it would be possible to differentiate visionary leadership roles from truth-tellers. The analysis might reveal a dearth of truth telling interactions and that visionary-type communications dominate the interactions within the social network, leading to bad decisions and failed missions.

Individuals could be evaluated in terms of how well they are able to fulfil different network leadership roles and recommended for the roles that they are best suited for. There are specific metrics associated with different types of leadership roles and these measures could derived from naturally occurring metadata that are the byproduct of e-mail interactions. Given these capabilities in the future, not only could there be a "real-time inventory and stocking system" for leadership skills and roles, but real-time systems for evaluating the performance of human assets and knowing when to replace or upgrade them. Such metrics will also be used to conduct forensic analyses of different missions where there have been leadership successes, failures, or the need for new kinds of leadership roles or combinations of roles. Given the explicitness of the leadership models, lessons learned from one networked organisation can be rapidly applied to another, thereby accelerating organisational learning and innovation adoption.

LEADERSHIP IN THE LIBRARY AND INFORMATION ENVIRONMENT

ANTECEDENTS

The subject of leadership has been described as a very imperative one that can never be over-flogged in management research. More imperative is the relevance of the theme in library and information management profession. While literature abound on the topic in management research, books on the subject as it relates to the library and information services are still terse. Western researchers even affirmed this and noted that not until the recent times that we have journal articles and short communications on the subject in LIS literature. General observation revealed that formal leadership training, if not totally absent in our library and information establishments, is very scarce.

EXIGENCIES

There is concern within the library profession that we are short of leaders. Why is this such a common lament. Those of us who are responsible for recruitment in our organisations often get together to scratch our heads and complain about the apparent lack of colleagues within the profession who will take up leadership roles. Why is this? The quote simply leads us to the first statement of exigency that:

* There is a dearth of library and information profession leaders.

Of course, leadership is also hard work – managing, persuading, motivating, inspiring others is not easy, although it can definitely be rewarding. I suspect many people are scared off by what is required....

The second statement of exigency is that:

* Leadership qualities, skills, and competencies are hard to come by.

One theory is that the typical value set of those who work in libraries are not compatible with managing people or managing physical resources such as budgets, or operating confidently in a political and business environment.

Some blame the library qualification providers for not attracting the right people.

The third statement of exigency is that:

* Even if people are not born leaders, the library and information schools should do better in teaching leadership skills to prospective library and information practitioners.

Librarianship as a profession has entered an area where its workforce is ageing and its leadership is becoming more "graying".

Fifty eight percent of librarians in the U.S. are projected to reach the retirement age of 65 between 2005 and 2019 and forty percent of library directors plan to retire in less than nine years. There is also an international trend of graying.

In Australia, over 52 per cent of librarians are currently more than 45 years old. If they retire, at the age of 60, then about half of the population of Australian librarians are expected to retire within the next 10 to 15 years.

The fourth statement of exigency as derived from the above is that:

* The library and information system need succession planning – Hence, the need for leaders.

To meet the demands of today's fast-paced and competitive business environment, people at all levels are being asked to step up and assume leadership behaviours . . . companies are investing millions of dollars annually in leadership development training to meet this challenge.

The fifth statement of exigency is that:

* The library and information system profession should take a cue from the business and corporate world by having leadership development agenda.

ISSUES IN LEADERSHIP IN THE LIBRARY AND INFORMATION ENVIRONMENT: FOCUS ON LIBRARY DIRECTORS

Despite all the theoretical bases for leadership, the leadership role of a leader cannot be divulged from his basic functions in a specific situation. Therefore, for practicability, this portion of this presentation will hang essentially on the propositions of Versosa as depicting the functional/leadership roles of the library leadership.

The highlights as submitted in her presentation are given as thus:

* Leadership is just one dimension of the managers work.

* It involves "the exercise of social influence by infusing the parent organisation with purpose and direction in order to achieve its goals.
* Leadership requires that the library director should influence members of the parent institutions to provide resources in order to:
  - Support expansion plans.
  - Accept the goals of the library as valid and deserving support.
* The 3 dimensions used to measure library leadership are:
  i. Leader activities.
  ii. Management of organisational change and
  iii. Reputational Effectiveness.

Leader Activities:

* Managerial role activities.
* Professional activities and involvement.
* Membership on community committees.
* Strategies for influencing the environment.

The managerial role/activities are further broken into six:

* Which involves directing the work of subordinates; integrating subordinates goals with the librarys goals and objectives; allocating human resources to tasks; evaluating subordinates job performance; resolving conflicts between subordinates and providing new staff with training.
* Involves attending social functions for contacts; attendance at conferences/meetings; maintaining informal communication networks; and relating with people outside.
* Includes initiating new ideas for services and operations; keeping up with professional trends/changes; keeping abreast of technological developments; scanning the environment for new opportunities to improve services/ operations; collecting information about users touring facilities to observe and reading reports of other units.
* Involves planning and implementing changes in the

library, initiating change in the library and solving problems by instituting changes in the library.

* Includes serving as an expert or advising people outside the library; keeping others abreast of developments in the library, attending to correspondences, and serving on committees, and representing the library.
* Changes in organisational domain *vis-a-vis* other community/cognate entities; Internal changes

REPUTATIONAL EFFECTIVENESS

Includes considerations of:

* Years in managerial positions.
* Libraries worked in.
* Continuing education.
* Professional journals scanned/read.
* No. of publications.
* Membership of Association, and
* Services to University/Parent Establishment.

THE LIBRARY/INFORMATION PROFESSIONALS LEADERSHIP AGENDA/STRATEGY

The following initiatives are desirable and could be found rewarding:

* Creation of awareness for need of leadership development skills among professionals.
* Self-development in leadership skills by Librarians and Information Professionals.
* Integration of leadership development into the library/information centre strategic planning.
* Leadership Development Programme to run through the ladder
* Library and Information Schools to integrate Leadership Skills development into their curricula.
* Need for librarians and information professionals to maintain strong network within and without their organisation to enhance development of skills and knowledge.

CONCLUSION

Leadership is essentially a subject of management research. It is however a theme that is relevant to all human endeavours. Business enterprises and corporations have embraced the application of leadership principles and have found them to be agents of productivity and profitability. The time is therefore ripe for the Library and Information Professionals, particularly in this part of the world, to take a cue from the latter s experiences to enhance professionalism, information service delivery as well as social/educational relevance of practitioners. The leadership qualities of a person create a niche for him and a combination of leadership competencies of managers in the workplace brings corporate success. It is also expedient to add that the phenomenon of the knowledge society has made cross-fertilisation of ideas imperative in the process of knowledge acquisition. This, without mincing words, is the surest way of survival in an extremely competitive world.

3

Planning

CONCEPT

Planning in organisations and public policy is both the organisational process of creating and maintaining a plan; and the psychological process of thinking about the activities required to create a desired goal on some scale. As such, it is a fundamental property of intelligent Behaviour. This thought process is essential to the creation and refinement of a plan, or integration of it with other plans, that is, it combines forecasting of developments with the preparation of scenarios of how to react to them. An important, albeit often ignored aspect of planning, is the relationship it holds with forecasting. Forecasting can be described as predicting what the future will look like, whereas planning predicts what the future should look like.

The term is also used for describing the formal procedures used in such an endeavor, such as the creation of documents, diagrams, or meetings to discuss the important issues to be addressed, the objectives to be met, and the strategy to be followed. Beyond this, planning has a different meaning depending on the political or economic context in which it is used. Two attitudes to planning need to be held in tension: on the one hand we need to be prepared for what may lie ahead, which may mean contingencies and flexible processes. On the other hand, our future is shaped by consequences of our own planning and actions. The counterpart to planning is spontaneous order. Planning is a process for accomplishing purposes. It is a blue print of business growth and a road map of development. It helps in deciding objectives both in quantitative and qualitative terms. It is setting of goals on the basis of objectives and keeping in the resources.

WHAT SHOULD A PLAN BE?

A plan should be a realistic view of the expectations. Depending upon the activities, a plan can be long range, intermediate range or short range. It is the framework within which it must operate. For management seeking external support, the plan is the most important document and key to growth. Preparation of a comprehensive plan will not guarantee success, but lack of a sound plan will almost certainly ensure failure. Planning can be summarised in 3 easy steps:

1. choosing a destination,
2. evaluating alternative routes, and
3. deciding the specific course of your plan.

PURPOSE OF A PLAN

Just as no two organisations are alike, so also their plans. It is therefore important to prepare a plan keeping in view the necessities of the enterprise. A plan is an important aspect of business.

It serves the following three critical functions:

* Helps management to clarify, focus, and research their business's or project's development and prospects.
* Provides a considered and logical framework within which a business can develop and pursue business strategies over the next three to five years.
* Offers a benchmark against which actual performance can be measured and reviewed.

IMPORTANCE OF THE PLANNING PROCESS

A plan can play a vital role in helping to avoid mistakes or recognise hidden opportunities. Preparing a satisfactory plan of the organisation is essential. The planning know the business and that they have thought through its development in terms of products, management, finances, and most importantly, markets and competition. Planning helps in forecasting the future, makes the future visible to some extent. It bridges between where we are and where we want to go. Planning is looking ahead.

FEATURES

On the basis of the definition of planning, its following features can be identified:

* Planning is a process rather than behaviour at a given point of time. This process determines the future course of action.
* Planning is future oriented It is primarily concerned with looking into future. It requires forecasting of future situation in which the organisation has to function. Therefore, correct forecasting of future situation leads to correct decisions about future course of actions.
* Planning involves selection of suitable course of action. This means that there are several alternatives for achieving a particular objective or set of objectives. However, all of them are not equally feasible and suitable for the organisation.
* Planning is undertaken at all levels of the organisation because all levels of management are concerned with the determination of future course of action. However, its role increases at successively higher levels of management. Moreover, planning at different levels may be different in the context that at the top management level, managers are concerned about the totality of the organisation and tries to relate it with the environment white-managers at lower levels may be involved in internal planning.
* Planning is flexible as commitment is based on future conditions, which are always dynamic. As such, an adjustment is needed between the various factors and planning.

* Planning is a pervasive and continuous managerial function involving complex processes of perception, analysis, conceptual thought, communication, decision, and action. The very pervasiveness of these planning elements makes it difficult to identify and observe them in detail.

IMPORTANCE

The importance of the planning function should have be clear to you.

We can outline the importance of planning function as follows:

* Planning provides a clear sense of direction to the activities of the organisation and to the job Behaviour of managers and others. It strengthens their confidence in understanding where the organisation is heading and what for, how best to make the organisation move along the chosen path, and when should they take what measures to achieve the goals of the organisation.
* Another source of importance of planning is that it permits managers to examine and analyse alternative course of action with a better understanding of their likely consequences. If managers have an enhanced awareness of the possible future effects of alternative courses of action, for making a decision or for taking any action, they will be able to exercise Judgement and proceed cautiously to choose the most feasible and favourable course of action.
* Planning forces managers to shake off their inertia and insular outlook; it induces them to look beyond those noses, beyond today and tomorrow, and beyond immediate concerns. It encourages them to probe and cut through complexities and uncertainties of the environment and to gain control over the elements of change.
* Planning tends to minimise the incidence of impulsive and arbitrary decisions and *ad hoc* actions; it obviates exclusive dependence on the mercies of

luck and chance elements; it reduces the probability of major errors and failures in managerial actions. It injects a measure of discipline in managerial thinking and organisational action. It improves the capability of the organisation to assume calculated risks. It increases the freedom and flexibility of managers withing well-defined limits.

* As stated earlier, planning is a prime managerial function which provides the basis for the other managerial functions. The organisational structure of task and authority roles is built around organisational plans. The functions of motivation, supervision, leadership and communication are addressed to implementation of plans and achievement of organisational objectives. Managerial control is meaningless without managerial planning. Thus, planning is the king-pin function around which other functions are designed.
* Planning is means of judicious allocation of strategic and scarce resources of the organisation in the best possible manner for achieving strategic goals of the organisation. The strategic resources include funds, highly competent executives, technological talent, good contacts with government, exclusive dealer network and so on. If the organisation enjoys a distinct advantage in possession of such resources, a careful planning is essential to allocate them into those lines which would strengthen the overall competitive position of the organisation.
* For an ongoing organisation, planning contributes towards a more efficient functioning of the various work units. There is better utilisation of the organisation's existing assets, resources and capabilities. It prompts managers to close gaps, to plug loopholes, to rectify deficiencies, to reduce wastage and leakages of funds, materials, human efforts and skills so as to bring about an overall improvement in resource use efficiency.

* Planning tends to improve the ability of the organisation to effectively adapt and adjust its activities and directions in response to the changes taking place in the external environment. An adaptive Behaviour on the part of the organisation is essential for its survival as an independent entity. For a business organisation, for example, adaptive Behaviour is critical in technology, markets, products and so on.
* While adaptation is a Behaviour in reaction and response to some changes in the outside world, it is not enough in some situations. In recognition of this fact, planning stimulates management to act, to take hold initiatives, to anticipate crises and threats and to ward them off, to perceive and seise opportunities ahead of other competitions, and to gain a competitive lead over others. For the purpose, some enterprises establish environmental scanning mechanism as part of their planning systems. Thereby such enterprises are able to direct and control change, instead of being directed and controlled by the pervasive external forces of change.
* Planning is an important process to bring about effective integration of the diverse decisions and activities of the managers not only at a point of time but also over a period of time. It is by reference to the framework provided by planning that managers make major decisions on organisational activities, in an internally consistent manner.

LIMITATIONS

Planning is an important function of management.

However, the planning may fail if the following limitations:

* Planning relates to future and future is always uncertain and so prediction about future is so much difficult. Moreover, planning are based on data/ information relating to past and as such planning

based on any wrong information may not be useful to the organisation.

* Formulation of plans involves too much cost which are in the form of time spend, money spent, etc., but some times there is little benefit from in plan and than it becomes a burden for the institution. If the plan is not useful than the amount or time spent on its formulation is a waste.
* Some plans are rigid and a manager faces difficulty while making any changes where as there may be continuous change in environment where as the quick decision is required as per the changed environment.
* Planning requires some time for thinking, analysing the situation and designing the final plan and so in case emergency decision is required it will take time and business will lose its opportunity. Moreover, delay in decision will further delay the action.
* People in organisation have to work strictly according to plan where as they may be able to give better performance in a way decided by themselves. Secondly they do not think beside the plan and performs their activities like a machine without using their psychology.
* There may be some changes in planning only up to some extent because measure changes in plan will further attract the changes in supporting plans also and as such the whole system is disturbed moreover changes in plans time and again will prove a wastage of time and money spent on previous plan.
* Planning are the results of thinking of human being. Information on the basis of which plan is formulated may not be free form bias or there may be some other errors which will further Reebok the better plan.
* Planning is too much theoretical and have a less practical use planning is more suitable when environment is suitable but due to unsuitability of

environment business has to take various quick steps/decision time and again and as such the importance of other resources which are used according to changing environment, is more than that of planning.

* Planning/target set at the lower side than the capability of or resources and target on over side than the capacity of the resources both are termed as improper planning because lower target will be easily achieved and as suggested, feel false sense of security. On the other hand over planned target beyond resources cannot be achieved even all effort both are the situation of improper plan.
* This may delay action if certain cases. But it is also true that, if sufficient time is not given to the planning process, the plans so produced may prove to be unrealistic. Similarly, planning involves costs of gathering and analysing information and evaluation of various alternatives. If the management is not willing to spend on planning, the result may not be good.
* The planner must possess the required initiative. He should be an active planner and should take adequate follow up measures to see that plans are understood and implemented properly.
* It is commonly experienced phenomenon in many organisations. Sometimes, planners themselves do like change and on other occasion, they do not think it desirable to bring change, as it will create resistance on the part of the workers. This attitude makes the planning process ineffective.
* This may deter the managers from taking initiative and doing innovative thinking. So, the planners must have sufficient discretion and flexibility in the enterprise. They should not always be required to follow the procedures rigidly.
* Some people consider present as more important than future because present is less uncertain. Such

persons are psychologically opposed to planning. But it should not be forgotten that dynamic managers always look ahead. Long-term well being of the enterprise cannot be achieved unless proper planning is done for future.

* Because of external factors, which are beyond the control of the planners. External stringencies are very difficult to predict. Sudden breakout of war, government controls, natural havocs and may other factors are beyond the control of management. They make the execution of plans very difficult.

THE PLANNING PROCESS

Normally, the emergency manager serves as the "planning coordinator" responsible for leading the jurisdiction's effort to develop an EOP. This chapter offers the emergency manager suggestions for the process of developing an EOP. This process may be more important and useful to the jurisdiction's emergency management community than the final product itself. The suggestions can be easily tailored to the specific needs of a jurisdiction.

PRINCIPLES

Developing an all-hazard plan for protecting lives and property in the jurisdiction may appear to be an extremely difficult challenge. It need not be if following principles are applied:

Don't Reinvent the Whee

Emergency operations planning need not start from scratch. Planners should take advantage of others' experience.

The State is a valuable resource for the local jurisdiction. States typically publish their own planning guides, conduct workshops and training courses, and assign their planners to work with local planners. FEMA supports State training efforts through its Emergency Management Institute (EMI), and offers courses. FEMA also publishes many documents relating to planning for specific functions and hazards.

If the jurisdiction has an EOP or other contingency plans, they are the place to start. Existing plans can point the planning coordinator to applicable authorities, perceptions of risk in the community, members of the jurisdiction's emergency response organisation, mutual aid agreements with other jurisdictions, and more. The planning coordinator should review the existing EOP for questionable assumptions, inaccuracies, inconsistencies, omissions, and vagueness. Critiques of recent emergency operations and exercises in the jurisdiction will help the planning coordinator develop a sense of what needs to be done.

Don't Go It Alone

The planning coordinator's is only one view. If a coordinated emergency response depends on teamwork, planning for response should involve the jurisdiction's emergency "team." Documentary research should be supplemented by interviews with key officials of the jurisdiction's response organisation: They may have information and insights that the planning coordinator lacks, as well as ideas that can spark creative solutions to problems. Key officials also determine what staff will be made available for planning meetings and what priority emergency planning issues will have in day-to-day work, so it is important to secure their commitment to the planning process.

FEMA recommends a team approach to planning for these reasons:

* The EOP is more likely to be used and followed if the tasked organisations have a sense of ownership, *i.e.*, their views were considered and incorporated.
* More knowledge and expertise are brought to bear on the planning effort.
* Closer professional relationships among response and recovery organisations in the planning process should translate into better coordination and teamwork in emergencies.

The planning team should be drawn from various groups that have a role or stake in emergency response. The list is not all-inclusive.

The important thing is for the planning coordinator to ensure that the planning team membership represents a good cross section of the organisations involved in the jurisdiction's emergency response effort:

* The Office of the Chief Executive.
* Law enforcement, fire/rescue, and emergency medical services (including dispatchers/911 at the local level), public health and safety, etc.
* Existing planning agencies (*e.g.*, community development, economic development, city planning commissions/municipal planners).
* Hazard mitigation planner/coordinator.
* Local Emergency Planning Committees (LEPC), for hazardous materials (HAZMAT) information.
* Public works agencies and utility companies.
* Social service agencies and volunteer organisations (*e.g.*, American Red Cross (ARC), Salvation Army, etc.,).
* Area hospitals, emergency medical service agencies, medical examiner, coroner, mortician, and other appropriate members of the medical community.
* Educational administrators.
* Public Information Officer (PIO).
* Local media.
* Industrial and military installations in the area.
* State aviation authority and/or others connected with provision of air support.
* Port authorities, U.S., Coast Guard station.
* The jurisdiction's Chief Financial Officer, auditor, and heads of any centralised procurement and resource support agencies.
* Jurisdiction's legal counsel.
* Labour and professional organisations.
* Organisations in the animal care and control community, including veterinary services.
* Amateur radio/CB groups, such as Radio Amateur Civil Emergency Service (RACES), Radio Emergency Associated Communications Teams (REACT), etc.,

* Emergency managers and agency representatives from neighbouring jurisdictions, to coordinate mutual aid needs.
* State and/or Federal representatives, as appropriate.

Don't Forget the Chief Executive Official (CEO)

Potential planning team members have many day-to-day concerns. For the team to come together, potential members must be convinced that emergency planning has a higher priority—and the person to convince them is the jurisdiction's chief executive. The emergency manager has to enlist the chief executive's support for and involvement in the planning effort. To do so, the emergency manager must show the chief executive what is at stake in emergency planning: share the hazard analysis for the jurisdiction, describe what government and especially the chief executive will have to do, Colour presentations with images from disasters like those that could befall the jurisdiction, discuss readiness assessments and exercise critiques, and remind the chief executive that planning ultimately facilitates his or her job in an emergency. Any backing available from the chief executive's office will help the emergency manager to obtain the respectful cooperation of other agency heads.

STEPS

Following are the basics for development and continual refinement of an EOP. They may be adapted to the needs of a jurisdiction.

Research

The first step is research. This consists of reviewing the jurisdiction's planning framework, analysing the hazards faced by the jurisdiction, determining the resource base, and noting characteristics of the jurisdiction that could affect emergency operations.

Review local and/or State laws, rules, regulations, executive orders, etc., that may be considered enabling legislation. Review Federal regulatory requirements. Review guidance, existing plans for the jurisdiction, and the plans of neighbouring jurisdictions. Review agreements with neighbouring jurisdictions, military installations, private sector organisations, etc., Become familiar with the plans of higher levels of government that may be called on to provide assistance.

Hazard analysis is the basis for both mitigation efforts and EOPs. From an emergency operations planning perspective, hazard analysis helps a planning team decide what hazards merit special attention, what actions must be planned for, and what resources are likely to be needed. Comprehensive hazard analysis merits its own document-length discussion.

However, for purposes of emergency operations planning, basic considerations of process, methods, and sources include the following:

* **Process and Methods.** Hazard analysis requires the planning team to:
  - Identify hazards, to know what kinds of emergencies have occurred or could occur in the jurisdiction.
    a. Begin with a list of hazards that concern emergency management in your jurisdiction. Laws, previous plans, and elected officials can help define the universe of hazards which the planning team should address in the all-hazard EOP. A list of "traditional" emergency management concerns might include: airplane crash, avalanche, dam failure, drought, earthquake, epidemic, flood, HAZMAT release (in transport or from a fixed facility), hurricane, landslide, mudslide, power failure (sustained), radiological release (in transport or from a fixed facility), subsidence, terrorism, tornado, train derailment, tsunami, urban conflagration, volcanic eruption, wildfire, and winter storm.
    b. For each of these potential emergencies, determine whether it has happened or could happen in the jurisdiction. Some can be

eliminated by common sense (*e.g.*, where mountains do no exist, volcanic eruption is not likely). For the rest, there are three lines of investigation: history (including statistical compilations), expert opinion, and maps—which summarise results of the first two.

- Profile hazards and their potential consequences, to have the information necessary for the next two steps (and to set the stage for other applications of the hazard analysis). The categories of information and the precision of the data will depend on several factors. One is the kinds of decisions the analysis is meant to support. For example, to decide that one hazard poses more of a threat than another may require only a qualitative estimate (*e.g.*, "High" vs. "Medium")—but to plan for health and medical needs the planning team would want to have an estimate for likely fatalities and injuries. Another factor is the availability of information and time. It may be necessary to take a long view of hazard analysis, and have each version build on the preceding one as part of a "research agenda" for emergency management.
- Develop information on each of the hazards identified for the community. Of particular interest are the hazard's frequency of occurrence (both historical and predicted or probable, as available), magnitude and intensity, location (if the hazard is associated with a facility or landscape feature) and spatial extent (either around the known location of the hazard or as an estimate for non-localised hazards like tornado), duration, seasonal pattern (based on month by month historical occurrence), speed of onset, and availability of warning.

  a. Develop information on the potential consequences of the hazard. This depends on identifying a vulnerable zone (if the hazard is localised) or relating the estimated spatial extent of the hazard to the jurisdiction (by a simple ratio of the hazard's extent to the jurisdiction's area, to get gross estimates of lives and property at risk, or by "overlaying" the estimated spatial extent of the hazard on a portion of the jurisdiction and determining what would be affected). Several kinds of consequences can be investigated; response planning would be concerned with effects on people (total affected, likely deaths and injuries), critical facilities and community functions, property, and sites of potential secondary hazards (*e.g.*, dams, chemical processing plants). The planning team can use both historical information and modeling to arrive at estimates for planning. In modeling, the general process is to consider what is exposed to a given intensity of the hazard, how susceptible it is to a type of damage or consequence (*e.g.*, death, for people; destruction, for property; days of service loss or repair time for critical facilities), and some measure of loss (*e.g.*, dollars, for property). Over time, collection of this information can be made easier by sectoring the jurisdiction (optimally, in sectors that will also be used for damage assessment) and developing a profile of each sector: *e.g.*, rough number of structures falling into different classes of construction, number of different kinds of critical facilities, rough number of people in different age groups or having special needs, etc.,

- Compare and prioritise risks, to determine which hazards merit special attention in planning (and other emergency management efforts). The planning team must consider frequency of the hazard and the likely or potential severity of its consequences, to develop a single indicator of the threat: This allows comparison and setting of priorities. While a mathematical approach is possible, it is easier to manipulate qualitative ratings (*e.g.*, "High", "Medium", "Low") or index numbers (*e.g.*, reducing quantitative information to a 1 to 3, 1 to 5, or 1 to 10 scale, based on defined thresholds) for different categories of information used in the ranking scheme. Some approaches involve consideration only of frequency and consequences, and treat the two categories as equally important. In other approaches, potential consequences receive more weight than frequency.

– Create and apply scenarios, to brainstorm needed hazardspecific planning provisions and estimate hazard-specific resource requirements. While it is important to have a sense of magnitudes involved (whether the single indicator used to rank hazards, or estimated numbers of people affected), these are static. Planning is concerned with actions that take place in time. For the top-ranked hazards, or hazards that rate above a certain threshold, the planning team should consider scenarios. Using information from the profile, the planning team should think about how the hazard occurrence would develop in the jurisdiction. Starting with a given intensity of the hazard, the team can imagine the hazard's development from initial warning (if available) to its impact on a specific part of the jurisdiction (as identified through analysis) and its generation of specific consequences (*e.g.*, collapsed buildings; loss of critical services and infrastructure; death, injury, or displacement). Through this initial brainstorming—which can be refined in formal tabletop exercises—the team will decide what actions and resources will become necessary. It will also become conscious of the planning assumptions to be used in functional annexes and hazard-specific appendices to the EOP.

- **Sources.** Sources of maps for hazards would include compilations of hazard information made by FEMA and State emergency management agencies, the U.S., Geological Survey (USGS) and State geological surveys, and the National Weather Service (NWS) and its local offices. For more localised hazards, maps from the Federal Insurance Administration (FIA), maps of 10- and 50-mile Emergency Planning Zones (EPZ) around nuclear power plants, and any maps of HAZMAT sites prepared by the LEPC would be useful. For historical investigation, many potential sources exist. Consult Federal or State hazard analyses, as appropriate, to see if the historical occurrence of the hazard is tabulated by jurisdiction. Also interview representatives from organisations on the planning team about their experience. Check local ARC disaster records. Check police, fire, and other responder records. Research area newspapers at the library. Check with utilities and businesses/facilities that have operated in the area for some time. Involve the local or State historical society, and perhaps area universities (*e.g.*, departments of history, sociology, geography, engineering). Professional or business associations (*e.g.*, of insurers, engineers and builders, etc.,) may have useful information. Long-time community residents can even contribute. For expert opinion on hazard potential, the sources are similar. Federal, State, and local agencies; academic, industrial, and public interest group researchers (or private consultants specialising in hazard analysis); and professional associations concerned with the hazards on your list should be able to help, either through interviews or publications. Sources for information on the community and possible consequences to it vary. Ideally, work already will have been done regarding potential consequences of certain facility-based hazards—and it is a matter of checking with the facility and the agency (local, State, regional, or federal) that regulates that kind of facility. For demographics, Census data are available, as are off-the-shelf computer products that organise such data by ZIP code. The planning team also should make extensive use of the information about the jurisdiction that is constantly developed within the jurisdiction. The local planning and zoning commission or department, for example, probably has extensive data on demographics, on land use, on numbers and types and—with the tax assessor and/or local realtors' association—value of buildings, and on the structural integrity of buildings (or at least on the code to which they were to be built, and what that code was and was not designed to do regarding hazard effects). The local public works (or civil engineering) department and utilities are the obvious sources for information on potential damage to and restoration time for the critical infrastructure threatened by hazard effects. The Chamber of Commerce may offer a perspective on damage to business and general economic loss. Other sources of information mentioned previously—emergency service logs and reports, universities, professional associations, etc., — also apply.

Agency heads and other potential members of the planning team should know what kinds of resources they can bring to emergency response and recovery. The problem is to quantify and list them, and compare the resources available to the resources needed for an effective emergency response. Shortfalls may require negotiating agreements with private suppliers or other jurisdictions. Determination of the resource base also should include a consideration of what facilities are vital to emergency operations and how they might be affected by hazards: Problems that cannot be mitigated should be taken into account in the EOP, not assumed away.

The planning team should note geographic and topographic features that may affect operations—for example, dependence on a single main transportation artery in and out of the jurisdiction. Planners also should identify special needs groups (non-English speakers, the aged, the disabled) and where they are concentrated (especially institutions such as nursing homes). Finally, the planning team should be alert to demographic and other trends in the jurisdiction that affect assumptions.

Development

* Develop a rough draft of the basic plan, functional annexes, and hazard-specific appendices to serve as a point of departure for the planning team.
* Develop agendas and invitation lists for first cycle of planning meetings; perhaps deliver invitations in person and conduct preliminary interviews with key officials.
* Brief the "CEO" and perhaps invite him or her as a keynote speaker.
* Conduct a presentation meeting, establish committees for parts of the EOP, appoint committee chairs, and schedule a follow-up meeting.
* Work with committees on successive drafts.
* Prepare necessary graphics (*e.g.*, maps, organisational charts).
* Produce a final draft and circulate the draft to the planning team for review and comment.
* Hold a meeting to incorporate final changes, discuss an implementation strategy and necessary distribution, and obtain (informal) commitments to provide information that could necessitate revision.

* Obtain concurrence from organisations with identified responsibilities for implementing the EOP.
* Present the EOP to local elected officials and obtain official promulgation of the EOP (advise the local media in advance).
* Print and distribute the EOP, with a copy (or press release) to local media. Maintain a record of the organisations and persons that received a copy (or copies) of the plan.

Validation

The written EOP should be checked for its conformity to applicable regulatory requirements and the standards of Federal or State agencies (as appropriate)—and for its usefulness in practice.

Further, conduct of a "table top" exercise involving the key representatives of each tasked organisation may serve as a practical and useful means to help validate the plan.

Consult the next level of government about its EOP review cycle. Plan reviews allow responsible agencies to suggest improvements in an EOP based on their accumulated experience. States may review local EOPs; FEMA Regional offices may assist States in the review of EOPs, upon request. Hazard-specific Federal Programmes (such as the REP Programme) require periodic review of certain sections of the all-hazard EOP, and may require review of associated SOPs.

To evaluate new or revised EOP, use functional and full scale emergency management exercises. Exercises offer the best way, short of emergencies, to determine if an EOP is understood and "works".

Maintenance

The EOP is a living document. Problems emerge, situations change, gaps become apparent, Federal requirements are altered—and the EOP must be adapted to remain useful and up to date.

A remedial action process can help a planning team identify, illuminate, and correct problems with the jurisdiction's

EOP. A remedial action process captures information from exercises, post-disaster critiques, self-assessments, audits, administrative reviews, and the like, which may indicate that deficiencies exist. It then brings members of the planning team together to discuss the problem, and to consider and assign responsibility for remedies. Remedial actions may involve revising planning assumptions and operational concepts, changing organisational tasks, or modifying organisational implementing instructions (SOPs). They also may involve refresher training on performance of tasks assigned by the EOP to an organisation's personnel. The final component of a remedial action process is a means to track and follow up the assigned actions. Establish a process for review and revision of the EOP. Review should be a recurring activity, accomplished on at least an annual basis. As appropriate, significant issues and problems identified through a remedial action process and/or the annual review should provide the information needed to allow the planning team to make the necessary revision(s) to the plan.

Ensure that each tasked organisation or individual develops the SOPs necessary to facilitate the accomplishment of assigned tasks. The EOP does not anticipate every detail of the tasks it describes—but the details are important to its implementation.

TYPES OF PLANS

Based on what the plans seeks to achieve and the method which the plan would like to adopt, plans can be classified as different types: Objectives, Strategy, Policy, Procedure, Method, Rule, Programme, Budget.

OBJECTIVES

The first step in planning is setting objectives. Objectives, therefore, can be said to be the desired future position that the management would like to reach. Objectives are very basic to the organisation and they are defined as ends which the management seeks to achieve by its operations. Therefore, an objective simply stated is what you would like to achieve, *i.e.*, the end result of activities. For example, an organisation may have an objective of increasing sales by 10 per cent or earning a reasonable rate of return on investment, earn a 20 per cent profit from business. They represent the end point of planning. All other managerial activities are also directed towards achieving these objectives. They are usually set by top management of the organisation and focus on broad, general issues. They define the future state of affairs which the organisation strives to realise. They serve as a guide for overall business planning. Different departments or units in the organisation may have their own objectives. Objectives need to be expressed in specific terms, *i.e.*, they should be measurable in quantitative terms, in the form of a written statement of desired results to be achieved within a given time period.

STRATEGY

A strategy provides the broad contours of an organisation's business. It will also refer to future decisions defining the organisations direction and scope in the long run. Thus, we can say a strategy is a comprehensive plan for accomplishing an organisation objectives.

This comprehensive plan will include three dimensions:

* Determining long term objectives,
* Adopting a particular course of action, and
* Allocating resources necessary to achieve the objective.

Whenever a strategy is formulated, the business environment needs to be taken into consideration. The changes in the economic, political, social, legal and technological environment will affect an organisations strategy. Strategies usually take the course of forming the organisations identity in the business environment. Major strategic decisions will include decisions like whether the organisation will continue to be in the same line of business, or combine new lines of activity with the existing business or seek to acquire a dominant position in the same market. For example, a company's marketing strategy has to address certain questions, *i.e.*, who are the customers?, what is the demand for the product?, which channel of distribution to use?, what is the pricing policy? and how do we advertise the product. These and many more issues need to be resolved while formulating a marketing strategy for any organisation.

POLICY

Policies are general statements that guide thinking or channellise energies towards a particular direction. Policies provide a basis for interpreting strategy which is usually stated in general terms. They are guides to managerial action and decisions in the implementation of strategy. For example, the company may have a recruitment policy, pricing policy within which objectives are set and decisions are made. If there is an established policy, it becomes easier to resolve problems or issues. As such, a policy is the general response to a particular problem or situation. There are policies for all levels and departments in the organisation ranging from major company policies to minor policies. Major company policies are for all to know, *i.e.*, customers, clients, competitors, etc., whereas minor polices are applicable to insiders and contain minute details of information vital to the employees of an organisation. But there has to be some basis for divulging information to others. Policies define the broad parameters within which a manager may function. The manager may use his/her discretion to interpret and apply a policy. For example, the decisions taken under a Purchase Policy would be in the nature of manufacturing or buying decisions. Should a company make or buy its requirements of packages, transport services, printing of stationery, water and power supply and other items? How should vendors be selected for procuring supplies? How many suppliers should a company make purchases from? What is the criteria for choosing suppliers. All these answers would be addressed by the Purchase Policy.

PROCEDURE

Procedures are routine steps on how to carry out activities. They detail the exact manner in which any work is to be performed. They are specified in a chronological order. For example, there may be a procedure for requisitioning supplies before production. Procedures are specified steps to be followed in particular circumstances. They are generally meant for insiders to follow. The sequence of steps or actions to be taken are generally to enforce a policy and to attain pre-determined objectives. Policies and procedures are interlinked with each other. Procedures are steps to be carried out within a broad policy framework.

METHOD

Methods provide the prescribed ways or manner in which a task has to be performed considering the objective. It deals with a task comprising one step of a procedure and specifies how this step is to be performed. The Methods may vary from task to task. Selection of proper method saves time, money and effort and increases efficiency. For imparting training to employees at various level from top management to supervisory, different methods can be adopted. For example for higher level management orientation programmes, lectures and seminars can be organised whereas at the supervisory level, on the job training methods and work-oriented methods are appropriate.

RULE

Rules are specific statements that inform what is to be done. They do not allow for any flexibility or discretion. It reflects a managerial decision that a certain action must or must not be taken. They are usually the simplest type of plans because there is no compromise or change unless a policy decision is taken.

BUDGET

A budget is a statement of expected results expressed in numerical terms. It is a plan which quantifies future facts and figures. For example, a sales budget may forecast the sales of different products in each area for a particular month. A budget may also be prepared to show the number of workers required in the factory at peak production times. Since, budget represents all items in numbers, it becomes easier to compare actual figures with expected figures and take corrective action subsequently. Thus, a budget is also a control device from which deviations can be taken care of. But making a budget involves forecasting, therefore, it clearly comes under planning.

It is a fundamental planning instrument in many organisations. Let us take an example of Cash Budget. The cash budget is a basic tool in the management of cash. It is a device to help the management to plan and control the use of cash. It is a statement showing the estimated cash inflows and cash outflows over a given period. Cash inflows would generally come from cash sales and the cash outflows would generally be the costs and expenses associated with the operations of the business. The net cash position is determined by the cash budget, *i.e.*, inflows minus (–) outflows = surplus or deficiency. The management has to hold adequate cash balances for various purposes. But at the same time, it should avoid excess balance of cash Since, it gives little or no return. The business has to assess and plan its need for cash with a degree of caution.

PROGRAMME

Programmes are detailed statements about a project which outlines the objectives, policies, procedures, rules, tasks, human and physical resources required and the budget to implement any course of action. Programmes will include the entire gamut of activities as well as the organisation's policy and how it will contribute to the overall business plan. The minutest details are worked out, *i.e.*, procedures, rules, budgets, within the broad policy framework.

4

Motivation

NATURE OF MOTIVATION

The concept of motivation focuses on explaining what "moves" behaviour. In fact, the term motivation is derived from the Latin word 'movere' , referring to movement of activity. Most of our everyday explanation of behaviour is given in terms of motives. Why do you come to the school or college? There may be any number of reasons for this behaviour, such as you want to learn or to make friends, you need a diploma or degree to get a good job, you want to make your parents happy, and so on. Some combination of these reasons and/or others would explain why you choose to go in for higher education. Motives also help in making predictions about behaviour. A person will work hard in school, in sports, in business, in music, and in many other situations, if s/he has a very strong need for achievement. Hence, motives are the general states that enable us to make predictions about behaviour in many different situations. In other words, motivation is one of the determinants of behaviour. Instincts, drives, needs, goals, and incentives come under the broad cluster of motivation.

The Motivational Cycle

Psychologists now use the concept of need to describe the motivational properties of behaviour. A need is lack or deficit of some necessity. The condition of need leads to drive. A drive is a state of tension or arousal produced by a need. It energises random activity. When one of the random activities leads to a goal, it reduces the drive, and the organism stops being active. The organism returns to a balanced state. Thus, the cycle of motivational events can be presented as shown in Fig. 4.1.

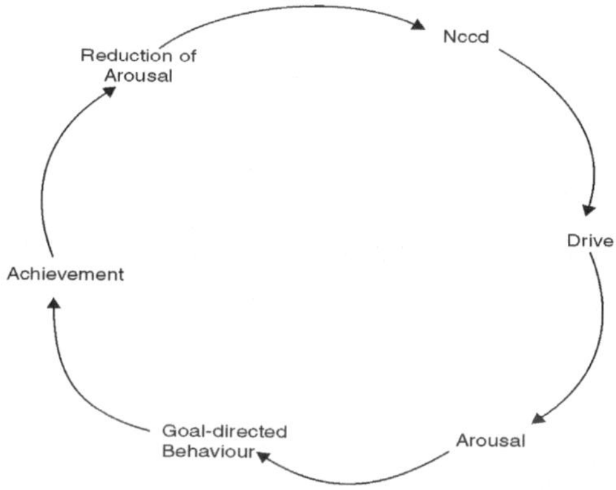

Fig. 4.1 The Motivational Cycle.

BIOLOGICAL MOTIVES

The biological or physiological approach to explain motivation is the earliest attempt to understand causes of behaviour. Most of the theories, which developed later, carry traces of the influence of the biological approach. The approach adhering to the concept of adaptive act holds that organisms have needs that produce drive, which stimulates behaviour leading to certain actions towards achieving certain goals, which reduce the drive.

The earliest explanations of motivation relied on the concept of instinct. The term instinct denotes inborn patterns of behaviour that are biologically determined rather than learned. Some common human instincts include curiosity, flight, repulsion, reproduction, parental care, etc. Instincts are innate tendencies found in all members of a species that direct behaviour in predictable ways. The term instinct most approximately refers to an urge to do something. Instinct has an "impetus" which drives the organism to do something to reduce that impetus. Some of the basic biological needs explained by this approach are hunger, thirst, and sex, which are essential for the sustenance of the individual.

Hunger

When someone is hungry, the need for food dominates everything else. It motivates people to obtain and consume food. Of course we must eat to live. But, what makes you feel hungry? Studies have indicated that many events inside and outside the body may trigger hunger or inhibit it. The stimuli for hunger include stomach contractions, which signify that the stomach is empty, a low concentration of glucose in the blood, a low level of protein and the amount of fats stored in the body. The liver also responds to the lack of bodily fuel by sending nerve impulses to the brain.

The aroma, taste or appearance of food may also result in a desire to eat. It may be noted that none of these alone gives you the feeling that you are hungry. All in combination act with external factors to help you understand that you are hungry.

Thus, it can be said that our food intake is regulated by a complex feedingsatiety system located in the hypothalamus, liver, and other parts of the body as well as the external cues available in the environment. Some physiologists hold that changes in the metabolic functions of the liver result in a feeling of hunger.

The liver sends a signal to a part of the brain called hypothalamus. The two regions of hypothalamus involved in hunger are - the lateral hypothalamus and the ventro-medial hypothalamus. LH is considered to be the excitatory area. Animals eat when this area is stimulated.

When it is damaged, animals stop eating and die of starvation. The VMH is located in the middle of the hypothalamus, which is otherwise known as hunger-controlling area which inhibits the hunger drive. Now can you guess about people who overeat and become obese, and people who eat very little or who are on a diet?

Thirst

What would happen to you, if you were deprived of water for a long time? What makes you feel thirsty? When we are deprived of water for a period of several hours, the mouth and throat become dry, which leads to dehydration of body tissues. Drinking water is necessary to wet a dry mouth. But a dry mouth does not always result in water drinking behaviour. In fact processes within the body itself control thirst and drinking of water. Water must get into the tissues sufficiently to remove the dryness of mouth and throat. Motivation to drink water is mainly triggered by the conditions of the body: loss of water from cells and reduction of blood volume. When water is lost by bodily fluids, water leaves the interior of the cells.

The anterior hypothalamus contains nerve cells called 'osmoreceptors', which generate nerve impulses in case of cell dehydration. These nerve impulses act as a signal for thirst and drinking; when thirst is regulated by loss of water from the osmoreceptors, it is called cellular-dehydration thirst. But what mechanisms stop the drinking of water? Some researchers assume that the mechanism which explains the intake of water is also responsible for stopping the intake of water. Others have pointed out that the role of stimuli resulting from the intake of water in the stomach must have something to do with stopping of drinking water. However, the precise physiological mechanisms underlying the thirst drive are yet to be understood.

Sex

One of the most powerful drives in both animals and human beings is the sex drive. Motivation to engage in sexual activity is a very strong factor influencing human behaviour. However, sex is far more than a biological motive.

It is different from other primary motives in many ways like:

* Sexual activity is not necessary for an individual's survival;
* Homeostasis (the tendency of the organism as a whole to maintain constancy or to attempt to restore equilibrium if constancy is disturbed) is not the goal of sexual activity; and
* Sex drive develops with age, etc.

In case of lower animals, it depends on many physiological conditions; in case of human beings, the sex drive is very closely regulated biologically, sometimes it is very difficult to classify sex purely as a biological drive. Physiologists suggest that intensity of the sexual urge is dependent upon chemical substances circulating in the blood, known as sex hormones. Studies on animals as well as human beings have mentioned that sex hormones secreted by gonads, *i.e.*, testes in males and the ovaries in females are responsible for sexual motivation. Sexual motivation is also influenced by other endocrine glands, such as adrenal and pituitary glands. Sexual drive in human beings is primarily stimulated by external stimuli and its expression depends upon cultural learning.

SOCIAL MOTIVES

Social motives are when people do or give things because they feel they have a sense of responsibility to their community.

People with social motives may have endured racial discrimination, poverty or may want to live in a selfless way:

* Social motives manifest themselves in different ways. There are people who work in soup kitchens because they were homeless at one time. Another person may focus on citisen advocacy because he experienced unfair treatment from law enforcement.
* Having a social motive for doing or giving is beneficial because it allows a person to be less self-centered and more focused on the needs of others. For example, if one grew up with a bias towards single mothers, social motives can gradually turn the bias into compassion.
* Some famous people are well-known for their social motives to help to the less fortunate in society. For example, Oprah Winfrey built a school for disadvantaged girls in South Africa so they can have quality education. Michael Jackson was a philanthropist throughout his career.

* If you're a person that seeks to advance the causes of the less fortunate, you can contribute even in small ways. Some ideas include donating items to the local food bank, visiting a battered women's shelter, bringing school supplies to a foster home or assisting the unemployed in a job search.
* A lot of good has been done in the U.S., because of people with social motives. For example, abolitionists crusaded for the end of slavery and female suffragists made it possible for women to vote.

PSYCHOSOCIAL MOTIVES

Social motives are mostly learned or acquired. Social groups such as family, neighbourhood, friends, and relatives do contribute a lot in acquiring social motives. These are complex forms of motives mainly resulting from the individual's interaction with her/his social environment.

Curiosity and Exploration

Often people engage in activities without a clear goal or purpose but they derive some kind of pleasure out of it. It is a motivational tendency to act without any specific identifiable goal. The tendency to seek for a novel experience, gain pleasure by obtaining information, etc., are signs of curiosity. Hence, curiosity describes behaviour whose primary motive appears to remain in the activities themselves. What will happen if the sky falls on us? Questions of this kind stimulate intellectuals to find answers. Studies show that this curiosity behaviour is not only limited to human beings, animals too show the same kind of behaviour. We are driven to explore the environment by our curiosity and our need for sensory stimulation. The need for varied types of sensory stimulations is closely related to curiosity. It is the basic motive, and exploration and curiosity are the expressions of it.

Our ignorance about a number of things around us becomes a powerful motivator to explore the world. We get easily bored with repetitive experiences. So we look for something new. In the case of infants and small children, this motive is very dominant. They get satisfaction from being allowed to explore, which is reflected in their smiling and babbling. Children become easily distressed, when the motive to explore is discouraged.

ACHIEVEMENT, AFFILIATION AND POWER [MASLOW'S HIERARCHY]

ACHIEVEMENT

You might have observed some students work very hard and compete with others for good marks/grades in the examination, as good marks/grades will create opportunities for higher studies and better job prospects. It is the achievement motivation, which refers to the desire of a person to meet standards of excellence. Need for achievement, also known as n-Ach, energises and directs behaviour as well as influences the perception of situations. During the formative years of social development, children acquire achievement motivation. The sources from which they learn it, include parents, other role models, and socio-cultural influences. Persons high in achievement motivation tend to prefer tasks that are moderately difficult and challenging. They have stronger-than-average desire for feedback on their performance, that is to know how they are doing, so that they can adjust their goals to meet the challenge.

AFFILIATION

Most of us need company or friend or want to maintain some form of relationship with others. Nobody likes to remain alone all the time. As soon as people see some kinds of similarities among themselves or they like each other, they form a group. Formation of group or collectivity is an important feature of human life. Often people try desperately to get close to other people, to seek their help, and to become members of their group. Seeking other human beings and wanting to be close to them both physically and psychologically is called affiliation. It involves motivation for social contact. Need for affiliation is aroused when individuals feel threatened or helpless and also when they are happy. People high on this need are motivated to seek the company of others and to maintain friendly relationships with other people.

POWER

Need for power is an ability of a person to produce intended effects on the behaviour and emotions of another person. The various goals of power motivation are to influence, control, persuade, lead, and charm others and most importantly to enhance one's own reputation in the eyes of other people. David McClelland described four general ways of expression of the power motive. First, people do things to gain feeling of power and strength from sources outside themselves by reading stories about sports stars or attaching themselves to a popular figure. Second, power can also be felt from sources within us and may be expressed by building up the body and mastering urges and impulses. Third, people do things as individuals to have an impact on others. For example, a person argues, or competes with another individual in order to have an impact or influence on that person. Fourth, people do things as members of organisations to have an impact on others as in the case of the leader of a political party; the individual may use the party apparatus to influence others. However, for any individual, one of these ways of expressing power motivation may dominate, but with age and life experiences, it varies.

MASLOW'S HIERARCHY OF NEEDS

Maslow's hierarchy of needs is a theory in psychology, proposed by Abraham Maslow in his 1943 paper 'A Theory of Human Motivation'. Maslow subsequently extended the idea to include his observations of humans' innate curiosity. His theories parallel many other theories of human developmental psychology, all of which focus on describing the stages of growth in humans.

Maslow studied what he called exemplary people such as Albert Einstein, Jane Addams, Eleanor Roosevelt, and

Frederick Douglass rather than mentally ill or neurotic people, writing that "the study of crippled, stunted, immature, and unhealthy specimens can yield only a cripple psychology and a cripple philosophy." Maslow studied the healthiest 1 per cent of the college student population. Maslow's theory was fully expressed in his 1954 book *Motivation and Personality*.

HIERARCHY

Maslow's hierarchy of needs is often portrayed in the shape of a pyramid, with the largest and most fundamental levels of needs at the bottom, and the need for self-actualisation at the top. The most fundamental and basic four layers of the pyramid contain what Maslow called "deficiency needs" or "d-needs": esteem , friendship and love, security, and physical needs.

With the exception of the most fundamental needs, if these "deficiency needs" are not met, the body gives no physical indication but the individual feels anxious and tense. Maslow's theory suggests that the most basic level of needs must be met before the individual will strongly desire the secondary or higher level needs. Maslow also coined the term Metamotivation to describe the motivation of people who go beyond the scope of the basic needs and strive for constant betterment. Metamotivated people are driven by B-needs, instead of deficiency needs.

Self-actualisation

"What a man can be, he must be?" This forms the basis of the perceived need for self-actualisation. This level of need pertains to what a person's full potential is and realising that potential. Maslow describes this desire as the desire to become more and more what one is, to become everything that one is capable of becoming. This is a broad definition of the need for self-actualisation, but when applied to individuals the need is specific. For example one individual may have the strong desire to become an ideal parent, in another it may be expressed athletically, and in another it may be expressed in painting, or inventions.

In order to reach a clear understanding of this level of need one must first not only achieve the previous needs, physiological, safety, love, and esteem, but master these needs. Maslow's descriptions of a self-actualised person's different needs and personality traits. Maslow also states that even though these are examples of how the quest for knowledge is separate from basic needs he warns that these "two hierarchies are interrelated rather than sharply separated". This means that this level of need, as well as the next and highest level, are not strict, separate levels but closely related to others, and this is possibly the reason that these two levels of need are left out of most textbooks.

Esteem

All humans have a need to be respected and to have self-esteem and self-respect. Also known as the belonging need, esteem presents the normal human desire to be accepted and valued by others. People need to engage themselves to gain recognition and have an activity or activities that give the person a sense of contribution, to feel accepted and self-valued, be it in a profession or hobby. Imbalances at this level can result in low self-esteem or an inferiority complex. People with low self-esteem need respect from others. They may seek fame or glory, which again depends on others.

Note, however, that many people with low self-esteem will not be able to improve their view of themselves simply by receiving fame, respect, and glory externally, but must first accept themselves internally. Psychological imbalances such as depression can also prevent one from obtaining self-esteem on both levels. Most people have a need for a stable self-respect and self-esteem.

Maslow noted two versions of esteem needs, a lower one and a higher one. The lower one is the need for the respect of others, the need for status, recognition, fame, prestige, and attention.

The higher one is the need for self-respect, the need for strength, competence, mastery, self-confidence, independence and freedom. The latter one ranks higher because it rests more on inner competence won through experience. Deprivation of these needs can lead to an inferiority complex, weakness and helplessness.

Love and Belonging

After physiological and safety needs are fulfilled, the third layer of human needs are social and involve feelings of belongingness.

This aspect of Maslow's hierarchy involves emotionally based relationships in general, such as:

* Friendship.
* Intimacy.
* Family.

Humans need to feel a sense of belonging and acceptance, whether it comes from a large social group, such as clubs, office culture, religious groups, professional organisations, sports teams, gangs, or small social connections. They need to love and be loved by others. In the absence of these elements, many people become susceptible to loneliness, social anxiety, and clinical depression. This need for belonging can often overcome the physiological and security needs, depending on the strength of the peer pressure; an anorexic, for example, may ignore the need to eat and the security of health for a feeling of control and belonging.

Safety Needs

With their physical needs relatively satisfied, the individual's safety needs take precedence and dominate Behaviour. These needs have to do with people's yearning for a predictable orderly world in which perceived unfairness and inconsistency are under control, the familiar frequent and the unfamiliar rare. In the world of work, these safety needs manifest themselves in such things as a preference for job security, grievance procedures for protecting the individual from unilateral authority, savings accounts, insurance policies, reasonable disability accommodations, and the like.

Safety and Security needs include:

* Personal security.

* Financial security.
* Health and well-being.
* Safety net against accidents/illness and their adverse impacts.

Physiological Needs

For the most part, physiological needs are obvious — they are the literal requirements for human survival. If these requirements are not met, the human body simply cannot continue to function.

Physiological needs include:

* Breathing.
* Nutrition.
* Water.
* Sex.
* Sleep.
* Homeostasis.
* Excretion.

Air, water, and food are metabolic requirements for survival in all animals, including humans. Clothing and shelter provide necessary protection from the elements. The intensity of the human sexual instinct is shaped more by sexual competition than maintaining a birth rate adequate to survival of the species.

CRITICISMS

In their extensive review of research based on Maslow's theory, Wahba and Bridgewell found little evidence for the ranking of needs Maslow described, or even for the existence of a definite hierarchy at all. Chilean economist and philosopher Manfred Max-Neef has also argued fundamental human needs are non-hierarchical, and are ontologically universal and invariant in nature—part of the condition of being human; poverty, he argues, may result from any one of these needs being frustrated, denied or unfulfilled. The order in which the hierarchy is arranged has been criticised as being ethnocentric by Geert Hofstede. Hofstede's criticism of Maslow's pyramid as ethnocentric may stem from the fact that

Maslow's hierarchy of needs neglects to illustrate and expand upon the difference between the social and intellectual needs of those raised in individualistic societies and those raised in collectivist societies.

Maslow created his hierarchy of needs from an individualistic perspective, being that he was from the United States, a highly individualistic nation. The needs and drives of those in individualistic societies tend to be more self-centred than those in collectivist societies, focusing on improvement of the self, with self-actualisation being the apex of self-improvement. Since, the hierarchy was written from the perspective of an individualist, the order of needs in the hierarchy with self-actualisation at the top is not representative of the needs of those in collectivist cultures. In collectivist societies, the needs of acceptance and community will outweigh the needs for freedom and individuality. Maslow's hierarchy has also been criticised as being individualistic because of the position and value of sex on the pyramid.

Maslow's pyramid puts sex on the bottom rung of physiological needs, along with breathing and food. It views sex from an individualistic and not collectivist perspective: *i.e.*, as an individualistic physiological need that must be satisfied before one moves on to higher pursuits. This view of sex neglects the emotional, familial and evolutionary implications of sex within the community.

ENTREPRENEURIAL MOTIVATION—MEANING

It is often said that a person cannot win a game that they do not play. In the context of entrepreneurship, this statement suggests that success depends on people's willingness to become entrepreneurs. Moreover, because the pursuit of entrepreneurial opportunity is an evolutionary process in which people select out at many steps along the way, decisions made after the discovery of opportunities—to positively evaluate opportunities, to pursue resources, and to design the mechanisms of exploitation—also depend on the willingness of people to "play" the game. In this paper, we argue that human motivations influence these decisions, and that variance across people in these motivations will influence who pursues entrepreneurial opportunities, who assembles resources, and how people undertake the entrepreneurial process.

In recent years, entrepreneurship research has focused largely on the environmental characteristics influencing firm foundings and the characteristics of entrepreneurial opportunities. Although this focus has greatly enhanced our understanding of the entrepreneurial phenomenon, it ignores the role of human agency. Entrepreneurship depends on the decisions that people make about how to undertake that process. We argue that the attributes of people making decisions about the entrepreneurial process influence the decisions that they make.

Although previous researchers have rightly criticised much of the existing empirical research on the role of human motivation in entrepreneurship, we argue that inadequate empirical work does not negate the importance of understanding the role of human motivation in the entrepreneurial process. In fact, even sociologists who have argued strongly against the usefulness of trait-based research in entrepreneurship implicitly acknowledge that motivation must matter to this process. Scholars write, entrepreneurial activity "can be conceptualised as a function of opportunity structures and motivated entrepreneurs with access to resources". We also believe that these criticisms have resulted in insufficient consideration of the role of the human motivation in the entrepreneurial process in recent entrepreneurship research.

Consequently, we are left with theories of entrepreneurship that do not consider variation in the motivations of different people. We believe that such an omission is problematic because, as Baumol eloquently argued, the study of entrepreneurship that does not explicitly consider entrepreneurs is like the analysis of Shakespeare in which "the Prince of Denmark has been expunged from the discussion of Hamlet." We identify several human motivations that influence the entrepreneurial process.

In our arguments, we explicitly assume that all human action is the result of both motivational and cognitive factors, the latter including ability, intelligence, and skills. We also assume that entrepreneurship is not solely the result of human action; external factors also play a role. However, environmental factors being held constant, we argue that human motivation plays a critical role in the entrepreneurial process. To this end, we suggest ways that researchers could develop more realistic explanations for how human motivation influences the entrepreneurial process than is the norm in the literature to date. We believe that this approach could overcome many of the criticisms of prior research on person-centric explanations for entrepreneurship. Finally, we offer suggestions on how empirical researchers should test these arguments in ways that overcome many of the criticisms of extant research on this topic.

We define entrepreneurship and present several arguments for why the study of entrepreneurship in general and consideration of the role of human motivation in the process in particular are important. We discuss opposing views of how opportunities may affect the relationship between motivation and entrepreneurship. We summarise the major mechanisms by which previous researchers believe motivation influences entrepreneurship. We identify what we believe are the major problems with prior research on motivation and entrepreneurship. We provide some recommendations for researchers conducting empirical research in this area. We offer some tentative conclusions about motivation and entrepreneurship.

WHAT IS ENTREPRENEURSHIP AND WHY STUDY IT FROM THE POINT OF VIEW OF HUMAN MOTIVATION

We believe that the study of the entrepreneurial process is important for several reasons. First, entrepreneurship drives innovation and technical change, and therefore generates economic growth. Second, as the Austrian economists have explained, entrepreneurial action is the process through which supply and demand are equilibrated. Third, entrepreneurship is an important process by which new knowledge is converted into products and services.

Fourth, entrepreneurship has become an important vocation and we need to understand its role in the development of human and intellectual capital. We adopt Shane and Venkataraman's definition of entrepreneurship as the process by which "opportunities to create future goods and services are discovered, evaluated, and exploited." As these authors have explained, this definition does not require viewing entrepreneurs as the founders of new organisations. An options trader can be an entrepreneur, as can a corporate salesman who discovers and pursues opportunities for the creation of new products. Moreover, this definition shows that entrepreneurship is a creative process. By rearranging resources in a new way, entrepreneurs engage in creative activity.

However, the degree of creativity involved in entrepreneurship varies across the types of resource recombination that occurs. For example, the creation of business to undertake space tourism may be more creative than the creation of a new restaurant in a strip mall. Entrepreneurship involves human agency. The entrepreneurial process occurs because people act to pursue opportunities. People differ in their willingness and abilities to act on these opportunities because they are different from each other. We argue that the variation among people in their willingness and ability to act has important effects on the entrepreneurial process.

Recent research has been relatively accepting of arguments that people vary in their willingness and ability to engage in the entrepreneurial process because of non-motivational individual differences. Researchers have shown that the willingness of people to pursue entrepreneurial opportunities depends on such things as their opportunity cost, their stocks of financial capital, their social ties to investors, and their career experience. We argue that motivational differences also influence the entrepreneurial process. For example, such things as variation across people in their perceptions of risk and opportunity influence entrepreneurial decisions.

People vary in how they view the risk of expending resources before knowing the distribution of outcomes. Similarly, the probability of success at the entrepreneurial process is low, and those people who are willing to proceed despite these odds might be more optimistic or higher in self-efficacy than people deterred by these odds. We consider the incorporation of this individual-level variation in motivation to be important to the entrepreneurial process. To isolate the effects of entrepreneurial motivation, other factors that could have a causal effect on the process and outcome of entrepreneurship need to be controlled. One category of control variables is the external environment.

These would include such things as:

* Political factors (*e.g.*, legal restrictions, quality of law enforcement, political stability, and currency stability);
* Market forces (*e.g.*, structure of the industry, technology regime, potential barriers to entry, market sise, and population demographics); and
* Resources (*e.g.*, availability of investment capital, Labour market including skill availability, transportation infrastructure, and complementary technology).

Most researchers either explicitly or implicitly agree that these categories of factors influence the entrepreneurial process and need to be controlled to measure the effect of motivations on the entrepreneurial process. While it is clear why the above factors need to be controlled if we are to fully understand how motivation is related to entrepreneurship, it is less clear how opportunities affect this relationship. Because the first two authors were unable to agree on the concept of opportunities, we present two versions of the relationship between opportunities and motivation. First, as suggested, present the view shared by Shane and Collins, then as suggested, present Locke's view.

ENTREPRENEURS, OPPORTUNITIES, AND THE EFFECTS OF MOTIVATION

Opportunities are aspects of the environment that represent potentialities for profit making. We follow Shane and

Venkataraman to define entrepreneurial opportunities as "situations in which new goods, services, raw materials, and organising methods can be introduced and sold at greater than the cost of their production." Since, potentialities are not yet actual, measuring them objectively and prospectively at the level of an individual entrepreneur poses daunting challenges. Entrepreneurs can pursue opportunities in any industry at any time.

For example, some entrepreneurs build successful new companies by contributing to the founding of a new industry, such as Robert Swanson in biotechnology. Other entrepreneurs build new companies in old and mature industries such as Sam Walton in retailing. Aggregate statistics show us that the general category of opportunities to which Sam Walton and Bob Swanson responded was not equal. The average value of new businesses created in retail is lower than the average value of new businesses created in biotechnology. Because human motivations are likely widely distributed across industry categories at the aggregate level, statistically significant differences in the mean value of businesses created in different industry categories suggest that the value of opportunities varies across industry.

This does not mean that entrepreneurs cannot successfully pursue opportunities in lowopportunity industries. Rather it means that the opportunities in these industries are simply less attractive to the average person. The value of opportunities also varies within industries. Because the opportunities that entrepreneurs identify and pursue have different economic value, the opportunities themselves influence entrepreneurial Behaviour. We believe that it is important for Behaviourally oriented entrepreneurship researchers to consider and measure the economic value of these opportunities in research about the motivations of entrepreneurs.

For example, in the early 1970s, Butler Lampson and Chuck Thacker, researchers at Xerox Parc, invented the Alto—the first personal computer. However, their design would have cost over US$10,000 to build. When Steve Jobs and Steve Wozniak came up with the design for the Apple computer, their design cost less than US$3000 to build. Because the number of people who would pay more than US$10,000 for a PC was much smaller than number of people who would pay US$3000, the financial value of the Jobs and Wozniak opportunity was greater than the value of the Xerox opportunity. One would expect that differences in the estimates of the value of the PC opportunity that resulted from the different solutions influenced the decisions of the different parties about their opportunities. Of course, although it is possible that Jobs and Wozniak possessed more of the relevant motives to pursue entrepreneurial opportunities than did Lampson and Thacker, researchers can only estimate the effect of these motives if they account for the differences in the two opportunities.

Although we argue that opportunities influence entrepreneurial behaviour, we do not argue that opportunities fully determine the process. Entrepreneurs are people and may make different decisions when confronted with similar opportunities. In addition to being influenced by the opportunity that Steve Jobs pursued at the time of founding, the development of Apple was likely influenced by Steve Jobs' motivations. Empirically, the objective and subjective parts of opportunity are difficult to separate. The mechanism for actualising an opportunity often initially exists mainly in the entrepreneur's mind, making the entrepreneur's idea for how to exploit the opportunity a personal interpretation of the opportunity.

This idea is basically what we would call vision. Such judgements may be mistaken; entrepreneurs sometimes believe that they have identified valuable opportunities when, in fact, no valuable opportunities actually existed, at least in the form in which they were conceptualised. Also, entrepreneurs may differ in how they interpret opportunities. For example, the development of the Internet has allowed entrepreneurs to develop new organising methods, such as "e-tailing", that were never before possible. Although a wide variety of entrepreneurs have responded to the opportunities to develop new organising methods that the Internet has generated, these entrepreneurs have developed approaches of different value in response to this organising opportunity. Some entrepreneurs have developed opportunities to compete with established retailers through e-tailing, while others have sought only to design web sites. Even though the way that opportunities are manifested in the entrepreneur's plans for exploitation are personal, the variance in their estimated value likely influences the decisions that people make in the entrepreneurial process and can confound attempts to measure the effects of motivation on this process. This is true even if the value is partially a function of the other decisions that the entrepreneur has made and partially a function of external forces.

MOTIVATION AND ENTREPRENEURSHIP: IMPORTANT MOTIVATIONAL CONCEPTS FROM PRIOR QUANTITATIVE RESEARCH

Previous research has explored several motivations and their effects on entrepreneurship. We discuss several of these concepts. However, we do not provide a complete review of prior empirical research for two reasons. First, the definitions of entrepreneurship used in previous empirical research on motivation and entrepreneurship are inconsistent with our definition, making it impossible to draw direct implications of prior work for research using our definition. Second, prior research has suffered from significant methodological problems that we discuss, making prior findings suggestive rather than conclusive, even for research that employs the same definition of entrepreneurship as was used in those studies. Therefore, we discuss previous empirical research only to illustrate the ways in which motivation can influence different aspects of the entrepreneurial process.

Need for Achievement

Within the research domain of personality traits and entrepreneurship, the concept of need for achievement has received much attention. McClelland argued that individuals who are high in nAch are more likely than those who are low in nAch to engage in activities or tasks that have a high degree of individual responsibility for outcomes, require individual skill and effort, have a moderate degree of risk, and include clear feedback on performance. Further, McClelland argued that entrepreneurial roles are characterised as having a greater degree of these task attributes than other careers; thus, it is likely that people high in nAch will be more likely to pursue entrepreneurial jobs than other types of roles. Johnson conducted a traditional review of various studies, which varied regarding samples, measurement of nAch, and definitions of entrepreneurship.

Based on this group of studies, Johnson concluded that there is a relationship between nAch and entrepreneurial activity—in this case, nAch distinguished firm founders from other members of society. In a similar review of studies, Fineman concluded that both projective and questionnaire measures of nAch significantly predict firm founding. Collins, Locke, and Hanges conducted the first and only meta-analysis of nAch and entrepreneurship studies, examining 63 nAch and entrepreneurship studies. The overall finding of the meta-analysis is that nAch is significantly related to founding a company.

The nAch both differentiated between entrepreneurs and others and predicted the performance of the founders' firms. Further, they found no significant differences in the predictive validity of three different measures of nAch. Moreover, Collins found that the relationship between nAch and entrepreneurial activity was moderated by several factors. First, nAch was a more robust predictor of group-level effects (*e.g.*, mean differences between firm founders and another profession, mean differences between high-performing and low-performing founders) than individuallevel effects (*e.g.*, predicting the performance of individuals). Second, they found that while nAch is a strong differentiator between firm founders and non-managerial employees, it is not a strong differentiator between firm founders and managers. Based on these results, Collins concluded that nAch is an effective tool for differentiating between firm founders and the general population but less so for differentiating between firm founders and managers. Further, they concluded that nAch might be particularly effective at differentiating between successful and unsuccessful groups of firm founders. Thus, nAch could play a very useful role in explaining entrepreneurial activity.

Risk Taking

Risk-taking propensity is another motivation of interest, which emerged from McClelland's original research on entrepreneurs. McClelland claimed that individuals with high achievement needs would have moderate propensities to take risk. This claim by McClelland is especially interesting for entrepreneurship research because the entrepreneurial process involves acting in the face of uncertainty. Liles argued that entrepreneurs often must accept uncertainty with respect to financial well-being, psychic well-being, career security, and family relations. Moreover, several theories of entrepreneurship view the entrepreneur as bearing residual uncertainty.

Scholar argued that individuals who have higher achievement motivation should prefer activities of intermediate risk because these types of activities will provide a challenge, yet appear to be attainable. On the other hand, individuals who score high on the motive to avoid failure will avoid intermediate risks. Instead, they will prefer easy and safe under- takings or extremely difficult and risky ones. Following the lead of Atkinson, risk-taking propensity has been defined in the entrepreneurship literature as the willingness to take moderate risks.

Despite these theoretical claims, previous research suggests that firm owners do not differ significantly from managers or even the general population in risk taking. For example, Litsinger failed to find any difference between motel owners and motel managers on risk preference. Kogan and Wallach found that firm founders clustered around the mean risk-taking score of the general population. In comparisons of firm founders and managers, neither Babb and Babb nor Palich and Bagby found significant differences between the two groups in terms of risk-taking propensity. However, none of the studies identified if firm founders were low, moderate, or high risk-takers.

Only Brockhaus tested for the actual level of risk taking, and he found that firm founders did prefer moderate risk but did not differ from managers in this regard. Only one study found a difference between firm founders and managers in this motivation. In a study of 239 New England business executives, Begley found that risk-taking propensity was the only trait on which founders and non-founders differed. Begley failed to identify whether the level of entrepreneurial risk taking was low, moderate, or high. While these empirical findings suggest that risk taking may or may not be an entrepreneurial motivation, self-efficacy may be confounding the findings.

Several recent evaluative studies using interviews and expert evaluations showed that firm founders objectively have a higher propensity for risk than do members of the general population, but that firm founders do not perceive their actions as risky. Similarly, Sarasvathy, Simon, and Lave found that when expert firm founders were asked to evaluate the same entrepreneurial simulations as bankers, the firm founders saw opportunities in information that the bankers thought indicated risk. Thus, the measurement of risk-taking propensity may be confounded with high self-efficacy.

Tolerance for Ambiguity

Schere argued that tolerance for ambiguity is an important trait for entrepreneurs because the challenges and potential for success associated with business start-ups are by nature unpredictable. Budner defined tolerance for ambiguity as the propensity to view situations without clear outcomes as attractive rather than threatening. Because entrepreneurs continually face more uncertainty in their everyday environment than do managers of established organisations, entrepreneurs who remain in their jobs are likely to score high on tests for this trait than would managers. There is mixed support for this prediction. Begley and Boyd found that firm founders scored significantly higher in tolerance for ambiguity than did managers, defined as non-founders working in business.

In smaller sample studies, both Schere and Miller and Drodge found that firm founders were significantly higher in tolerance for ambiguity than were managers. Finally, based on a review of four additional studies, Sexton and Bowman identified tolerance for ambiguity as a distinguishing psychological characteristic between firm founders and managers. However, several studies did not match these findings.

Babb and Babb found no significant difference in tolerance for ambiguity between founders and non-founders of rural businesses in Northern Florida. Similarly, Begley found no significant differences between New England firm founders and managers on their tolerance for ambiguity. This inconsistency in findings and potential methodological problems in the research that provides support for the tolerance of ambiguity proposition suggests that we do not yet know if tolerance of ambiguity is a motivation that affects any part of the entrepreneurial process.

Locus of Control

Another motivational trait that has received attention is locus of control—the belief in the extent to which individuals believe that their actions or personal characteristics affect outcomes. Individuals who have an external locus of control believe that the outcome of an extent is out of their control, whereas individuals with an internal locus of control believe that their personal actions directly affect the outcome of an event. As McClelland discussed earlier, individuals who are high in nAch prefer situations in which they feel that they have direct control over outcomes or in which they feel that they can directly see how their effort affects outcomes of a given event. This point was extended by Rotter who argued that individuals with an internal locus of control would be likely to seek entrepreneurial roles because they desire positions in which their actions have a direct impact on results. The research on locus of control suggests that firm founders differ from the general population in terms of locus of control. Shapero found that firm founders from Texas and Italy were more "internal" than other groups of professions reported by Rotter.

This same pattern holds with female firm founders versus the general female population and with Black firm founders versus the general Black population. While locus of control orientation differs between firm founders and the general public, most studies have not found a difference between firm founders and managers on locus of control, a result similar to the situation with studies on nAch. For example, Babb and Babb found no differences in locus of control between founders and managers in small businesses in Northern Florida. Similarly, Brockhaus found that managers and owners of new businesses did not differ on locus of control. In a longitudinal study of students, Hull, Bosley, and Udell found that locus of control did not differentiate between students who went on to work in managerial positions and those who started their own business.

Finally, in the studies of New England entrepreneurs, Begley and Begley and Boyd found that locus of control did not distinguish between founders and managers. We suspect that one reason for the difference between firm founder and the general population, but not between founders and managers, is the similarity between founding a company and managing. Defining entrepreneurial situations as starting a company rather than working for others might not capture the real differences between entrepreneurial and non-entrepreneurial situations. For example, serving as a manager in a rapidly growing high-technology company might demand greater entrepreneurial motivations than starting a corner grocery store.

Self-efficacy

Self-efficacy is the belief in one's ability to muster and implement the necessary personal resources, skills, and competencies to attain a certain level of achievement on a given task. In other words, self-efficacy can be seen as task-specific self-confidence. Self-efficacy for a specific task has been shown to be a robust predictor of an individual's performance in that task and helps to explain why people of equal ability can perform differently. An individual with high self-efficacy for a given task will exert more effort for a greater length of time, persist through set backs, set and accept higher goals, and develop better plans and strategies for the task. A person with high self-efficacy will also take negative feedback in a more positive manner and use that feedback to improve their performance.

These attributes of self-efficacy may be important to the entrepreneurial process because these situations are often ambiguous ones in which effort, persistence, and planning are important. One study directly assessed the effect of self-efficacy on some dimension of the entrepreneurial process. Baum assessed firm founders in the architectural woodworking industry on a number of variables including general traits and motives, specific skills and competencies, situation-specific motivation, vision, and strategic action. In a LISREL model, Baum found that self-efficacy had a strong positive relationship with realised growth. In fact, it was the single best predictor in the entire array of variables.

Goal Setting

Tracy, Locke, and Renard conducted a study of the owners of small printing firms. Both concurrent and longitudinal measures of four aspects of performance were obtained: financial performance, growth, and innovation. The quantitative goals the entrepreneurs had for each outcome were significantly related to their corresponding outcomes, both concurrently and longitudinally. Baum, Locke, and Smith also found that growth goals were significantly related to the subsequent growth of architectural woodworking firms. Although there have been other studies of entrepreneurial goals, to our knowledge, only these two have related quantitative measures of goal difficulty to performance.

PROBLEMS WITH PREVIOUS RESEARCH ON HUMAN MOTIVATION AND ENTREPRENEURSHIP AND SUGGESTED SOLUTIONS TO THESE PROBLEMS

Despite the importance of including individual-level factors in a comprehensive explanation for the entrepreneurial process, previous studies of entrepreneurial motivation have often led to disappointing results. However, we believe that researchers should not conclude from this failure that human motivation is irrelevant to the entrepreneurial process. Rather, we suggest that there are specific reasons for the limited results obtained in previous research.

Controls for Opportunities

Previous research has suffered from a lack of control for the variation in the opportunities that different entrepreneurs pursue. To accurately measure the effects of motivation on entrepreneurial decisions, researchers need to control the effects of opportunities. As Venkataraman argued, a valuable opportunity for an individual is one that generates a level of profit that exceeds the entrepreneur's opportunity cost, a premium for the illiquidity of money, time, and effort expended, and a premium for bearing risk and uncertainty. Because some opportunities will exceed this threshold by a greater amount than will others, the nature of the opportunity will influence entrepreneurial decisions.

Researchers need to know the magnitude of the force exerted by the opportunities themselves to accurately estimate the effect of the individual motivations on entrepreneurial decisions. In the absence of such controls, one cannot know if the effects observed represent the effects of individual motivations or are artifacts of unobserved correlation between the opportunities and the people who pursue them. Prior research has generally failed to control the effect of opportunities by examining entrepreneurs pursuing different opportunities without explicitly modeling the value of the different opportunities pursued. In addition, prior studies have generally compared managers with firm founders.

However, human motivations can influence the tendency of people to engage in entrepreneurial activities only if those activities are possible. If people have not discovered entrepreneurial opportunities or have discovered opportunities but cannot act on those discoveries, it is impossible to determine if their individual motivations make them more or less likely than others to act on entrepreneurial opportunities. Therefore, one cannot tell from studies that compare managers to firm founders whether certain motivations influence people to make entrepreneurial decisions unless researchers have ensured that the managers have discovered opportunities and have measured the value of those opportunities. Otherwise, researchers might only capture the fact that some managers have all of the right motivations, but no opportunities in which to use them.

We offer four suggestions to researchers interested in examining the effect of motivations on entrepreneurial decisions about how to deal with variation in opportunities. First, researchers could explore settings in which potential entrepreneurs pursue reasonably identical opportunities. For example, every year, many potential entrepreneurs evaluate and pursue opportunities to purchase McDonald's franchises.

When a person applies to be a McDonald's franchisee or company-owned outlet manager, one applies only to be part of the system rather than to select a particular outlet. Therefore, the opportunities to which people respond in this setting are identical. By comparing the motivations of a sample of people seek to be McDonald's franchisees with people who seek to be McDonald's company-owned outlet managers, researchers can determine the contributions of particular motivations on the decision to entrepreneur. Second, as a variety of researchers are beginning to do, scholars could employ experimental designs in which potential entrepreneurs are asked to make a series of entrepreneurial decisions in a controlled simulation. By measuring the motivations of potential entrepreneurs and examining the correlation between the motivations and the decisions made in these simulations, researchers could determine how motivations influence entrepreneurial decisions.

Third, the most obvious means of controlling opportunity are to use a sample of entrepreneurs within the same industry and country and to measure aspects of the environment that might vary within industry and region. We recommend these approaches to limiting other sources of variance than motivations from studies of motivation and entrepreneurship. Fourth, as some researchers are beginning to do, scholars could employ third parties to code the value of potential opportunities. For example, researchers could explore the propensity of inventors to found companies based on their inventions. Because all inventors are at risk of exploiting their inventions through firm formation, this setting provides a useful context in which to explore the decision to entrepreneur. By partialing out the externally evaluated value of the opportunities, researchers could determine whether motivations influence the decision to entrepreneur, net of the effects of the value of the opportunity.

Entrepreneurship as a Process

Much of the prior research has looked at entrepreneurship as a profession that certain types of people adopt, rather than as a process that occurs over time. This approach is problematic because the appropriate conceptual lens through which to look at entrepreneurship is as a dynamic process. Because entrepreneurship is episodic and much entrepreneurial action is not long lasting, it is unrealistic to model motivation as dividing entrepreneurs and other members of society into two groups. In fact, relatively little of the motivation research on entrepreneurship has considered the effects of motivation on specific steps in the entrepreneurial process. Most studies on motivation and entrepreneurship adopt static designs that seek to determine if firm founders are different from each other, managers, or the general population at the moment the two groups are measured.

This approach makes two problematic assumptions. First, it assumes that a given motivation influences all steps in the entrepreneurial process equally, and that the effects of a given motivation do not select out some people at earlier stages in the process. Second, it assumes that, at the moment in which the founders are compared to the others, the founders who are still in charge of the organisations that they founded represent the population of people who engage in entrepreneurial activity. Because entrepreneurship is a process, with tremendous selection at each step, we believe that these assumptions are quite faulty.

The motivations that allow progression from opportunity recognition to resource assembly might not lead from financial assembly to first sales. For example, to assemble resources, a person might need to be highly confident. Those people lacking sufficient overconfidence to assemble resources are selected out of the entrepreneurial process. If there is very little variation in over-confidence among the people who have resources and seek to reach first sales, overconfidence will have no effect on achieving first sales. For these reasons, we believe that it may not be possible to examine the direct effects of a lead entrepreneur's motivations on the financial performance of a new company that the individual founds.

The effects of motivation might be captured by the intervening variables in any causal model of the effects of motivation on firm performance. For example, those higher in nAch might be more likely to obtain venture capital financing. However, once venture capital financing is measured, there is no effect of nAch on firm performance. We offer several specific suggestions for how researchers could better think about how motivations influence the entrepreneurial process. First, researchers could incorporate motivations into a dynamic evolutionary perspective on entrepreneurship by using motivations to distinguish those individuals who select out at different steps in the entrepreneurial process. For example, motivations could separate those individuals who positively evaluate opportunities from those who do not, those who obtain outside funding from those who do not, those who continue to pursue opportunities from those who abandon the effort, or those who pursue rapid rather than slow growth.

The pursuit of opportunity provides a good example. As Aldrich and Zimmer explain, "opportunities are irrelevant unless taken advantage of, and people vary widely in their ability to seise opportunities". We agree, but would argue that people also differ widely in their motivation to seise opportunities. It would be interesting to know if certain motivations predispose people to take action in response to the discovery of opportunities. One might argue, for example, that people higher in self-efficacy will be more likely to seek financing to exploit opportunities than will people lower in self-efficacy.

Because the process of financing exposes a person's entrepreneurial ideas to the scrutiny of skeptical others, those people willing to expose their ideas to scrutiny might have to be more confident than those who will not. Second, researchers could theorise more deeply about how motivation might impact entrepreneurial decisions. Rather than falling back on the stock idea that firm founders must be fundamentally different types of people from other members of society, we suggest researchers consider how motivations might influence some people to make different decisions from others in the entrepreneurial process.

For example, inventors higher in selfefficacy might found firms to exploit their inventions while inventors lower in self-efficacy might license their technology to others. Similarly, entrepreneurs with a greater need for independence might self-finance new firms, whereas those with a lesser need for independence might seek venture capital. We also suggest that it is not necessarily important for entrepreneurship researchers to show that specific motivations influence the financial performance of new firms. If financial performance of a new firm is conditional on the ability of an entrepreneur to create the firm, and that act of creation depends heavily on human motivation, then human motivation matters to entrepreneurship even if motivation has no direct effect on the performance of the newly founded firm.

In fact, we would expect that the more significant a firm that an entrepreneur founds, the less their motivations influence the firm formation process. For example, the more significant the new firm that an entrepreneur builds, the less influence they will have personally on day-to-day operations, and the less that we would expect the financial performance of the firm to be affected by their personal motivations.

Meta-analysis

The third criticism of previous research is the failure to use meta-analysis. The ability to combine the results of scores or hundreds of individual studies into a single statistic was not always available to researchers. This sometimes led people who conducted narrative reviews to underestimate the effect of the variable being considered; for example, non-significant results in single studies may be due to sampling error rather than invalidity. Although metaanalytic results are not available for all the motivations we discuss, such data, where available, throw new light on some motivations.

Wrong Motives

A fourth criticism of extant research is its tendency to study the wrong motives. Some motives are more relevant to entrepreneurial activity than others. For example, risk-taking propensity as measured by self-perception and tolerance for ambiguity has long been assumed to be an entrepreneurial motive, but the evidence so far is only equivocal. Regarding risk, perhaps the problem has been that people cannot perceive the riskiness of their own actions, or that what is risky to one person is not risky to another. For example, several recent studies using interviews and expert evaluations showed that entrepreneurs objectively have a higher propensity for risk than either entrepreneurs or the general population but that entrepreneurs do not perceive their actions as risky. Thus, the effects of risk-taking propensity may be confounded with the high self-efficacy of entrepreneurs.

We suggest that researchers better define the motives that they think are important and focus on more precise measures of them. One way to do that would be for researchers to go back to the underlying psychological literature and examine how researchers have dealt with the nuances of theorising about and measuring the same motives in other settings. If psychologists have figured a way around the problems of using self-perceptions in the measurement of risky Behaviour, like drug usage, those same techniques can be brought to bear on the measurement of risky behaviour in entrepreneurial settings. We believe that another important step for research on motivation and entrepreneurship would be for researchers to develop more complete models of the entrepreneurial process before examining the effects of particular motives on particular activities. A fuller understanding of the role of motivations in the overall process would require consideration of factors other than motives. We suggest that researchers develop explanations that include the variety of such influences.

Indirect Effects

A fifth criticism has been the failure to look for indirect effects of motivational traits. Most, though not all, researchers have assumed that traits and motives have direct effects on outcomes and this may be true to some extent. However, an increasing body of literature is revealing that traits affect action indirectly through other mechanisms. For example, in the general realm of work, conscientiousness is a reliable predictor of performance, but there is considerable evidence that the effects of conscientiousness on work performance are mediated by situation-specific factors such as goal setting and goal commitment. Similarly, Bandura has argued that locus of control is not a strong, direct predictor of performance in a task; and studies have shown that the effects of self-efficacy mediate the effects of locus of control when self-efficacy is added to the equation. Therefore, locus of control effects reported in the entrepreneurship literature might be proxying unobserved self-efficacy.

One recent study to have taken the approach of considering indirect effects of motivation in the setting of entrepreneurial action is that of Baum, who studied the growth of small companies in the architectural woodworking industry. They included variables from five separate domains: traits and motives, skills and abilities, situation-specific motivation, business strategies, and environmental factors. They combined the measures within each domain into single indexes and related these indexes to each other and to venture growth. All the domains played a role in venture growth but the effects of motives were all indirect. Motives worked through skills, situation-specific motivation, and strategies to affect growth. Given the indirect effects observed in this study, we suggest that researchers consider such indirect patterns in their explanations for the effect of motivation on entrepreneurial action.

Definitions

A sixth criticism has stemmed from a lack of consistent definitions of entrepreneurship. In general, the definition of what constitutes entrepreneurial activity varies significantly across studies. For example, McClelland viewed managerial positions of certain types such as sales as one that demanded entrepreneurial skills, whereas much of the recent work in the applied field of management has sought to compare entrepreneurs to managers. Therefore, it is unclear if the samples from these different studies are comparable, or even represent entrepreneurship in a meaningful way. This point, of course, brings us back to the importance of a common definition of entrepreneurship. As we indicated earlier, we advocate the definition proposed by Shane and Venkataraman. Whether researchers adopt this particular definition, however, is less important than the existence of a common definition. Without a common definition, it will not be possible to accumulate findings that are comparable from study to study.

HOW MOTIVATIONS INFLUENCE ENTREPRENEURSHIP

We suggest how human motivations might influence the entrepreneurial process. We offer this example to help future researchers design empirical tests of the role of motivation in entrepreneurship.

We begin with the set of human motivations that psychologists have shown to influence many aspects of human Behaviour. These include the motivations that we described earlier in the study, in particular, nAch, locus of control, desire for independence, passion, and drive. We propose that entrepreneurship is a process that begins with the recognition of an entrepreneurial opportunity and is followed by the development of an idea for how to pursue that opportunity, the evaluation of the feasibility of the opportunity, the development of the product or service that will be provided to customers, assembly of human and financial resources, organisational design, and the pursuit of customers. We suggest that some or all of the motivations influence the transition of individuals from one stage of the entrepreneurial process to another. In some cases, all of the motivations might matter.

In other cases, only some of the motivations might matter. The relative magnitudes of how much each motivation matters will likely vary, depending on the part of the process under investigation. In fact, it is quite plausible that motivations that influence one part of the process have all of their effects at that stage in the process and have no effects on later stages in the process. In this example, motivations are not the only things that influence these transitions. Cognitive factors, including knowledge, skills, and abilities, certainly matter. All action is the result of the combination or integration of motivation and cognition. First, the entrepreneurs need to have some knowledge, especially of the industry and of any relevant technology that is critical to success.

They can hire people with certain specialised skills that they lack, but they must possess enough expertise to know that they are doing the right thing. Second, the entrepreneur must have skills. The necessary skills will depend on the circumstances, but they may include such factors as selling and bargaining, leadership, planning, decision-making, problem solving, team building, communication, and conflict management. Third, the entrepreneur needs to have the requisite abilities, including intelligence. Possessing the necessary KSAs enables the entrepreneurs to develop a viable vision, including a strategy for the organisation and to carry it out successfully.

Motivation helps the entrepreneur to acquire such KSAs in the first place and provide the impetus and energy to implement the needed actions. The human capital literature in entrepreneurship has begun to show the effect of certain types of knowledge and skills on the start-up and resource assembly parts of this process. The opportunities themselves certainly matter. Prior research has shown that such things as the possession of a patented technology make individuals more likely to engage in the entrepreneurial process. One would expect that identification of a large market or a high margin product would do the same.

First, opportunities may interact in interesting ways with the attributes of people. Second, as much of the macro-level research has shown, the willingness to engage in entrepreneurial activities depends on such things as the legal system of the country in which the entrepreneur operates, the age of the industry, the availability of capital in the economy, the condition of capital markets, and the state of the overall economy. We believe that these factors are important, but that it might also be interesting to know whether motivations of particular people lead to different types of entrepreneurial action under different environmental conditions.

Motivations might be more or less stronger than these other factors in the degree that they influence particular transition points. In addition, there might be important and interesting interaction effects between motivations and opportunities, KSAs, and environmental factors. The relative importance of different categories of factors, their independent and combined effects, and their relative importance at different stages of the entrepreneurial process are clearly important theoretical and empirical questions that remain largely unexplored. We hope that researchers will begin to explore them because they appear to us to be central issues in the field of entrepreneurship.

MOTIVATION FACTORS AND THEORIES

MOTIVATION FACTORS

* When we look at the psychology of human Behaviour we can begin to understand certain

baseline motivations which draw adults to on line social networks. Abraham Maslow published his theory of human motivation in 1943. Its popularity continues unabated. Like his colleague Carl Rogers, Maslow believed that actualisation was the driving force of human personality, Motivation and Personality. Maslow's great insight was to place actualisation into a hierarchy of motivation. Self-actualisation, as he called it, is the highest drive, but before a person can turn to it, he or she must satisfy other, lower motivations like hunger, safety and belonging. The hierarchy has five levels.

* Physiological (hunger, thirst, shelter, sex, etc.).
* Safety (security, protection from physical and emotional harm).
* Social (affection, belonging, acceptance, friendship)
* Esteem (also called ego). The internal ones are self respect, autonomy, achievement and the external ones are status, recognition, and attention.
* Self-actualisation (doing things).

Maslow points out that the hierarchy is dynamic; the dominant need is always shifting. The hierarchy does not exist by itself, but is affected by the situation and the general culture. Satisfaction is relative. Douglas McGregor makes it the building block for his Theory X and Theory Y.

A 1990s example of self actualisation may be surfing the Internet. Empirical research has confirmed the first three levels, but has not done so for the fourth and fifth levels of esteem and self-actualisation. Some have noted that Maslow's hierarchy follows the life cycle. A newborn baby's needs are almost entirely physiological. As the baby grows, it needs safety, then love.

Toddlers are eager for social interaction. Teenagers are anxious about social needs; young adults are concerned with esteem and only more mature people transcend the first four levels to spend much time self actualising. Based on the observations across numerous networking platforms and reflect on the past definitions of human motivation we can see that social networks on line provide a primary motivation for adults in the category of self actualisation, or doing things.

Maslow defines self actualisation as growth-motivated rather than deficiency-motivated:

* Based on observations and interview as suggested, provide a general categorisation of the factors that enhance individual growth for adults participating in on line social networks. Each of these factors will be defined in greater detail in future articles post.
* With all the hype, craze and media coverage of social networking platforms, *,i.e.,* Facebook and Linkedin, many adults are drawn to the medium to learn what the hype is all about.
* Once adults enter networks and learn the "tools of the trade" many are amazed to find the presence of other adults they know and many they don't already engaged with the medium.
* Adults begin to find association with groups, causes, forums, media and other affinities which relate to their interest both personally and professionally.
* The predominant business segment using social networks today is employment recruiters. However, as the medium and adult participation has grown there is an exponential growth of business opportunities that adults are learning to facilitate using social networks as the medium.
* Adults, and their businesses, are applying creative ways to use the technology behind social computing to extend its value to both personal and professional needs.
* When you consider the creative possibilities of social networks adults expect to the formation of some economic and social value to be derived from their participation whether currently or in the future.

The expectation of individual growth and satisfaction is high.These factors combined with the media hype over social networking are the motivating issues which are driving millions of adults to the medium at annual growth rates of 70 per cent and more. The opportunity to capitalise economically is emerging quickly. Word of mouth will fuel growth rates faster than any other technological medium in our past.

THEORIES OF MOTIVATION

Contribution of Robert Owen

Though Owen is considered to be paternalistic in his view, his contribution is of a considerable significance in the theories of motivation. During the early years of the nineteenth century, Owen's textile mill at New Lanark in Scotland was the scene of some novel ways of treating people. His view was that people were similar to machines. A machine that is looked after properly, cared for and maintained well, performs efficiently, reliably and lastingly, similarly people are likely to be more efficient if they are taken care of. Robert Owen practiced what he preached and introduced such things as employee housing and company shop. His ideas on this and other matters were considered to be too revolutionary for that time.

Jeremy Bentham's "The Carrot and the Stick Approach"

Possibly the essence of the traditional view of people at work can be best appreciated by a brief look at the work of this English philosopher, whose ideas were also developed in the early years of the Industrial Revolution, around 1800. Bentham's view was that all people are self-interested and are motivated by the desire to avoid pain and find pleasure. Any worker will work only if the reward is big enough, or the punishment sufficiently unpleasant. This view - the 'carrot and stick' approach - was built into the philosophies of the age and is still to be found, especially in the older, more traditional sectors of industry.

The various leading theories of motivation and motivators seldom make reference to the carrot and the stick. This metaphor relates, of course, to the use of rewards and penalties in order to induce desired Behaviour. It comes from the old story that to make a donkey move, one must put a carrot in front of him or dab him with a stick from behind. Despite all the research on the theories of motivation, reward and punishment are still considered strong motivators. For centuries, however, they were too often thought of as the only forces that could motivate people. At the same time, in all theories of motivation, the inducements of some kind of 'carrot' are recognised. Often this is money in the form of pay or bonuses. Even though money is not the only motivating force, it has been and will continue to be an important one. The trouble with the money 'carrot' approach is that too often everyone gets a carrot, regardless of performance through such practices as salary increase and promotion by seniority, automatic 'merit' increases, and executive bonuses not based on individual manager performance. It is as simple as this: If a person put a donkey in a pen full of carrots and then stood outside with a carrot, would the donkey be encouraged to come out of the pen ? The 'stick', in the form of fear-fear of loss of job, loss of income, reduction of bonus, demotion, or some other penalty–has been and continues to be a strong motivator.

Yet it is admittedly not the best kind. It often gives rise to defensive or retaliatory Behaviour, such as union organisation, poor-quality work, executive indifference, failure of a manager to take any risks in decision making or even dishonesty. But fear of penalty cannot be overlooked. Whether managers are first-level supervisors or chief executives, the power of their position to give or with hold rewards or impose penalties of various kinds gives them an ability to control, to a very great extent, the economic and social well-being of their subordinates.

Abraham Maslow's "Need Hierarchy Theory"

One of the most widely theories of motivation is the hierarchy of needs theory put forth by psychologist Abraham Maslow. Maslow saw human needs in the form of a hierarchy, ascending from the lowest to the highest, and he concluded that when one set of needs is satisfied, this kind of need ceases to be a motivator. As per his theory this needs are: These are important needs for sustaining the human life. Food, water, warmth, shelter, sleep, medicine and education are the basic physiological needs which fall in the primary list of need satisfaction. Maslow was of an opinion that until these needs were satisfied to a degree to maintain life, no other motivating factors can work.

These are the needs to be free of physical danger and of the fear of losing a job, property, food or shelter. It also includes protection against any emotional harm. Since, people are social beings, they need to belong and be accepted by others. People try to satisfy their need for affection, acceptance and friendship. Once people begin to satisfy their need to belong, they tend to want to be held in esteem both by themselves and by others. This kind of need produces such satisfaction as power, prestige status and self-confidence. It includes both internal esteem factors like self-respect, autonomy and achievements and external esteem factors such as states, recognition and attention.

Maslow regards this as the highest need in his hierarchy. It is the drive to become what one is capable of becoming, it includes growth, achieving one's potential and self-fulfilment. It is to maximise one's potential and to accomplish something.

From the standpoint of motivation, the theory would say that although no need is ever fully gratified, a substantially satisfied need no longer motivates. So if you want to motivate someone, you need to understand what level of the hierarchy that person is on and focus on satisfying those needs or needs above that level. Maslow's need theory has received wide recognition, particularly among practicing managers. This can be attributed to the theory's intuitive logic and ease of understanding. However, research does not validate these theory. Maslow provided no empirical evidence and other several studies that sought to validate the theory found no support for it.

"Theory X and Theory Y" of Douglas McGregor

McGregor, in his book "The Human side of Enterprise" states that people inside the organisation can be managed in two ways. The first is basically negative, which falls under the category X and the other is basically positive, which falls under the category

Y. After viewing the way in which the manager dealt with employees, McGregor concluded that a manager's view of the nature of human beings is based on a certain grouping of assumptions and that he or she tends to mold his or her Behaviour towards subordinates according to these assumptions.

Under the assumptions of theory X:

* Employees inherently do not like work and whenever possible, will attempt to avoid it.
* Because employees dislike work, they have to be forced, coerced or threatened with punishment to achieve goals.
* Employees avoid responsibilities and do not work fill formal directions are issued.
* Most workers place a greater importance on security over all other factors and display little ambition.

In contrast under the assumptions of theory Y:

* Physical and mental effort at work is as natural as rest or play.
* People do exercise self-control and self-direction and if they are committed to those goals.
* Average human beings are willing to take responsibility and exercise imagination, ingenuity and creativity in solving the problems of the organisation.
* That the way the things are organised, the average human being's brainpower is only partly used.

On analysis of the assumptions it can be detected that theory X assumes that lower-order needs dominate individuals and theory Y assumes that higher-order needs dominate individuals. An organisation that is run on Theory X lines tends to be authoritarian in nature, the word "authoritarian" suggests such ideas as the "power to enforce obedience" and the "right to command". In contrast Theory Y organisations can be described as "participative", where the aims of the organisation and of the individuals in it are integrated; individuals can achieve their own goals best by directing their efforts towards the success of the organisation. However, this theory has been criticised widely for generalisation of work and human Behaviour.

Contribution of Rensis Likert

Likert developed a refined classification, breaking down organisations into four management systems:

* 1st System – Primitive authoritarian.
* 2nd System – Benevolent authoritarian.
* 3rd System – Consultative.
* 4th System – Participative.

As per the opinion of Likert, the 4th system is the best, not only for profit organisations, but also for non-profit firms.

Frederick Herzberg's Motivation-hygiene Theory

Frederick has tried to modify Maslow's need Hierarchy theory. His theory is also known as two-factor theory or Hygiene theory. He stated that there are certain satisfiers and dissatisfiers for employees at work. Intrinsic factors are related to job satisfaction, while extrinsic factors are associated with dissatisfaction. He devised his theory on the question: "What do people want from their jobs ?" He asked people to describe in detail, such situations when they felt exceptionally good or exceptionally bad. From the responses that he received, he concluded that opposite of satisfaction is not dissatisfaction. Removing dissatisfying characteristics from a job does not necessarily make the job satisfying. He states that presence of certain factors in the organisation is natural and the presence of the same does not lead to motivation. However, their non-presence leads to demotivation. In similar manner there are certain factors, the absence of which causes no dissatisfaction, but their presence has motivational impact.

Examples of Hygiene factors are:

* Security, status, relationship with subordinates, personal life, salary, work conditions, relationship with supervisor and company policy and administration.

Examples of Motivational factors are:

* Growth prospectus job advancement, responsibility, challenges, recognition and achievements.

Contributions of Elton Mayo

The work of Elton Mayo is famously known as "Hawthorne Experiments". He conducted Behavioural experiments at the Hawthorne Works of the American Western Electric Company in Chicago. He made some illumination experiments, introduced breaks in between the work performance and also introduced refreshments during the pause's.

On the basis of this he drew the conclusions that motivation was a very complex subject. It was not only about pay, work condition and morale but also included psychological and social factors.

Although this research has been criticised from many angles, the central conclusions drawn were:

* People are motivated by more than pay and conditions.
* The need for recognition and a sense of belonging are very important.
* Attitudes towards work are strongly influenced by the group.

Vroom's Valence x Expectancy Theory

The most widely accepted explanations of motivation has been propounded by Victor Vroom. His theory is commonly known as expectancy theory.

The theory argues that the strength of a tendency to act in a specific way depends on the strength of an expectation that the act will be followed by a given outcome and on the attractiveness of that outcome to the individual to make this simple, expectancy theory says that an employee can be motivated to perform better when their is a belief that the better performance will lead to good performance appraisal and that this shall result into realisation of personal goal in form of some reward.

Therefore an employee is:

* Motivation = Valence x Expectancy.

The theory focuses on three things:

* Efforts and performance relationship.

* Performance and reward relationship.
* Rewards and personal goal relationship.

This leads us to a conclusion that:

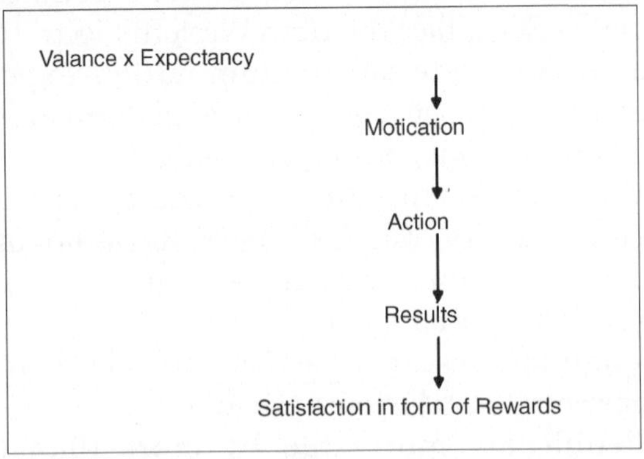

The Porter and Lawler Model

Lyman W. Porter and Edward E. Lawler developed a more complete version of motivation depending upon expectancy theory.

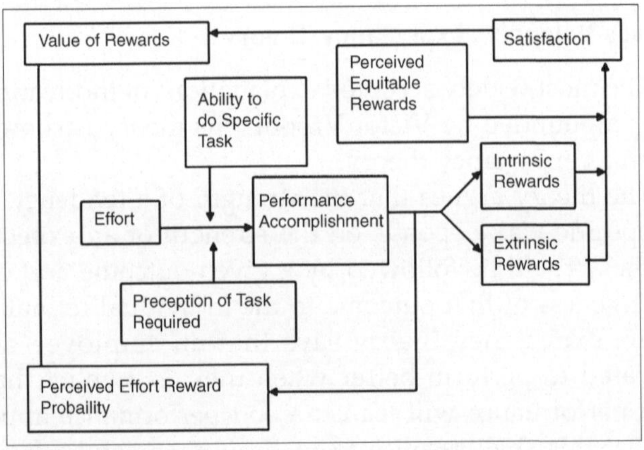

Actual performance in a job is primarily determined by the effort spent. But it is also affected by the person's ability to do the job and also by individual's perception of what the required task is.

So performance is the responsible factor that leads to intrinsic as well as extrinsic rewards. These rewards, along with the equity of individual leads to satisfaction. Hence, satisfaction of the individual depends upon the fairness of the reward.

Clayton Alderfer's ERG Theory

Alderfer has tried to rebuild the hierarchy of needs of Maslow into another model named ERG, *i.e.*, Existence–Relatedness–Growth. The existence group is concerned mainly with providing basic material existence. The second group is the individuals need to maintain interpersonal relationship with other members in the group. The final group is the intrinsic desire to grow and develop personally.

The major conclusions of this theory are:

* In an individual, more than one need may be operative at the same time.
* If a higher need goes unsatisfied than the desire to satisfy a lower need intensifies.
* It also contains the frustration-regression dimension.

McClelland's Theory of Needs

David McClelland has developed a theory on three types of motivating needs:

* Need for Power.
* Need for Affiliation.
* Need for Achievement.

Basically people for high need for power are inclined towards influence and control. They like to be at the center and are good orators. They are demanding in nature, forceful in manners and ambitious in life. They can be motivated to perform if they are given key positions or power positions. In the second category are the people who are social in nature. They try to affiliate themselves with individuals and groups. They are driven by love and faith. They like to build a friendly environment around themselves. Social recognition and affiliation with others provides them motivation. People in the third area are driven by the challenge of success and the fear of failure. Their need for achievement is moderate and they set for themselves moderately difficult tasks. They are analytical in nature and take calculated risks. Such people are motivated to perform when they see atleast some chances of success. McClelland observed that with the advancement in hierarchy the need for power and achievement increased rather than Affiliation. He also observed that people who were at the top, later ceased to be motivated by this drives.

Equity Theory

As per the equity theory of J. Stacey Adams, people are motivated by their beliefs about the reward structure as being fair or unfair, relative to the inputs. People have a tendency to use subjective Judgement to balance the outcomes and inputs in the relationship for comparisons between different individuals. Accordingly:

$$\frac{\text{Out comes by a Person}}{\text{Inputs by a Person}} = \frac{\text{Out comes by Another Person}}{\text{Input by Another Person}}$$

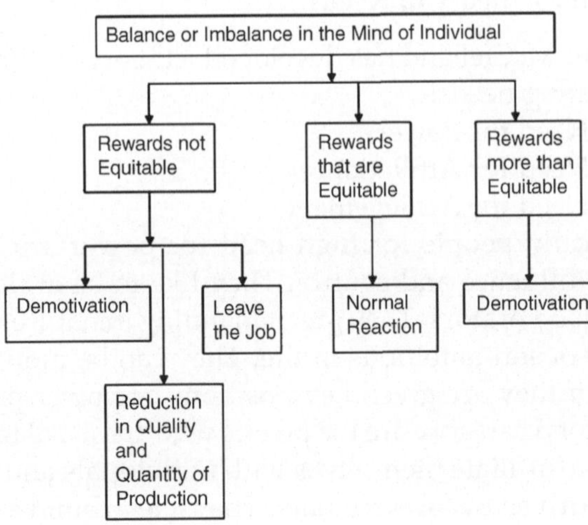

If people feel that they are not equally rewarded they either reduce the quantity or quality of work or migrate to some other organisation. However, if people perceive that they are rewarded higher, they may be motivated to work harder.

Reinforcement Theory

B.F. Skinner, who propounded the reinforcement theory, holds that by designing the environment properly, individuals can be motivated. Instead of considering internal factors like impressions, feelings, attitudes and other cognitive Behaviour, individuals are directed by what happens in the environment external to them.

Skinner states that work environment should be made suitable to the individuals and that punishments actually leads to frustration and de-motivation. Hence, the only way to motivate is to keep on making positive changes in the external environment of the organisation.

Goal Setting Theory of Edwin Locke

Instead of giving vague tasks to people, specific and pronounced objectives, help in achieving them faster. As the clarity is high, a goal orientation also avoids any misunderstandings in the work of the employees. The goal setting theory states that when the goals to be achieved are set at a higher standard than in that case employees are motivated to perform better and put in maximum effort. It revolves around the concept of "Self-efficacy", *i.e.*, individual's belief that he or she is capable of performing a hard task.

Cognitive Evaluation Theory

As per this theory a shift from external rewards to internal rewards results into motivation. It believes that even after the stoppage of external stimulus, internal stimulus survives. It relates to the pay structure in the organisation. Instead of treating external factors like pay, incentives, promotion etc and internal factors like interests, drives, responsibility etc, separately, they should be treated as contemporary to each other.

The cognition is to be such that even when external motivators are not there the internal motivation continues. However, practically extrinsic rewards are given much more weightage.

OBJECTIVES AND ACHIEVEMENTS OF MOTIVATION

MAIN OBJECTIVES OF MOTIVATION

Self-preservation, whether this is pointed directly to survivial or towards our image of ourselves painted by our beliefs and ideals. What I mean by this is that we have in our mind a view point of who we are and we trive to accomplish this in either advancement or a continuation of our currant state. This personal view point might look down upon theft, and so seeing a theft we might feel "motivated" to call police, in order to up keep our currant view of what kind of person we see ourselves as.

ACHIEVEMENT

Over the years, behavioural scientists have noticed that some people have an intense desire to achieve something, while others may not seem that concerned about their achievements. This phenomenon has attracted a lot of discussions and debates. Scientists have observed that people with a high level of achievement motivation exhibit certain characteristics. Achievement motivation is the tendency to endeavor for success and to choose goal oriented success or failure activities.

Achievement motivation forms to be the basic for a good life. People who are oriented towards achievement, in general, enjoy life and feel in control. Being motivated keeps people dynamic and gives them self-respect. They set moderately difficult but easily achievable targets, which help them, achieve their objectives. They do not set up extremely difficult or extremely easy targets. By doing this they ensure that they only undertake tasks that can be achieved by them. Achievement motivated people prefer to work on a problem rather than leaving the outcome to chance.

It is also seen that achievement motivated people seem to be more concerned with their personal achievement rather than the rewards of success. It is generally seen that achievement motivated people evidenced a significantly higher rate of advancement in their company compared to others. Programmes and courses designed, involves seven "training inputs." The first step refers to the process through which achievement motivation thinking is taught to the person. The second step helps participants understand their own individuality and goals. The third assist participants in practicing achievement-related actions in cases, role-plays, and real life. A fourth refers to practicing of achievement-related actions in business and other games.

A fifth input encourages participants to relate the achievement Behaviour model to their own Behaviour, self-image, and goals. The sixth Programme facilitates participants to develop a personal plan of action. Finally, the course provides participants with feedback on their progress towards achieving objectives and targets. Achievement motivation as a branch of study has greatly established its prominence. A number of companies are now training their employees in the same.

ENTREPRENEURIAL COMPETENCIES

Every career draws on the competencies of an individual. Some of these competencies may be general and some peculiar to the chosen career. You may understand competencies to mean abilities and skills. However, we would desist from calling these as personality traits as such a conceptualisation only reinforces the mistaken belief that entrepreneurs are born rather than made. We believe that recognition of these competencies as abilities and skills makes entrepreneurship as a teachable and learnable behaviour. We orient you towards a set of entrepreneurial competencies developed by the Entrepreneurship Development Institute of India Ahemdabad. These competencies were identified by a thorough research procedure based on critical analysis of the case studies of the successful entrepreneurs.

ENTREPRENEURIAL COMPETENCIES IDENTIFIED BY THE EDI

* Acting out of choice rather than compulsion, taking the lead rather than waiting for others to start.

* A mindset where one is trained to look for business opportunities from everyday experiences. Recall 'oranges' example.
* A 'never say die' attitude, not giving up easily, striving Information seeking continuously until success is achieved.
* Knowing who knows, consulting experts, reading of relevant material and an overall openness to ideas and information.
* Attention to details and observance of established standards and norms.
* Taking personal pains to complete a task as scheduled.
* Concern for conservation of time, money and effort.
* Breaking up the complex whole into parts, close examination of the parts and inferring about the whole *e.g.*, simultaneously attending to production, marketing and financial aspects (parts) of the overall business strategy (the whole).
* Observing the symptoms, diagnosing and curing.
* Not being afraid of the risks associated with business and relying on one's capabilities to successfully manage these.
* Conveying emphatically one's vision and convincing others of its value.
* Eliciting support of others in the venture.
* Providing leadership.
* Ensuring the progress of the venture as planned.
* Believing in employee well being as the key to competitiveness and success and initiating programmes of employee welfare.

The self-administered questionnaire in the annexure to this chapter would help you measure where you stand on these competencies. Given that these competencies matter in entrepreneurial success. EDI estimates that development of these competencies can substantially bring down incidence of business failures/industrial sickness.

DEVELOPING COMPETENCIES

'Awareness,' they say, is the first step towards 'improvement' and 'success.' Now that you are aware of the critical competencies for entrepreneurial success and also have a measure of your scores on these, it is appropriate that you also think in terms of how to improve your scores. Suppose, you find yourself lacking in the competency - 'opportunity spotting,' you may start practicing to think like an entrepreneur. With just a little change in perspective, the world changes for you. Similarly you may work on the other competencies as well.

MOTIVATION AND PRODUCTIVITY IN THE LIBRARY

Employee motivation is important in libraries, as in any other organisation. This chapter attempts to identify the place of motivation in developing human resources in the library. This attempt begins with the need to define human resources, human resources development, and motivation, and to discuss theories of motivation and the literature of motivation as they pertain to libraries.

THE CONCEPT OF HUMAN RESOURCES

UNECA conceptualises human resources as the body of knowledge, skills, attitudes, physical, and managerial efforts required to manipulate land, capital, and technology, to produce goods and services for human consumption and welfare.

Human resources includes:

* Technical skill and abilities acquired from education, training, and experience. It indicates the ability to use knowledge, methods, and techniques in the performance of library tasks.
* Human skills, which is the ability to work with and through people. It includes the understanding of motivation and the application of effective leadership.
* Conceptual skill, which incorporates the ability to understand the complexity of the overall organisation.

Human resources includes two major activities. The first is recruitment, selection, compensation, discipline, appraisal, and welfare of employees. The second is working with employees to improve their efficiency and productivity. The activities that enable individuals and groups to acquire new knowledge and skills and assume new roles and responsibilities are usually referred to as human resources development.

HUMAN RESOURCES DEVELOPMENT

Nadler defines human resources development as a "series of organised activities conducted within a specified time and designed to produce Behaviour change" in individuals and organisations. The key point is learning. Ojo remarks that, the "organised activities contained in the definition provided above embraced a carefully developed learning activity with identifiable components of objectives, actions, and evaluation. These conditions must exist in all forms of human resources development." Ideally, human resources development should provide solutions to problems such as a shortage of employees, employees who are inadequately skilled and efficient, high turnover, organisational expansion, career planning, and training needs.

MOTIVATION IN THE DEVELOPMENT OF HUMAN RESOURCES IN THE LIBRARY

A library is an organisation whose mission is to provide information to its users. The library staff are the human resources, who provide information services using library resources. How well the services are provided depends on how well the human resources are motivated and developed.

Motivation is crucial to the development of human resources in the library in the following ways:

* Maslow's hierarchy of needs is apparent in library employment. Acquiring a job and looking for job security help satisfy physiological and safety needs. When those needs are satisfied, employees look to their need for belonging and self-esteem. The need

for self-esteem and self-actualisation are represented in library human resources development efforts that focus on training, creativity, problem-solving, and so on.

* The maintenance and motivational factors of Herzberg's two-factor theory play important roles in the development of human resources in the library. Herzberg's believed that motivators must be build into the job. These include responsibility, autonomy, respect and recognition from superiors, a sense of wellbeing, and the opportunity to have one's ideas adopted.
* Equity theory indicates likewise has a place in the library. Workers compare their pay, work schedules, benefits, or any reward with what is being received by other employees. Unless the reward system is carefully administered, it could result in problems of perceived or actual inequity.
* Expectancy theory can be used in the development of human resources in libraries. The logic of expectancy theory is that individuals exert effort for a performance that results in preferred rewards. Expectancy can be influenced by selecting individuals with particular skills and abilities, providing training, and providing support to achieve a particular level of performance.

STRATEGIES FOR INCREASING MOTIVATION

Job Enrichment

The idea of quality work life has received attention for several decades. Workers become increasingly dissatisfied and frustrated by routine tasks. The result may be lower output, poor attitude, lower quality, absenteeism, high turnover, and pressure for better conditions and greater participation in decision-making. Herzberg contributed the theory of job enrichment as a motivational technique. Job enrichment provides employees with an opportunity to grow psychologically and mature in a job. Job enrichment attempts to make the job itself motivational. Research indicates that jobs higher in enrichment factors result in higher satisfaction; however, research also indicates that enriched jobs require more training time and result in slightly higher anxiety and stress. Job enrichment increases a job's range and depth, which refers to the number of activities and the autonomy, responsibility, discretion, and control.

Merit Pay

The money that employees receive is actually a package made up of salary, and other fringe benefits such as transport, housing, furniture, medical allowance. Others include meal subsidy and utility allowances. The motivation theories discussed, suggest that and fringe benefits can have some influence on effort and persistence. The money that employees receive is actually a package of salary and benefits. Theories of motivation suggest that salary and benefits have influence on effort and persistence. Pay has the potential to satisfy each of the five needs in Maslow's hierarchy. In Herzberg's two-factor model pay is a maintenance factor that should not contribute significantly to motivation. In expectancy theory, pay can satisfy a variety of needs and influence choice and Behaviour, while in equity theory, pay is a major outcome that one compares with other employees. A number of studies reveal that, in order to motivate, a salary plan must demonstrate that good performance leads to higher levels of pay, minimise any negative consequences of good performance, and relate other rewards to good performance.

Flexible Working Hours

Libraries are faced with an increasingly diverse workforce that includes nursing mothers, single parents with young children, employees with very different responsibilities, and those taking classes or pursuing degrees to improve skills and abilities or for self-improvement. The concept of flexible working hours has motivational appeal to many library staff. Flexible time is intended to ensure that the work of the organisation is accomplished and, at the same time, to permit library staff and their supervisors to establish work schedules that recognise individual and family needs. Research indicates that flexible scheduling can be motivational in that job satisfaction is improved and absenteeism reduced. The ability to accommodate employee needs is a healthy and positive approach to motivation.

MOTIVATING EMPLOYEES IN ACADEMIC LIBRARIES IN TOUGH TIMES

Organisational effectiveness is largely determined by the quality of the employees and how the organisation develops them. Therefore, it is natural that high performing organisations try to recruit and retain the right people and provide them with training and professional development opportunities. However, abilities, skills, personality, and organisational support alone might not lead to individual job performance that contributes to overall organisational effectiveness if people are not motivated. It is possible that some employees choose not to perform even if they have the right qualifications.

Managers face tough motivational challenges especially in economic downturns and it seems helpful to know key organisational Behaviour studies' findings related to human motivation. However, the goal is not manipulating and making people do what managers want them to do, but making people reach their highest job performance potential and getting them excited to do so. The author's literature review revealed that motivation analyses in libraries as workplaces are limited and have been focused on content theories or what motivates people.

This chapter attempts to build on the former analyses and explain applications of motivation theories that describe the motivation factors, motivation processes, effective job design, and conditions for sustaining motivation in the academic library workplace.

CONTENT THEORIES: WHAT MOTIVATES PEOPLE

The motivation theories that deal with the content of what motivates people are referred to as content theories or static-content theories as they look at only one point in time and do not predict Behaviour. The most well-known theories in this area include Maslow's hierarchy of needs, Alderfer's ERG theory, McClelland's theory of socially acquired needs, and Herzberg's motivator- hygiene theory. Maslow organised the needs underlying human motivation in a hierarchy on five levels: physiological needs, security needs, social needs, ego or self-esteem needs, and self-actualisation needs.

He further proposed that lower-level needs such as physiological needs and security needs must be satisfied before the individual can address higher-level needs. Although there is little evidence to support the concept of hierarchical progression and all individuals cannot be motivated in the same way, managers can attempt to influence their performance by satisfying employees' needs. Table 4.1 shows some possible applications in academic library work environment.

Alderfer's ERG Theory, on the other hand, provides an alternative to Maslow's theory and is based on a 3-fold conceptualisation of human needs: existence, relatedness, and growth. It does not assume lowerlevel satisfaction as a prerequisite for the emergence of higher-level needs. To test his theory, Alderfer surveyed 110 bank employees at several job levels.

Although the results indicated stronger support for the ERG theory than Maslow's theory, both theories are similar in that people shape their actions to satisfy unfulfilled needs. McClelland identified three basic needs that people develop in the society: the need for achievement, power, and affiliation. He argued that each individual is likely to have developed a dominant orientation Towards one of these needs based on our life experiences. An obvious implication for managers might be to draw out those employees with a high need for achievement.

Table. 4.1 Maslow's Hierarchy of Needs and Applications in Academic Libraries.

Level	Needs	Examples in the Academic Library Workplace
1	Physiological	* Clean Air * Enough work space * Ergonomically-designed workstations * Appropriate lighting * Appropriate temperature * Convenient and reasonable foodservice facilities * Water fountains
2	Security	* Safe workplace * Stable wages and salaries * Job security * Health insurance * Retirement benefits
3	Social Affiliation	* Employee social activities * Teamwork * Friendship * Sense of belonging * Affection
4	Self-esteem	* Recognition * Awards * Prestige * Autonomy
5	Self-actualisation	* Well-being of others * Accepting self * Meaningful work

However, McClelland suggested that motivation is changeable and that people can be taught to have certain needs through training Programmes. Herzberg's motivator-hygiene theory is different from other content theories as it suggested that motivation is composed of two dimensions:

* Hygiene Factors or the conditions surrounding the job and can prevent dissatisfaction; and
* Motivators, or the factors associated with the work itself and influence employees to grow and develop.

The hygiene factors include such things as salary, supervision, policies, working conditions, relationship, and job securities. The motivators include promotion, growth opportunities, responsibility, recognition, and achievement. The main implication of this theory is that for employees to be truly satisfied and perform above minimum standards, motivators had to be built into the job.

PROCESS THEORIES: HOW DOES MOTIVATION OPERATE

Although the static-content theories can provide a basic understanding of what energises people, they are not sufficient to explain the complex nature of human motivation as people respond differently to their needs. Factors other than unfulfilled needs also influence motivation, and various process theories were developed to explain how motivation operates.

Expectancy theory, which is also known as VIE theory, assumes that motivation is a function of three components; for an individual to be motivated:

* The reward must be valued by the person;
* The person must believe that higher performance will result in greater rewards (instrumentality); and
* That additional effort will lead to higher performance (expectancy).

For example, if an employee perceives that high performance might not be achieved even after hours of effort due to lack of skills or self-efficacy, even if he or she desires promotion, the person might not feel motivated enough to achieve the goal. Therefore, providing appropriate training, clarifying expectations, and providing guidance are important to strengthen this effort-performance link. Another example might be that if an individual believes that rewards might be given to people with higher seniority regardless of their performance, getting the reward might be perceived as unlikely for junior staff, thus undermining the person's motivation to perform.

Finally, if an employee can perform well but does not value the reward provided, *e.g.*, a gift certificate to a restaurant that the person does not care for, the person is likely to be less motivated. Goal-setting theory is another process theory and suggests the idea that setting goals can be a cause of high performance. Locke argued that a person's conscious intentions (goals) are the primary determinants of task-related motivation.

Managers should:

* Set specific goals;
* Make goals sufficiently difficult (but not too difficult);
* Involve employees in goal setting to ensure commitment;
* Provide feedback; and
* Link goal accomplishment with rewards that are valued by the employee.

This theory can be applied in various library tasks. For example, instead of asking employees to do their best in enhancing information fluency, the goal might be "implementing information fluency Programmes in at least 10 courses next semester." To gain goal commitment, it will be important for managers to provide clear direction and guidance to employees in addition to building their self-efficacy. Organisational justice theories suggest that people's perception of fairness within the organisation regarding how and what decisions are made about the distribution of outcomes affects motivation.

Justice theories are important given the current economy where many organisations have been forced to lay off people. Questions such as "Are we restructuring our organisation in a fair manner?" and "Were the layoffs perceived as fair by employees?" are important for managers. The outcomes of justice perceptions can have an economic impact on the organisation such as absenteeism, withdrawal, theft, sabotage, or even lawsuits against employers. Justice theories consider both procedural justice and distributive justice. Distributive justice theory is also referred to as equity theory and suggests that people compare the ratio of their inputs (effort) and outcomes (rewards) to the input-outcome ratios of other comparable individuals.

The research on equity theory is also more definitive on the reactions of people who perceive that they are under-rewarded. If an individual views a relationship as unequal, an attempt will be made to restore equality either by trying to gain greater rewards or by putting forth less effort. For example, if an employee feels that everyone gets promoted at the same rate regardless of their amount of inputs, he or she who feels under-rewarded might reduce the amount of the effort. At the same time, the employee will not think it is unfair if another employee who contributes more to the organisation receives more reward.

Colquitt *et al.* conducted a meta-analysis of justice theories and concluded that there was a strong negative correlation (r = –.51) between distributive justice and withdrawal, suggesting that if an employee views a relationship as unequal, he or she is likely to lose interest in the work or leave the organisation. They also concluded that there was a strong positive correlation (r =.56) between procedural justice and performance, suggesting that employees are likely to perform better if procedures are perceived as fair.

Other business literature also suggests that procedural justice increases performance significantly as managers gain trust, commitment, and voluntary cooperation from their employees. It is possible that some managers might be fair in terms of distributing rewards such as recognition, promotion, pay raise, authority, responsibility, and resources, but not so in terms of process. Fair process involves engaging employees, providing opportunities for them to speak up, explaining why final decisions are made as they are, and clarifying expectations.

Fair process is lost when information is filtered and managers retain power by withholding what they know to themselves. It is important for employees to be treated with sincerity and respect, and adequate explanation needs to be provided. When the process is perceived to be fair, most people will realise that compromises are occasionally necessary and accept outcomes that might not be in their favour.

JOB CHARACTERISTICS THEORY: HOW CAN WE MAKE JOBS INTERESTING

Job design and job enrichment also affect human motivation and it will be helpful to know the characteristics that make jobs interesting. The job characteristics model developed by Hackman and Oldham identified five core job dimensions that should be enriched when jobs are re-designed:

* *Skill variety*—the degree to which a job requires a variety of activities that draw on different skills and talents of the employee.
* *Task identity*—the degree to which the job requires completion of a task, from beginning to end.
* *Task significance*—the degree to which the job has a significant impact on the lives of other people.
* *Autonomy*—the degree to which the job provides substantial freedom, independence, and discretion to the individual in scheduling work and determining the procedures to be used.
* *Feedback*—the degree to which workers are provided with direct and clear information about their performance.

As the core dimensions are enhanced, the job characteristics model posits that they influence three critical psychological states:

* Experienced meaningfulness of work, which is increased by skill variety, task identity, and task significance;
* Experienced responsibility for work outcomes, which is enhanced by autonomy; and
* Knowledge of results, which is provided by effective feedback mechanisms.

For example, providing credits to individuals rather than to the department when preparing path-finders, instruction handouts, or other documents will provide opportunities for those employees involved to receive direct feedback from library users and establish client relationships with them. In addition, open lines of communication between employees and managers need to be incorporated into the workplace culture. The more people know how well they are doing, the better equipped they are to take appropriate corrective action. In terms of increasing autonomy, the first step will be to hire people who can do their jobs properly without close supervision.

Second, the individuals will need to be trained to do their jobs effectively. Finally, it should be clear that high-quality performance is expected. Loading jobs vertically by giving employees greater responsibility for their jobs and allowing them to make their own decisions, instead of micro-managing, increase the level of autonomy and sense of accountability that results in higher motivation. At the same time, employees should not be given a great deal of autonomy in any organisations where marginal work tends to be accepted without question.

Autonomy will work only when everyone involved buys into the importance of performing at a high level. One approach in increasing autonomy might be to ask employees what goals they want to accomplish and what resources or support is needed as self-setting goals are naturally self-committed. It is important to note that the job characteristics model recognises the limitation that not everyone wants and benefits from enriched jobs and that people with a high need for personal growth benefit the most. In that sense, it will be essential for managers to hire people who are interested in growing professionally in the work instead of people who are attracted to the work because of work conditions or benefits.

ENVIRONMENTALLY-BASED THEORIES: HOW CAN WE REINFORCE AND MAINTAIN MOTIVATION

Let's now think about some of the ways in which motivation can be sustained. If we are rewarded for behaving in a certain way, we begin to make the connection between the Behaviour and the reward and continue to engage in the Behaviour. As B.F. Skinner's operant conditioning theory explains, Behaviours with positive consequences are strengthened and acquired, and Behaviours with negative consequences are eliminated. The positive consequences, such as recognition and reward, need to be tied directly to desired Behaviours and be given immediately and continuously so that the connection between the Behaviour and reinforcer is established.

For example, staff recognition needs to be provided with an explanation of desirable Behaviour. It should also be repeated if the staff continues to improve the work instead of choosing different employees to be rewarded when in fact the same employee performed the best. Additionally, rewards need to be distributed consistently so that recognition of good work will become part of the organisational culture. It is also important to know what you are rewarding.

For example, if you reward someone because she or he answered the largest number of reference questions, the employee and possibly others might try to enhance the number of reference questions instead of focusing on the quality of the service and other ways that reference service can be improved. As social learning theory suggests, people acquire new Behaviours by observing the rewards and punishments given to others.

If you want to increase teamwork but continue distributing rewards according to individual performance only, your desired outcome, *i.e.*, teamwork will not be reinforced. In addition, if an individual performs fine in one area but not so in another, the explanation for the reward needs to be very clear so that the desirable Behaviour is strengthened while the undesirable Behaviour is not. When providing rewards, it will be helpful to know the difference between extrinsic and intrinsic rewards. Extrinsic rewards are contrived and some of them incur direct cost.

They include such things as promotion, monetary reward, gifts, and bonuses. Intrinsic rewards involve no direct cost, and the examples include compliments, public recognition, opportunities, and a smile. Thus, intrinsic rewards are closely related to the work itself and are motivators in the context of Herzberg's motivator. Therefore, intrinsic motivation is synonymous with a desire to work hard solely for the pleasure of task accomplishment. On the other hand, extrinsic motivation encourages us to complete the task to receive the reward.

In other words, rewards motivate people to get rewards. Scholars research implies that the feedback and social reinforcers, such as recognition and attention, may have as strong an impact on performance as pay. Their research also indicates that extrinsic rewards can undermine an individual's intrinsic motivation. However, this is not to suggest that extrinsic incentives are unimportant. Good pay, benefits, and good working condition are often significant factors to attract and retain best people and cannot be ignored.

CONCLUSIONS

This chapter described applications of various motivation theories in the academic library workplace. Although those theories might not accurately explain Behaviour in all situations, they can still be helpful for managers who try to increase motivation among staff in academic libraries. Need theories can be used to satisfy employees' physical and psychological needs and hopefully to motivate them by enhancing their sense of self-esteem and self-actualisation. Hygiene-Motivator theory makes us realise that job conditions such as pay and benefits alone might not motivate people.

Therefore, it will be important for managers to provide motivators such as growth opportunities, sense of responsibility and accomplishment, and recognition as well as providing good working conditions. Expectancy theory suggests that managers need to provide rewards that are valued by their employees and that the employees need to feel they can achieve their goals and high-performance will result in the reward. Goals need to be specific, sufficiently difficult, accepted by the employee, and self-set if possible so that the employee becomes naturally committed.

In addition, process and reward distribution needs to be fair to enhance trust, job performance, and motivation. We also learned that characteristics of jobs affect human motivation. Jobs with a variety of activities, task identity, task significance, autonomy, and feedback mechanisms tend to increase motivation. Autonomy does not mean that employees can do whatever they want; instead, it involves hiring the right people, providing training, explaining that high-performance is expected, enriching jobs, providing respect and independence, and rewarding appropriately. Direct feedback channels should be established between service users and the employees who contributed to the work as well as between the employees and their supervisors.

Providing appropriate credits to work is important so that "thank you" notes and other feedback arrive to the people who were involved. Rewarding excellent work is essential to reinforce and maintain employee motivation. Intrinsic rewards such as compliments, public recognition, professional and opportunities are motivators according to the content theory and can be as effective as extrinsic rewards such as monetary reward and gifts, which might motivate employees to win the reward rather than to focus on the work itself. Nevertheless, extrinsic rewards encourage risk taking and for people to do extraordinary things and cannot be ignored. At the same time, it will be important for managers to be mindful of those employees who get disappointed when their effort does not lead to rewards.

Distributing rewards consistently instead of providing them only when accomplishment is visible will help strengthen trust within the organisation. Although most theories were tested in corporate settings, it appears they are also applicable in academic or non-profit workplaces. Peter Drucker wrote that "Non-profits need management precisely because they don't have a bottom line" and argued that non-profit organisations often end up becoming pioneers in the most crucial area—the motivation and productivity of knowledge workers—as non-profits start with the mission, which business will have to learn from them. It seems that the key for the successful management is to clarify the mission of the organisation, hire people who have the right skills and agree with the mission, set goals, provide development opportunities, explain accountability, build trust through fair process, give autonomy and feedback, and provide appropriate rewards. Service excellence can be achieved even in times of budget constraints.

5

Coordination

OVERVIEW

The term 'coordination' refers to syntactic constructions in which two or more units of the same type are combined into a larger unit and still have the same semantic relations with other surrounding elements.

The units may be words, phrases, subordinate clauses, or full sentences:

* My husband supports and adores Juventus Turin.
* My uncle or your in-laws or the neighbours will come to visit us.
* I realise that you were right and that I was mistaken.
* The pope dissolved the Jesuit order, and all the Indian missions were abandoned.

All languages appear to possess coordination constructions of some kind, but there is a lot of cross-linguistic variation. Individual languages may possess a wealth of different coordinate constructions that relate to each other in complex ways. It is the purpose of this chapter to introduce and discuss a wide range of conceptual distinctions that are useful for describing the cross-linguistic and language-internal variation.

This entails the use of a large number of technical terms, each of which is explained and illustrated as it is introduced. The particle or affix that serves to link the units of a coordinate construction is called coordinator. The coordinator is printed in boldface. By far the most frequently occurring coordinator is 'and' but coordinate constructions can also involve various other semantic types of linkers, such as 'or', 'but' and 'for'. 'And' - coordination is also called conjunctive coordination, 'or' - coordination is also called disjunctive coordination, 'but' - coordination is called adversative coordination, and 'for' - coordination is called causal coordination.

Examples of each of these four types are given in:

1. (conjunction) Snow-white ate and drank.
2. (disjunction) She was a countess or a princess.
3. (adversative coordination) The dwarfs were ugly but kind.
4. (causal coordination) She died, for the apple was poisoned.

The units combined in a conjunctive coordination are called conjuncts, and more generally, the units of any coordination will be called coordinands here. Adversative coordination is always binary, *i.e.*, it must consist of two coordinands. Ternary or other multiple coordinations are impossible here.

This is illustrated in:

* The queen tried to kill Snow-white but Snow-white escaped but she went through much hardship.

* The mountain climbers were tired but happy but bankrupt.

By contrast, conjunctions and disjunctions can consist of an indefinite number of coordinands.

The examples in show six coordinands each:

* You can vote for Baranov or Wagner or Lefèvre or McGarrigle or Ramírez or Abdurrasul.

* Cameroon, Nigeria, Niger, Libya, Sudan, and the Central African Republic have a common border with Chad.

Languages differ with respect to the number and the position of the coordinators used in coordinate constructions.

For instance, while English generally shows the pattern A co-B, Kannada shows the pattern A-co B-co:

* So:mas&e:kharan-u: pe:t5e-ge ho:-d-aru. Narahari-
and Somashekhara-and market-DAT go-PAST-3PL
'Narahari and Somashekhara went to the market.'

The patterns of coordinator placement and the types of linkers are discussed here. Many languages have several alternative patterns for a given semantic type of coordination, as illustrated in the English examples. Coordination with the two-part coordinator both ... and describes the coordinands as contrasting in some way: is appropriate, for instance, if the hearer expects only one of them to make the trip.

These constructions will be called contrastive coordination in this chapter:

* Both Franz and Sisi will travel to Trieste.
* Franz and Sisi will travel to Trieste.

Moreover, many languages have special coordinators for negative contexts, as in the English example. This sentence is roughly equivalent semantically with, but again it has a more emphatic, contrastive Flavour.

The construction in will be called contrastive negative coordination:

* Neither Brahms nor Bruckner reached Beethoven's fame.
* Brahms and Bruckner did not reach Beethoven's fame.

Contrastive and negative coordinate constructions are discussed below: We saw in above that a coordinate construction can consist of different types of coordinands: words, phrases, clauses or sentences. But as the definition of coordination says, each coordinand must be of the same type within a coordinate construction.

Because the coordinands are syntactically different or at least semantically different:

* Guglielmo wrote to his bishop and to the pope.
* Guglielmo wrote a letter of protest and to the pope.
* Guglielmo spoke with the abbot and with the cardinal.
* Guglielmo spoke with eloquence and with the cardinal.

Different languages may require different coordinators depending on the syntactic type of the coordinands.

Types of coordinands and their relevance for the structure of coordination are discussed below: In addition to the major semantic distinctions that we saw in, numerous more fine-grained distinctions can be made. For example, many languages distinguish between two types of disjunction: interrogative disjunction and standard disjunction.

Mandarin Chinese uses two different coordinators for these two cases, haishi and huozhe:

1. You want I help you or want self do 'Do you want me to help you, or do you want to do it yourself?'
2. We at here eat or eat restaurant all OK 'We can either eat here or eat out.'

Next we discuss some special types of conjunction. Since, conjunction is the most frequent kind of coordination, it exhibits the greatest formal diversity.

The most prominent "special type" of conjunction involves the use of a comitative marker, as in Hausa, where da means both 'with':

* I went to the market with Audu.
* Go market 'Dauda and Audu went to the market.'

In addition to coordinations in which each coordinand is a regular syntactic constituent many languages allow non-constituent coordination. For the sake of clarity, the coordinands are enclosed in square brackets in these examples:

* [Robert cooked the first course] and [Maria the dessert].
* Ahmed [sent a letter to Zaynab] or [a postcard to Fatima].
* [Martin adores], but [Tom hates Hollywood movies].

The first coordinand is an ordinary constituent but the second coordinand is not. Only the second coordinand is an ordinary constituent. In order to assimilate non-constituent coordinations to patterns found elsewhere in the grammar, linguists have often described them in terms of ellipsis. That is, abstract underlying structures such as those in are posited which show ordinary constituent coordination.

In a second step, a rule of ellipsis of identical elements deletes the words underlined in resulting in the surface patterns:

* Robert cooked the first course and Maria cooked the dessert.
* Ahmed sent a letter to Zaynab or sent a postcard to Fatima.

* Martin adores Hollywood movies, but Tom hates Hollywood movies.

Finally, we discuss ways of delimiting coordination against less grammaticalised constructions and, perhaps most importantly, against subordination and dependency. The latter two notions will be discussed briefly here. The primary contrast is that between coordination and dependency. In a coordination structure of the type A(-link-)B, A and B are structurally symmetrical in some sense, whereas in a dependency structure of the type X(-link-)Y, X and Y are not symmetrical, but either X or Y is the head and the other element is a dependent.

When the dependent element is a clause, it is called subordinate clause. Although the distinction between coordination and dependency is of course fundamental, it is sometimes not evident whether a construction exhibits a coordination relation or a dependency relation.

The best-known distinctive property of coordinate structures is that they obey the coordinate structure constraint, which prohibits the application of certain rules such as extraction of interrogative words from coordinate structures.

This is illustrated, where the:

* Sentences show the basic structure, and the;
* Sentences show fronting of who.

As the examples make clear, only the dependency structures allow extraction:

* Dependency (subordination):
  - (basic sentence) You talked to someone before Joan arrived.
  - (who extraction) Who did you talk to _ before Joan arrived.
* Coordination:
  - (basic sentence) You talked to someone and then Joan arrived.
  - (who extraction) *Who did you talk to _ and then Joan arrived.

* Dependency:
  - (basic sentence) You saw Marvin with someone.
  - (who extraction) Who did you see Marvin with –.
* Coordination:
  - (basic sentence) You saw Marvin and someone.
  - (who extraction) *Who did you see Marvin and _.

Obeying the coordinate structure constraint is a formal property of constructions that is sometimes taken as the decisive criterion for coordinate status. As suggested, work with a primarily semantic definition of coordination, as given at the beginning of this section. The reason for this is that only semantically-based notions can be applied cross-linguistically – formal criteria are generally too language-particular.

DEVELOPMENT AND COORDINATION OF LIBRARY SERVICES TO STATE GOVERNMENT

In recent years the sise, complexity, pervasiveness and burgeoning growth of the federal government have made it a prime focus of the nation's news media, and it consequently has captured the attention of the general public. A similar expansion has occurred at the level of state government, but without as much commentary or analysis by the press. One author refers to the "surprising discovery that the largest growth sector in the 1960s and 1970s is not national Defence, automobile manufacturing, or even the federal government" but is instead state and local government. When the broadened scope of responsibilities, services and agency functions are considered, the changing nature and importance of state government is even more impressive. Like the federal government, state governments have responded to the needs of a population beset by accelerating technological, social, economic, cultural, and political change. Thus there are state agencies, com- missions, committees, bureaus, councils, and departments whose responsibilities and concerns range from atomic energy to drug addiction treatment, and from medical care to the aged to the development of the arts.

This expanding scope of interests has meant that the business of state government, in all its facets, requires an expanding variety of information sources and services. Like the rest of society in this postindustrial era, state government has become heavily information-dependent. How have state libraries responded to the burgeoning information needs of state government? Almost every state library gives some kind of information service to other agencies of state government and, indeed, many have been doing so Since, the early days of the Republic. The standards for Library functions at the state level makes clear the state library's responsibility to provide quality services to other agencies of state government.

The ways in which state libraries fulfil this responsibility, the variety of services offered, the intensity of effort, and the degree of coordination with other agencies varies widely among the fifty states. As early as 1966, Phillip Monypenny noted a variety of provisions to supply service to legislative, executive and judicial branches of state government, with varying degrees of coordination between law libraries, historical societies, archives, departmental libraries, and general state library agencies.

Some indication of the variety of such services offered by state library agencies may be gained from the 1977 Simpson survey, where state library agencies listed the following: library services to state government, consultant services to state agency libraries, research library for state agencies, special collection for state agencies, cooperation with agency and departmental libraries, reference services to state agencies and officials, centralised purchasing for agency libraries, centralised processing for agency libraries, audiovisual production and direction for state agencies, legislative reference library, reference services to legislature, special administrative and legislative library, legislative research, computerised on- line bill status, state law library as part of state library, current awareness services, depository for state publications, depository for historical records, distribution of state publications, index of state publications, published checklist of state documents, records management service for state government, consultant services to state institutions, and library services to state institutions.

State library collections range in sise from the large and comprehensive libraries of New York, Illinois and California, to the more typical 100,000-200,000 volume collections held by many states. A few state libraries, such as Maryland's, do not maintain collections, but provide reference service by other means. In addition to the services and collections of the state library itself, agency or departmental libraries exist in many states. Although reliable and up to date data on these are difficult to obtain, a US Office of Education (USOE) survey conducted in late 1977 of special libraries serving state government will provide such data when compiled and published.

It is known, however, that the number of such libraries varies from state to state (New York has nearly fifty, Texas twenty-three, New Jersey thirteen). Similarly, the collection sise, budget and number and level of staffing will vary widely from state to state, from major and sizable libraries (most typically court or law libraries) to office collections with part-time or no library staff. The literature on the activities of state library agencies during the past fifteen years has clearly dealt more with statewide library development and extension services than with other functions.

A similar bias was observed by Ralph Blasingame in a survey of library studies conducted between 1965 and 1969 based on an ERIC bibliography. He reported that only seven of the eighty-nine studies listed were concerned with services to state institutions (none specifically with services to state government), while two-thirds were studies of public libraries. A reading of the literature indicates that information services to state government have not been the leading edge of "state library" Programme development during this period.

This emphasis on statewide library Programmes is not surprising in view of the passage of the Library Services Act of 1956, and the attendant in- flux of federal funds to support this type of development. Forced to respond to pressure from the field and anxious to seise the opportunity to effectuate long-sought improvements in statewide planning and library system development, many state libraries clearly have not given the same attention to the development of information services to state government. Regulations of the federal Library Services and Construction Act specifically prohibited use of federal funds for service to state government.

Several states, however, have commissioned studies during this period designed to improve information service to state government. Studies in South Dakota, Ohio, Indiana and New York do indicate a growing concern and offer recommendations for implementation of Programmes in this area. Michael Jackley, in a 1965 analysis of the functions of the South Dakota Library Commission, opted for greater centralisation. His recommendations take the form of central purchasing of library materials, with those appropriate to departmental libraries being placed on permanent loan with the departmental library as a branch of the central agency. Better access to materials held by archives, history and law would be promoted by close coordination with these agencies and the central library.

He suggested that those agencies of state government whose major function is research, such as the Legislative Research Council, should be housed with the state library on the Capitol grounds. Blasingame, in a 1968study for Ohio, advocated that the Information Resources and Services Division of the state library become a govern-mental service unit with three new staff positions. Each of these new staff members would work with a specific group of logically chosen state agencies in order to become knowledgeable about the concerns and problems of these groups. This would enable the state library to provide strong leadership in planning the development of information services in state agencies, and provide individual advice and assistance to those agencies with their own libraries.

Duplication of effort and materials would be avoided, and maximum exploitation of existing resources inspired. Recommendations by Genevieve Casey were made in 1970 in a study for the Indiana State Library.

Detailed recommendations for the coordination of services to the legislature and to state agencies include: consultant services to agencies desiring aid in cataloging and classifying materials; better circulation procedures; the provision of more sophisticated bibliographical services; centralised purchasing and processing; periodical print- outs and centralised records in the state library of the holdings of agencies; some form of current awareness service, with staff members working with administrators and librarians in the agencies assessing information needs and helping to establish acquisition policies; the use of existing TWX facilities by state employees; contracting for access to the collection and services of the Indiana University Medical Library for all state employees, especially those in the fields of health and environment; and the evaluation of the state library collection in terms of state government.

To provide guidance in establishing priorities for comprehensive information services, a council of persons responsible for department libraries and staff libraries in institutions would meet regularly with state library staff to discuss common problems and concerns. Work with large state agencies might be organised with small advisory councils within the agencies to work directly with the staff member from the state library responsible for that agency. Financial arrangements could take the form of either in- creased budget for the state library to support additional services to agencies, or an inter-accounting mechanism between the library agency and departments receiving special services. The state library would require additional funds in any case, primarily for new staff to implement these activities, but also for materials and equipment. In 1974, the New York State Library undertook a major review of information services to state government in other states. To obtain up- to-date information on existing patterns of service from the other forty- nine state library agencies, a brief but pointed questionnaire was developed and distributed in autumn 1974.

Follow up visits were made to Texas, North Carolina and Ohio in this study, and additional data were gathered from

Washington State. These visits provided information on both innovative Programmes and the varying approaches to state agency services taken in each of the states. The Texas State Library, employing a former public library consultant, has emphasised cooperative activities with other state agency libraries in Austin, resulting in the development of a lively organisation called State Agency Libraries of Texas (SALT). SALT publishes a news-letter, holds regular meetings and workshops, and has developed a number of cooperative projects, including a union list of serials and a Texas state documents project.

Building on the recommendations of the Blasingame report summarised above, the Ohio State Library has expanded its services in recent years through an aggressive campaign to create awareness.

Acting Head, Information and Reference Division:

* Active marketing of the information provision capabilities of the State Library of Ohio is emphasised -through "sales calls," by pre- sentations before department groups, through orientation and familiarisation classes and tours, with follow-through in the form of individualised current awareness services which provide an ordering tool to the recipient. In the last year, more than a third of the circulation to state government personnel can be traced to the stimulus provided by the direct mail current awareness Programme. An important positive aspect is the system for delivery to the requestor whether he is remotely sited or contiguous to the library.

Like Texas and Ohio, the North Carolina State Library created a special unit to provide service to state agencies, entitled the "Library Services to State Agencies Branch." The Programme differs from Texas's and Ohio's reference-centered operations in that a considerable portion of the unit's thrust is in the area of technical services. In 1973-74, this unit provided cataloging, consultative and other support services to fourteen agency libraries, including the large Public Health Service library, the Department of Public Instruction, and newly organised libraries in the Labour and State Personnel departments. In the latter instance, the state library provided the necessary in-service training to assist the agency in starting the new library and the department provided staff, furnishings, shelving and a card catalogue. Central to an understanding of the Washington State arrangement is the fact that the state librarian is a cabinet officer reporting directly to the governor, and the state library is responsible for all library services for state government (except law), no matter where the facility served is located.

The former Washington State Librarian, described the Programme in refreshingly non-bureaucratic language:

> * Some departments want us to operate fully and where they can generate federal funds for the service we enter into a "contract".... We pay no attention to the actual dollars so generated but render the service as needed. In some instances the department prefers to have the library staff on its payroll. . . . All materials are purchased and processed by us so that our catalog reflects the total information resource. The staffs are given orientation here so they realise we are back-up to their limited collection. The collections are weeded frequently and materials returned here for final decision as to retention. Some offices around the state have small collections but we encourage the employees to use their local public library and to call us directly. In addition to subscribing to key professional publications, we Xerox tables of contents and route them around. People write their names by the article desired and we send a Xerox copy which they can keep or throw away. It is a very wide ranging, flexible and effective programme.

Special consultative services are also available to state agencies by contract and have resulted in a comprehensive bibliography on disasters in Washington State for the Department of Emergency Services, and a combined subject index for environmental impact statements for the Department of Ecology. The New York State Library, building on an 86-year history of special services to the legislature, established a Legislative and Governmental Services unit in 1977, directed by a member of the top-level administration. This unit will promote library services to state agencies aggressively, provide special research and bibliographic support, and conduct orientation and other Programmes for legislative and agency staff. Publications currently issued by the unit include Legislative trends (an annotated list of state library acquisitions on topics of interest to the legislature), Spotlight (guides to basic resources in selected subject fields), Topics on top (short bibliographies on topics of current interest), and comprehensive literature searches on requested subjects. Resources offered include free search services on twenty-six computerised data banks.

Despite the considerable variety of state library Programmes, certain general norms or patterns emerge which suggest the following elements as essential in developing an effective Programme of state library services to state agencies:

* *Attitude:* An aggressive, outreach approach is needed, based on a commitment to service and a wide-ranging, well-defined Programme to meet the needs of state agencies, officials and employees.
* *Organisation:* The state library should serve as the hub or center of library activity for state government, and should create a special office or unit which will provide leadership, coordination and the necessary monitoring of the programme. At the least, it should assign one or more staff members to carry out this outreach Programme on a continuing and preferably full-time basis. Staff should be carefully chosen for many of the same qualities which characterise successful field consultants, as well as for their perception of reference and bibliographic needs, and of the operation and structure of state government.
* *Agency Involvement:* As many agencies as possible should be involved, not only in the planning of service patterns, but in their refinement and

evaluation as well. Even if the cooperating agency has no library *per se,* it should assign someone to work with the state library coordinator.

* *Shared Activities/Shared Financing:* Services which are beyond the capability of the individual cooperating agency should be explored care- fully and implemented as practicable, including centralised ordering and processing of library materials, union lists and other methods of bibliographic control, central computerised data banks with terminal access as required, cooperative storage and materials retirement plans, etc. Shared financing on some unit cost basis, by means of contractual or other arrangements, is desirable and tends to stimulate mutual involvement, respect and commitment, and provides a basis for evaluating cost-effectiveness.
* *Visibility, Direct Contact with Administration:* In order to gain the support of the administration and the legislature, the state library and its Programme of service to state government needs visibility, a voice and some degree of clout. This may be achieved organisationally, with cabinet rank for the state librarian or with strong advisory groups who can make their voices heard by the power structure. It may like- wise be achieved personally, through the visibility and personal dynamics of the chief state library officer and the programme specialists; and functionally, through the provision of services of demonstrable value and reliable quality. All these avenues may be necessary and should be bulwarked with an effective public relations Programme including publicity, orientation workshops and appropriate accountability through regular reports.

The data assembled in this chapter indicate that state library agencies generally accept information service to state government as a primary responsibility. Although this function does not appear to have been the "leading edge" of state library Programme development in recent years, there is evidence of increased interest and innovative activity in a number of states. As state government expands its interests, as legislative, judicial and executive agencies become increasingly information dependent, and as the relationship of information availability to cost-effectiveness and productivity becomes clearer, it may be expected that information service to state government will become an increasingly critical area of state library agency activity.

6

Staffing

CONCEPT AND IMPORTANCE OF STAFFING

CONCEPT

Staffing is one of the important management functions which is mainly concerned with proper arrangement and management of the required manpower for the organisation. After having prepared plans, as well as the structure of organisation for seeking the objectives, various positions are created. Effectiveness is not uni dimensional or one sided. To be effective in work setting people must do many things well and they as people must derive same value from their efforts. to have an effective staffing process, it requires as a first step the explicit specification of exactly what is that people must do well and what they will be offered in reward for doing it. - Benjamin Schneider Staff function of the management consists of the following features:

* To prepare manpower planning.
* To determine manpower requirements of organisation in terms of quantity and quality.
* To make all necessary arrangement for acquiring needed human force through proper and effective recruitment and selection.
* To maintain human force in organisation for a period of time.
* To formulating effective Labour policies for long period.

* To implementing the Labour policies in various projects.
* To develop manpower to its maximum by providing scientific training and conducting various development programmes.

IMPORTANCE OF STAFFING

* Staffing function is very closely related to other managerial areas of the business. It greatly influences the direction and control in the organisation. The effectiveness of other managerial functions depends on the effectiveness of the staffing function.
* Staffing function helps to build proper human relationships in the organisation. Smooth human relations is the key to better communication and co-ordination of managerial efforts in an organisation.
* Skilled and experienced staff is the best asset of a business concern. The staffing function helps developing this asset for the business. It inculcates the corporate culture into the staff which in turn ensures smooth functioning of all the managerial aspects of the business.
* Staffing decisions have long term effect on the efficiency of an organisation. Qualified, efficient and well motivated staff is an asset of the organisation. Staffing function assumes special significance in the context of globalisation which demands high degree of efficiency in maintaining competitiveness.
* Staff selection should be based on the ability of the prospective employees to meet the future challenges that the organisation need to address. Therefore the potential contribution of the staff in their anticipated future roles should also be taken into account in staff selection.

STAFFING AS PART OF HUMAN RESOURCE MANAGEMENT

It is a function which all managers need to perform. It is

a separate and specialised function and there are many aspects of human relations to be considered. It is the job of managers to fill positions in their organisation and to make sure that they remain occupied with qualified people. Staffing is closely linked to organising Since, after the structure and positions have been decided, people are required to work in these positions.

Subsequently, they need to be trained and motivated to work in harmony with the goals of the organisation. Thus, staffing is seen as a generic function of management. The staffing function deals with the human element of management. Managing the human component of an organisation is the most important task because the performance of an organisation depends upon how well this function is performed. The success of an organisation in achieving its goals is determined to a great extent on the competence, motivation and performance of its human resources. It is the responsibility of all managers to directly deal with and select people to work for the organisation. When the manager performs the staffing function his role is slightly limited. Some of these responsibilities will include placing the right person on the right job, introducing new employees to the organisation, training employees improving their performance, developing their abilities, maintaining their morale and protecting their health and physical conditions. In small organisations, managers may perform all duties related to employees salaries, welfare and working conditions. But as organisations grow and number of persons employed increases, a separate department called the human resource department is formed which has specialists in managing people.

The management of human resources is a specialised area which requires the expertise of many people. The number of human resource specialists and sise of this department gives an indication of the sise of the business as well. For a very large company, the Human Resources Department itself will contain specialists for each function of this department. Human Resource Management includes many specialised activities and duties which the human resource personnel must perform.

These duties are:

* Analysing jobs, collecting information about jobs to prepare job descriptions.
* Defending the company in law suits and avoiding legal complications.
* Developing compensation and incentive plans.
* Handling grievances and complaints.
* Maintaining labour relations and union management relations.
* Providing for social security and welfare of employees.
* Recruitment, *i.e.*, search for qualified people
* Training and development of employees for efficient performance and career growth.

STAFFING PROCESS

* The very first step in staffing is to plan the manpower inventory required by a concern in order to match them with the job requirements and demands. Therefore, it involves forecasting and determining the future manpower needs of the concern.
* Once the requirements are notified, the concern invites and solicits applications according to the invitations made to the desirable candidates.
* This is the screening step of staffing in which the solicited applications are screened out and suitable candidates are appointed as per the requirements.
* Once screening takes place, the appointed candidates are made familiar to the work units and work environment through the orientation programmes. placement takes place by putting right man on the right job.
* Training is a part of incentives given to the workers in order to develop and grow them within the concern. Training is generally given according to the nature of activities and scope of expansion in it. Along with it, the workers are developed by

providing them extra benefits of indepth knowledge of their functional areas. Development also includes giving them key and important jobs as a test or examination in order to analyse their performances.

* It is a kind of compensation provided monetarily to the employees for their work performances. This is given according to the nature of job-skilled or unskilled, physical or mental, etc. Remuneration forms an important monetary incentive for the employees.
* In order to keep a track or record of the behaviour, attitudes as well as opinions of the workers towards their jobs. For this regular assessment is done to evaluate and supervise different work units in a concern. It is basically concerning to know the development cycle and growth patterns of the employeesin a concern.
* Promotion is said to be a non-monetary incentive in which the worker is shifted from a higher job demanding bigger responsibilities as well as shifting the workers and transferring them to different work units and branches of the same organisation.

RECRUITMENT: MEANING AND SOURCES

Acquiring and retaining high-quality talent is critical to an organisation's success. As the job market becomes increasingly competitive and the available skills grow more diverse, recruiters need to be more selective in their choices, Since, poor recruiting decisions can produce long-term negative effects, among them high training and development costs to minimise the incidence of poor performance and high turnover which, in turn, impact staff morale, the production of high quality goods and services and the retention of organisational memory.

At worst, the organisation can fail to achieve its objectives thereby losing its competitive edge and its share of the market. Traditionally, Public Service organisations have had little need to worry about market share and increasing competition Since, they operate in a monopolistic environment. But in recent time, the emphasis on New Public Management/ Public Sector Management approaches has forced public organisations to pay closer attention to their service delivery as consumers have begun to expect and demand more for their tax dollars.

No longer are citisens content to grumble about poorly-produced goods and services and the under-qualified, untrained employees who provide them. As societies become more critical and litigious, public service organisations must seek all possible avenues for improving their output and providing the satisfaction their clients require and deserve.

The provision of high-quality goods and services begins with the recruitment process. Recruitment is described as "the set of activities and processes used to legally obtain a sufficient number of qualified people at the right place and time so that the people and the organisation can select each other in their own best short and long term interests". In other words, the recruitment process provides the organisation with a pool of potentially qualified job candidates from which judicious selection can be made to fill vacancies. Successful recruitment begins with proper employment planning and forecasting.

In this phase of the staffing process, an organisation formulates plans to fill or eliminate future job openings based on an analysis of future needs, the talent available within and outside of the organisation, and the current and anticipated resources that can be expended to attract and retain such talent. Also related to the success of a recruitment process are the strategies an organisation is prepared to employ in order to identify and select the best candidates for its developing pool of human resources.

Organisations seeking recruits for base-level entry positions often require minimum qualifications and experience. These applicants are usually recent high school or university/ technical college graduates many of whom have not yet made clear decisions about future careers or are contemplating engaging in advanced academic activity. At the middle levels, senior administrative, technical and junior executive positions are often filled internally. The push for scarce, high-quality talent, often recruited from external sources, has usually been at the senior executive levels. Most organisations utilise both mechanisms to effect recruitment to all levels.

THE RECRUITMENT PROCESS

Successful recruitment involves the several processes of:

* Development of a policy on recruitment and retention and the systems that give life to the policy;
* Needs assessment to determine the current and future human resource requirements of the organisation. If the activity is to be effective, the human resource requirements for each job category and functional division/unit of the organisation must be assessed and a priority assigned;
* Identification, within and outside the organisation, of the potential human resource pool and the likely competition for the knowledge and skills resident within it;
* Job analysis and job evaluation to identify the individual aspects of each job and calculate its relative worth;
* Assessment of qualifications profiles, drawn from job descriptions that identify responsibilities and required skills, abilities, knowledge and experience;
* Determination of the organisation's ability to pay salaries and benefits within a defined period;
* Identification and documentation of the actual process of recruitment and selection to ensure equity and adherence to equal opportunity and other laws.

Documenting the organisation's policy on recruitment, the criteria to be utilised, and all the steps in the recruiting process is as necessary in the seemingly informal setting of in house selection as it is when selection is made from external sources. Documentation satisfies the requirement of procedural transparency and leaves a trail that can easily be followed for audit and other purposes.

Of special importance is documentation that is in conformity with Freedom of Information legislation, such as:

* Criteria and procedures for the initial screening of applicants;
* Criteria for generating long and short lists;
* Criteria and procedures for the selection of interview panels;
* Interview questions;
* Interview scores and panellists' comments;
* Results of tests;
* Results of reference checks.

Recruitment Strategies and Processes

Recruitment may be conducted internally through the promotion and transfer of existing personnel or through referrals, by current staff members, of friends and family members. Where internal recruitment is the chosen method of filling vacancies, job openings can be advertised by job posting, that is, a strategy of placing notices on manual and electronic bulletin boards, in company newsletters and through office memoranda. Referrals are usually word-of-mouth advertisements that are a low-cost-per-hire way of recruiting. Internal recruitment does not always produce the number or quality of personnel needed; in such an instance, the organisation needs to recruit from external sources, either by encouraging walk-in applicants; advertising vacancies in newspapers, magazines and journals, and the visual and/or audio media; using employment agencies to "head hunt"; advertising on-line via the Internet; or through job fairs and the use of college recruitment.

Public service agencies enjoy greater exposure to scrutiny than most private sector organisations; therefore, openness and transparency in recruitment and selection practices are crucial. The discussion that follows will identify some of the options available for attracting applicants to the public service job market and discuss strategies for managing the process.

POSTING VACANCIES

As indicated earlier, job posting refers to the practice of publicising an open job to employees and listing its attributes, such as criteria of knowledge, qualification, skill and experience. The purpose of posting vacancies is to bring to the attention of all interested persons the jobs that are to be filled.

Before posting a vacancy, management needs to decide whether:

* It intends to retain the job in its present form and with its present title, remuneration and status;
* Selected attributes of the job, for example, skill or experience, will change;
* There are sufficient qualified, potential applicants serving in other positions within the organisation who may be potential candidates for that job;
* The existing organisational policy on recruitment is still applicable;
* The organisations stands to benefit more, in the long-term, from recruiting applicants from external sources.

Also necessary is the availability of a functional human resource information system that supports recruitment.

An effective, computerised system would:

* Flag imminent vacancies throughout the organisation to ensure that the recruitment process is timely;
* Ensure that no candidates are lost but, instead, move through the process and are kept informed of their status;
* Ensure that good candidates whose applications are pending are kept in touch to maintain their interest in the organisation;
* Assist in analysing hiring, transfer and exit trends and provide other data that are helpful in planning, evaluating and auditing the recruitment process;
* Identify any adverse impacts of the recruitment process on vulnerable groups;
* For internal recruiting, control the internal job posting process, generate the notices, and then match internal applicant qualifications with job specifications;

* Where jobs are not being posted, generate a list of qualified internal candidates.

An organisation needs to analyse the benefits and disadvantages of recruiting its personnel through internal or external sources and, where the latter is selected, whether formal or informal systems should be used.

Recruiting from Internal Sources

There are sound reasons for recruiting from sources within the organisation:

* The ability of the recruit is known so it is easy to assess potential for the next level. By contrast, assessments of external recruits are based on less reliable sources, such as references, and relatively brief encounters, such as interviews.
* "Insiders" know the organisation, its strengths and weaknesses, its culture and, most of all, its people.
* Promotions from within build motivation and a sense of commitment to the organisation. Skilled and ambitious employees are more likely to become involved in developmental activities if they believe that these activities will lead to promotion.
* Internal recruitment is cheaper and quicker than advertising in various media and interviewing "outsiders". Time spent in training and socialisation is also reduced.

At the same time, several disadvantages exist:

* Sometimes it is difficult to find the "right" candidate within and the organisation may settle for an employee who possesses a less than ideal mix of competencies.
* If the vacancies are being caused by rapid expansion of the organisation there may be an insufficient supply of qualified individuals above the entry level. This may result in people being promoted before they are ready, or not being allowed to stay in a position long enough to learn how to do the job well.

* Infighting, inbreeding, and a shortage of varied perspectives and interests may reduce organisational flexibility and growth, and resistance to change by those who have an interest in maintaining the *status quo* may present long term problems.
* In times of rapid growth and during transitions, the organisation may promote from within into managerial positions, regardless of the qualifications of incumbents. Transition activities and rapid organisational growth often mask managerial deficiencies; it is not until the growth rate slows that the deficiencies become apparent and, then, the organisation finds it difficult, if not impossible, to undo the damage. The resulting cost of remedial training can prove prohibitive.

Recruiting from External Sources

External recruiting methods can be grouped into two classes: informal and formal. Informal recruiting methods tap a smaller market than formal methods. These methods may include rehiring former employees and choosing from among those "walk-in" applicants whose unsolicited résumés had been retained on file. The use of referrals also constitutes an informal hiring method. Because they are relatively inexpensive to use and can be implemented quickly, informal recruiting methods are commonly used for hiring clerical and other base-level recruits who are more likely than other groups to have submitted unsolicited applications.

Former students who participated in internship programmes may also be easily and cheaply accessed. Formal methods of external recruiting entail searching the labour market more widely for candidates with no previous connection to the organisation. These methods have traditionally included newspaper/magazine/journal advertising, the use of employment agencies and executive search firms, and college recruitment.

More often, now, job/career fairs and e-Recruiting are reaching the job seeker market. Posting vacancies externally through the various arms of the media or via employment agencies reaches a wider audience and may turn up a greater number of potential candidates from which the organisation can choose.

At the same time, this method is relatively expensive and time-consuming as the organisation works through initial advertisements, short-listing, interviewing and the other processes that precede selection. Even then, there is no guarantee that the results will be satisfactory to the organisation, Since, the cost of advertising often limits the frequency and duration of the job posting, as well as the amount of information made available, thus making it difficult for a job seeker to accurately judge the worth of the position being offered.

In addition, the organisation may hire a candidate who fails to live up to the high potential displayed during the selection process. Recruiting firms/employment agencies are gaining in popularity, especially in the search for management level/executive talent. Recruiting via this medium is expensive, whether the organisation uses a contingency firm or has one on retainer. Executive search firms tend to match candidates to jobs faster that most organisations can, on their own, primarily because the recruiting firms/employment agencies possess larger databases of, and wider access to, persons and have a greater awarene of the location of competencies needed by the client agencies.

Of course, it is possible to for an organisation to reduce the risks and high costs of recruitment by maintaining a small cadre of full-time, permanent employees and meeting an unexpected and temporary need for staff through the use of *ad hoc* and short-term contract workers who come to the position already trained. It is frequently said that the best jobs are not advertised; their availability is communicated by word of mouth. Networking, therefore, continues to be a viable mechanism for recruiting, especially at the senior management level in certain industries. In many instances, networking is a strategy used by the recruitment firms/ employment agencies.

ON-LINE APPLICATIONS/RECRUITING ON THE INTERNET

Using the Internet is faster and cheaper than many traditional methods of recruiting. Jobs can be posted on Internet sites for a modest amount, remain there for periods of thirty or sixty days or more - at no additional cost - and are available twenty-four hours a day. Candidates can view detailed information about the job and the organisation and then respond electronically. Most homes and workplaces are now using computerised equipment for communication; the Internet is rapidly becoming the method of choice for accessing and sharing information. First-time job seekers are now more likely to search web sites for job postings than to peruse newspapers, magazines and journals. The prevalence of eadvertising has made it easier.

The Internet speeds up the hiring process in three basis stages:

* Faster posting of jobs.
  - The submission of information to the media house and its appearance in print disappears. On the internet, the advertisement appears immediately and can be kept alive for as long as the recruiter requires it.
* Faster applicant response.
  - Jobs posted on the Internet and requiring responses via the same medium receive responses on the same day.
* Faster processing of résumés.
  - An applicant sending a résumé electronically can immediately have the application processed, receive an acknowledgement, be screened electronically, and have details of the application and résumé despatched to several managers at the same time.

On-line recruiting also provides access to passive job seekers, that is, individuals who already have a job but would apply for what appears a better one that is advertised on the Internet. These job seekers may be of a better quality Since, they are not desperate for a job change as are the active job seekers who may be frustrated, disgruntled workers looking for a new position. Companies that are likely to advertise on-line usually have a Web site that allows potential candidates to learn about the company before deciding whether to apply, thus lowering the incidence time-wasting through the submission of unsuitable applications.

The Web site can be used as a tool to encourage potential job seekers to build an interest in joining the organisation. Job web sites offer unlimited space which can be used, by management, to sell the organisation. The site can then be used, not only to post vacancies, but also to publicise the organisation. That will allow candidates to become more familiar with the company, know what skills the company is looking for and get to know about its culture. Most importantly, the system will provide a proper path to securing quick responses to job openings. On-line recruiting facilitates the decentralisation of the hiring function by making it possible for other groups in the organisation to take responsibility for part of the function.

* Some applicants still place great value on face-to-face interactions in the hiring process. Such applicants are likely to ignore jobs posted, impersonally, on-line.
* Companies are overwhelmed by the volume of résumés posted on the Internet. This can, in fact, lengthen the short-listing process. If the screening process is not well done, the quantity of applications/ résumés logged-on may be more of a hindrance to the process that an aid to selection.

Job seekers who demand confidentiality in the recruitment process may be reluctant to use the Internet as a job search mechanism.

For effectiveness in the use of the strategy of e-Recruiting, companies are advised to:

* Use specialised Job Sites that cater to specific industries; interested in joining the company;
* Take advantage of the fact that Internet job advertisements have no space limitations so

recruiters can use longer job descriptions to fully describe the company, job requirements and working conditions offered;

* Use valid Search Engines that will sort candidates effectively, but will not discriminate against any persons or groups;
* Create attention-grabbing newspaper advertisements that prompt people to visit the company's Web site. They will then see all vacancies that are advertised;
* Encourage employees to e-mail job advertisements to friends;
* Design and implement a successful e-Recruitment strategy.

COLLEGE RECRUITMENT

College recruiting – sending an employer's representatives to college campuses to prescreen applicants and create an applicant pool from that college's graduating class – is an important source of management trainees, promotable candidates, and professional and technical employees. To get the best out of this hiring strategy, the organisation and its career opportunities must be made to stand out.

Human resource professionals are aware that few college students and potential graduates know where their careers will take them over the next fifteen to twenty years. Therefore many of the an opportunity for recruiters to select the potential employees with the personal, technical and professional competencies they require in their organisation. The personal competencies identified may include, *inter alia,* a positive work ethic, strong interpersonal skills, leadership capacity and an ability to function well in a work team. The opportunity to discuss a student's current strengths and potential future value to an organisation cannot be replicated in any other setting. Two major advantages of this strategy are the cost (which is higher than word-of-mouth recruiting but lower than advertising in the media or using an employment agency), and the convenience (Since, many candidates can be interviewed in a short time in the same location with space and administrative support provided by the college itself).

Unfortunately, suitable candidates become available only at certain times of the year, which may not always suit the needs of the hiring organisation. Another major disadvantage of college recruiting is the lack of experience and the inflated expectations of new graduates and the cost of hiring graduates for entry-level positions that may not require a college degree. To make college recruiting effective, the recruiting organisation must first determine how many and which schools should be targeted. It may prove cost-effective to do intensive recruiting in a few, carefully-selected institutions, establishing a presence and building the organisation's reputation among students and faculty.

Timely and frequent dissemination of literature, the offer of internships and the award of prises for academic and/or social prowess help to advertise the organisation as a preferred place of employment. Subsequent invitations to the organisation's offices, made to students identified as potential employees, may serve to solidify the firm's image. Public Service organisations are usually unable to compete financially with their Private Sector counterparts and are therefore less likely to pay competitive salaries.

However, most public service agencies provide their employees with a wealth and range of experiences that are available nowhere else. It is for that reason that many college graduates use the Public Service as an employer of first resort to gain the experiences that will make them marketable in the short term. The strategies may not work as smoothly for public service recruiters, Since, the laws that govern their organisations' recruitment practices may be more stringent than those that apply in private sector companies. There may also be questions about the legality of the on-line application form. If this strategy were to be employed, public service recruiters must first decide on the criteria that should guide the process. The Public Service is seldom immediately seen as an attractive employer, mainly because salaries are uncompetitive.

Except for those students who have a commitment to public service, the top ten percent of college graduates will select the Private Sector as the employer of choice, partly because of the prestige value but primarily because of the remuneration package and because the recruiters may have been more successful in marketing their company. Therefore, it is understood that many of the graduates who enter the Public Service will stay for a short time and either return to school or proceed to another sector once they have acquired the requisite skills and experience that make them marketable. Recruitment and retention strategies in the Public Service must, therefore, reflect this reality and efforts made to get the most out of college graduates before they move on; conversely, the organisation may need to plan to recruit those students whose academic records suggest that they will remain in an organisation that pays less.

Retention strategies will focus on ensuring opportunities for intense training and development for skill enhancement and personal satisfaction. College recruitment also offers opportunities for internships. These programmes may provide the organisations with quality employees at low cost per hire. Some interns are hired at low cost (perhaps minimum wage) and are offered work experience.

Interns are able to have business skills, check out potential employers, and learn more about employers' likes and dislikes before making final career choices. Some of the better interns are recruited after graduation. College recruitment is relatively expensive and time consuming for the recruiting company. The process involves screening the candidate, that is, determining whether he/she is worthy of further consideration and marketing the company as a preferred place of employment. An alternate strategy for college recruitment is the career planning workshop.

These activities are usually (but not exclusively) associated with adolescent school leavers. They do not immediately produce ready candidates for the job market but provide the opportunity for an organisation to present itself as an employer worthy of consideration. Co-ordinators of career planning workshops co-opt professionals and organisations to present career options to potential school leavers in a controlled setting so as to lay out the range of possibilities to young job seekers. Career planning workshops are used mainly as information-giving tools which the school leaver can use to make informed career choices. Some organisations use the workshops as a base for internships.

Job Fairs

The concept of a job fair is to bring those interested in finding a job into those companies who are searching for applicants. Job fairs are open fora at which employers can exhibit the best their companies have to offer so that job seekers can make informed choices. They are considered one of the most effective ways for job seekers to land jobs. At the job fair, employers have a large pool of candidates on which to draw, while job seekers have the opportunity to shop around for dozens – sometimes hundreds – of employers, all in one place.

Notwithstanding the fact that the atmosphere at the fair is more relaxed than at an interview, employers are still on the look out for qualified, potential employees who have interest, dedication and initiative.

Maintaining Fairness/Equity in the Recruitment Process

It is often difficult to ensure and maintain fairness/equity in the recruitment process although, in every jurisdiction, there are laws that protect individuals and vulnerable groups from the negative impact of discriminatory practices. Where necessary, systems, detailed procedures and processes exist or must be established to minimise discrimination.

Each country designates/identifies a group or groups for special notice; women, visible minorities and the disabled are usual targets. The Government of Canada, in articulating its "Employment Equity Act and Regulations", identified four designated groups as employment equity targets: women, Aboriginal people, members of visible minority groups, persons with disabilities.

In the legislation, managers' responsibilities for employment equity are stated as:

* Ensuring effective overall performance and continuous progress of the employment equity goals within the operation;
* Achieving, fostering and maintaining a representative workforce;
* Showing leadership in employment equity and demonstrating commitment to it by ensuring that discrimination and stereotyping are not tolerated; and
* Informing and educating employees in the organisation about employment equity and diversity.

The Australian Public Service Commission, in ensuring that there were no infringements against individuals rights, issued general guidelines on workplace diversity, some of which related to recruitment:

* Integrate workplace diversity with the agency's goals and business.
* Reflect agency workplace diversity objectives in workplace agreements and certified agreements.
* Integrate workplace diversity principles into human resources policies and practices.
* Include implementation of workplace diversity objectives in the corporate plan, business plan and client service charters.
* Ensure information about employment opportunities is available in accessible formats.
* Review recruitment and selection processes to ensure that current and potential employees are not discriminated against.

Gather information on demographics. It is the goal of every jurisdiction to minimise or eliminate any instance of obvious discrimination against individuals or groups. In discussing policies on employment equity, scholor explains: "Employment equity policies and Programmes are about fairness in the workplace, not about reverse discrimination. Fairness is achieved when no one is denied employment opportunity and no one benefits for reasons unrelated to ability. Employment equity Programmes attempt to change the composition of the Workforce so that employees better reflect the community. The facts (both historical and current) show that members of the four designated groups face discrimination, enjoy less access to educational Programmes and training, and are often denied employment and promotions even when they have the necessary skills and experience."

The University's policies give special attention, *inter alia,* to the existence of systemic barriers and instances of intentional discrimination in the process of recruitment. Service Commissions were enshrined in the Independence Constitutions of the territories of the Commonwealth Caribbean and given *inter alia,* the power to recruit/appoint persons into the Public Service and, in so doing, reduce the influence of politicians on the staffing process.

In order to discharge their authority for making appointments, the Commissions have influenced the development of legislation and regulations that circumscribe the practice of recruitment, primarily to ensure that no discrimination attends the exercise.

To this end, entry into the Public Service follows the procedures of:

* Application on prescribed forms;
* Selection on the basis of seniority of application; application of age limits for entry into certain defined grades/classes; the use of written examinations and/or competitive interviews as the basis for permanent appointment to certain grades/classes.

The rules established by the Commissions enforce compliance in an attempt to minimise or eliminate the possibility of bias in staffing on the basis of race/ethnicity, creed, age, social status or physical disability.

SELECTION—PROCESS

In the context of evolution, certain traits or alleles of genes segregating within a population may be subject to selection.

Under selection, individuals with advantageous or "adaptive" traits tend to be more successful than their peers reproductively—meaning they contribute more offspring to the succeeding generation than others do. When these traits have a genetic basis, selection can increase the prevalence of those traits, because offspring will inherit those traits from their parents. When selection is intense and persistent, adaptive traits become universal to the population or species, which may then be said to have evolved. Scientists who do experimental genetics employ artificial selection experiments that permit the survival of organisms with user-defined phenotypes.

Artificial selection is widely used in the field of microbial genetics, especially molecular cloning. Whether or not selection takes place depends on the conditions in which the individuals of a species find themselves. Adults, juveniles, embryos, and even eggs and sperm may undergo selection. Factors fostering selection include limits on resources (nourishment, habitat space, mates) and the existence of threats (predators, disease, adverse weather). Biologists often refer to such factors as selective pressures. Natural selection is the most familiar type of selection by name. The breeding of dogs, cows and horses, however, represents "artificial selection". Sub-categories of natural selection are also sometimes distinguished. These include sexual selection, ecological selection, stabilising selection, disruptive selection and directional selection. Selection occurs only when the individuals of a population are diverse in their characteristics—or more specifically when the traits of individuals differ with respect to how well they equip them to survive or exploit a particular pressure. In the absence of individual variation, or when variations are selectively neutral, selection does not occur.

Meanwhile, selection does not guarantee that advantageous traits or alleles will become prevalent within a population. Through genetic drift, such traits may become less common or disappear. In the face of selection even a so-called deleterious allele may become universal to the members of a species. This is a risk primarily in the case of "weak" selection (*e.g.*, an infectious disease with only a low mortality rate) or small populations. Though deleterious alleles may sometimes become established, selection may act "negatively" as well as "positively." Negative selection decreases the prevalence of traits that diminish individuals' capacity to succeed reproductively (*i.e.*, their fitness), while positive selection increases the prevalence of adaptive traits. In biological discussions, traits subject to negative selection are sometimes said to be "selected against," while those under positive selection are said to be "selected for," as in the sentence Desert conditions select for drought tolerance in plants and select against shallow root architectures.

TYPES AND SUBTYPES OF SELECTION

Patterns of Selection

Aspects of selection may be divided into effects on a phenotype and their causes. The effects are called patterns of selection, and do not necessarily result from particular causes (mechanisms); in fact each pattern can arise from a number of different mechanisms. Stabilising selection favours individuals with intermediate characteristics while its opposite, disruptive selection, favours those with extreme characteristics; directional selection occurs when characteristics lie along a phenotypic spectrum and the individuals at one end are more successful; and balancing selection is a pattern in which multiple characteristics may be favoured.

Mechanisms of Selection

Distinct from patterns of selection are mechanisms of selection; for example, disruptive selection often is the result of disassortative sexual selection, and balancing selection may result from frequency-dependent selection and overdominance.

EMPLOYEE SELECTION PROCESS

Employee Selection is the process of putting right men on right job. It is a procedure of matching organisational requirements with the skills and qualifications of people.

Effective selection can be done only when there is effective matching.

By selecting best candidate for the required job, the organisation will get quality performance of employees. Moreover, organisation will face less of absenteeism and employee turnover problems. By selecting right candidate for the required job, organisation will also save time and money. Proper screening of candidates takes place during selection procedure.

All the potential candidates who apply for the given job are tested. But selection must be differentiated from recruitment, though these are two phases of employment process. Recruitment is considered to be a positive process as it motivates more of candidates to apply for the job. It creates a pool of applicants.

It is just sourcing of data. While selection is a negative process as the inappropriate candidates are rejected here. Recruitment precedes selection in staffing process. Selection involves choosing the best candidate with best abilities, skills and knowledge for the required job.

The Employee selection process takes place in following order:

* It is used to eliminate those candidates who do not meet the minimum eligiblity criteria laid down by the organisation. The skills, academic and family background, competencies and interests of the candidate are examined during preliminary interview. Preliminary interviews are less formalised and planned than the final interviews. The candidates are given a brief up about the company and the job profile; and it is also examined how much the candidate knows about the company. Preliminary interviews are also called screening interviews.
* The candidates who clear the preliminary interview are required to fill application blank. It contains data record of the candidates such as details about age, qualifications, reason for leaving previous job, experience, etc.,

* Various written tests conducted during selection procedure are aptitude test, intelligence test, reasoning test, personality test, etc. These tests are used to objectively assess the potential candidate. They should not be biased.
* It is a one to one interaction between the interviewer and the potential candidate. It is used to find whether the candidate is best suited for the required job or not. But such interviews consume time and money both. Moreover the competencies of the candidate cannot be judged. Such interviews may be biased at times. Such interviews should be conducted properly. No distractions should be there in room. There should be an honest communication between candidate and interviewer.
* Medical tests are conducted to ensure physical fitness of the potential employee. It will decrease chances of employee absenteeism.
* A reference check is made about the candidate selected and then finally he is appointed by giving a formal appointment letter.

TRAINING AND DEVELOPMENT: CONCEPT, IMPORTANCE AND METHODS OF TRAINING

Changes in technology, especially information technology, generate knowledge spreading up at tremendous speed, as well as its quick obsolence. In the period between 1900 and 1950, the amount of human knowledge doubled, and Since, then it has doubled every 5 to 8 years. Knowledge is becoming obsolete so quickly that all of us need do double our knowledge every 2 to 3 years in order to keep up with the changes. On the other hand, the increasing complexity, turbulency and uncertainty of the environment requires different and greater knowledge. Modern business requires more and more knowledge and skills that are still inadequatly present in the formal school education, *i.e.*, the gap between business reqiurements and the knowledge acquired at school is growing.

The period of mass producing is over and the customers are very selective. Increased consumer demands require new solutions and knowledge. Due to increasing competition, the organisation is required to constantly revise its product and service mix, managerial methods, and to increase productivity. Modern conditions of dynamic competition, sophisticated information technology, knowledge economy, market globalisation, has changed the relation to importance of human resources in organisation. These conditions actualise the human capital as the strategic resource of every organisation. Differences between the organisations exist exactly due to the differences between human capital, *i.e.*, the organisations human resources, ways of their management and development.

In a more and more global, complex and turbulent environment, knowledge is the only reliable source of competitive advantage. Traditional factors of manufacturing as the soil, Labour and capital did not disappear, but their significance is not primary anymore. Knowledge is viewed as the key of realisation of a competitive advantage. And therefore the question of where the corporative knowledge is located, how to release it and develop to achieve organisational goals has become very important.

Since, the organisational knowledge is largely located inside the human mind, *i.e.*, the head of employees, as carriers of knowledge and activities, human resources are becoming the key factor of business success. Organisational development is always conditioned by human knowledge and skills. That is why, contemporary organisations pay more and more attention to the development of their emplozees. Thus, employee education and training are becoming an optimal answer to complex business challenges, and the management of human resources is taking central role in modern management.

Through the process of employee training and development, the management of human resources provides constant knowledge innovation, creates conditions for mutual knowledge and experience exchange and proactive behaviour, in this way contributing to competitive advantage and satisfaction of all participants in business procedures. As a consequence of these procedures a learning organisation has formed. The aim of this chapter is to point to the fact that education and development of human potential are the basic factor for creation of basis for transformation from traditional to a learning company. Learning organisation is organisation that promotes learning of all of its members and it transforms permanently. Individuals and societies that do not have enough knowledge are in inferior position, compared to societies and organisations that have it and even permanently acquire new knowledge. That is the reason why we say that success is not among the educated but among those that are learning permanently, and everything changes except knowledge acquirement, which is constant.

EMPLOYEE TRAINING AND DEVELOPMENT

Understanding the phenomenon of employee training and development requires understanding of all the changes that take place as a result of learning. As the generator of new knowledge, employee training and development is placed within a broader strategic context of human resources management, *i.e.*, global organisational management, as a planned staff education and development, both individual and group, with the goal to benefit both the organisation and employees. To preserve its obtained positions and increase competitive advantage, the organisation needs to be able to create new knowledge, and not only to rely solely on utilisation of the existing. Thus, the continous employee training and delopment has a singnificant role in the development of individual and organisational performance.

The strategic procedure of employee training and development needs to encourage creativity, ensure inventiveness and shape the entire organisational knowledge that provides the organisation with uniqueness and differentiates it from the others. Education is no longer the duty and privilege of those in higher positions and skilled labour, but it is becoming the duty and need of everyone. The larger the organisations, the more funds they spend on education and provide their employees with greater and diverse possibilities of education and development.

Understanding the tremendous significance of education for the modern organisation and confident that it represents a good and remunirative investment, present day organisations set aside more and more resources for this activity. Most of the organisations invest 3 to 5 per cent of their revenue into adult education. It is estimated that the organisations that desire to keep the pace with changes need to provide their employees with 2 per cent of total annual fund of working hours for training and education. Thus, it is necessary to accept the model of permanent, continuous learning.

That truth has been known for more than two centuries. Denis Diderot, a French philosopher and literate of the Age of Enlightment, wrote the following: "Education shouldn't be finished when an individual leaves school, it should encompass all the ages of life . . . to provide people in every moment of their life with a possibility to maintain their knowledge or to obtain new knowledge". The only way for present day organisations to survive is the imperative to innovate or perish.

Since, this depends on the knowledge the organisation possesses, this imperative could be read as: learn faster than competition. The logical sequence is: knowledge creation – innovation – competitive advantage. If knowledge is good, is it not true that the more knowlegde we have, the better we are? Many organisations which consider knowledge as a good thing are trapped into the pitfall of gathering as much knowledge as possible. Knowledge that is not necessary is exatly what it is: unnecessary. And the efforts to obtain it are wasted efforts.

The only important knowldege is the knowledge with strategic importance to the company, knowledge that helps to increase the value of the company, knowledge with significance to the strategy of the company. It is not about knowledge for the sake of knowledge, but rather knowledge according to the needs, applicable knowledge, knowledge to create innovation and competitive advantage. Obtaining knowledge, learning, education, all could have a real effect on the quality of labour only if they are harmonised with the needs of a particular organisation, its goals and the goals of its employees.

The further choice of educational contents and educational methods, and the efficiency of educational effectiveness control depend on clearly defined educational goals and needs, answers to the questions of which knowldege is necessary to realise the strategy and the survival of the organisation in general, which employees need to possess this knowledge and will this knowledge solve certain problems. Employee training and development does not imply only obtaining new knowledge, abilities and skills, but also the possibility to promote entrepreneurship, introduce employees to changes, encourage the changes of their attitude, introduce the employees to important business decisions and involve them actively in the process of decision making.

To precisely define expectations and attract skilled workforce, more and more employment advertisings offer a certain number of annual hours or days for education. The most wanted resources are the people with particular knowledge, skills and abilities. Managers must learn to manage them, and the organisations to employ and retain them. Knowledge based organisations must preserve their competitive advantage by retaining skilled workforce, workers of knowledge, strengthening their motivation and improving the reward and compensation systems according to the workers' performances.

Within the context of learning organisation, it is not sufficient for the worker only to add value to the organisation based on his knowledge, but he also has to receive knowledge. He gives as much knowledge as he receives. For the present day employees the wage by itself is not a sufficient incentive, but they also need investment into themselves in a sense of investing in their knowledge. Empolyees no longer work for money alone, nor can they be influenced by traditional attractive financial packages.

CONCEPT OF A LEARNING ORGANISATION

Every individual should appreciate lifelong learning, and every successful organisation has to become a permanently learning organisation. Many successful organisations describe themselves as learning organisation or one of their strategic goals is to become such an organisation. Companies such as Coca-Cola, Motorola, General Electrics and Cisco have assigned vice presidents for knowledge, learning or intellectual capital whose task is to create knowledge management systems that enable them to quickly adopt development tendencies, influencing in that way the customers, competitors, distributors and suppliers.

The organisation is not only the user of knowledge, but also its creator. Peter Senge described in the book named "The Fifth Discipline", the learning organisation implies free flow of knowledge, *i.e.*, lifting of all barriers on developing knowledge and new ideas at the very beginning. In the future it will not be possible to "unthread things from above" and for all the others to follow the "big brother's" instructions anymore. The top organisations of the future will be distinguished by their knowledge about how to encourage engagement and develop the learning potential on each organisational level. Peter Senge's model of a learning organisation is very interesting Since, it recognises the organisation as a whole, *i.e.*, in his organisation, through their functions and sectors within the organisation, all the employees influence the course of business procedures, and the knowledge creation, consequently the creation of new values both for the organisation and its customers. With this definition, Senge has made significant qualitative progress compared to the classical organisation, Since, he emphasised the necessity of ability development through the process of learning.

Besides Senge, Chris Argyris was a great populariser of a learning organisation as well. In his book "Teaching smart people how to learn", he says: "Any company that aspires to succeed in the tougher business environment must first resolve a basic dilemma: success in the marketplace increasingly depends on learning, yet most people don't know how to learn.

What's more, those members of the organisation that many assume to be the best at learning are, in fact, not very good at it. I am talking about the well-educated, highpowered, highly committed professionals who take up key leadership positions in the modern corporation." Organisations learn only through the learning individuals. Individual learning does not guarantee organisational learning. But without it there is no organisational learning as well. The ablity to learn faster than the competitors may be the only sustainable competitive advantage.

Thus, the learning organisation is the organisation that learns and encourages people to learn in the organisation. It motivates information exchange between employees and creates staff with different knowledge. Chris Argiris explains this: "On the other hand, there is a problem of existence of individuals within the organisation who know how to learn, but that doesn't create automatically conditions for the organisation to learn as well. This is due to the indisputable view that knowledge is still the only private property the man owns. This means that individual learning, and even learning of all the employees, doesn't imply the existence of a learning organisation. To have a learning organisation, it is necessary to know how to transfer individual into organisational knowledge, *i.e.*, into organisational learning." The starting point of knowledge management concept is in the fact that power does not come from knowledge, but from the exchange of knowledge.

It starts from the synergic effect. By exchanging knowledge, combining individual knowledge, we get much more qualitative knowledge than the individual knowledge. Obtaining and sharing knowledge is the core of the learning organisation. The reasons to become a learning organisation are the following: people are developing (greater motivation, flexibility of employees, people are more creative, improved social interaction), better working teams and groups (knowledge sharing, mutual dependence), benefiting organisations (greater work productivity, more qualitative products/services/ procedures, competitive advantage, profit).

APPROACH TO TRAINING AND DEVELOPMENT WITHIN OUR ORGANISATIONS AND NEED FOR TRANSFORMATION

Unfortunately, the procedures of employee training and development within our organisations are undeveloped. They are mainly performed occasionally, and not connected with organisational strategy, nor do they have some strategic significance. They are mostly enforced when such business problems occur or are perceived that are considered relievable or solvable by organising a training, course or seminar for some of the employees. Employees view the training as an imposed obligation, rather than a way to maximise their potential and they do not realise that by improving their performances and innovation of their knowledge they may contribute to better business results of the organisation they belong to. Unfortunately, top managers do not realise this as well. From their relationship with the employees it is plain to see that the employees are still treated as an expense, rather than an investment worthy of investing. In our organisations there is no culture of obtaining and sharing of knowledge. Many of our managers are under the influence of prejudices such as: training is expensive, training is an expense burdening the current business, it is not rewarding, training is for the young, etc., Knowledge is expensive, but ignorance is even more expensive.

Human possibilites to learn are unlimited, unless idviduals do not limit their abilities within their minds. Many studies have shown that investing in employee training and development has larger business effects than investing in equipment and other material resources. Our organisations must harmonise their approach to employee development with the changes. Employee training and development has to be connected with the organisational goals and strategy, they need to fulfil the new reqiurements of the environment.

Employee training and development needs to become a managerial function. It is a managerial challenge to consider the employees of the organisation from a strategic perspective (future orientedness) and constantly monitor and encourage the development of new skills and knowledge as the foundation of organisational development. This is not about assigning the employees to appropriate jobs, but rather about the constant dynamic of encouraging and discovering new possibilities. This is a new type of leadership, significantly different from the classical model of organisational management.

The leaders are no longer expected to be all-knowing bosses and supervisors, but rather moderators and inspirators. Since, people do not share the information which is the source of their power instictively, the leaders need to recognise, attract and release knowledge in the organisation. One of the main challegnes of modern organisations therefore is how to manage the process of knowledge transfer. "The answer is that wisdom, just because it is the most important, doesn't need to be located inside a tall building where the chief executive and his main assistants hang their hats (and soon their heads as well – unless they join the revolution of the mind). This pictoresque answer of Tom Peters refers to decentralisation and substantivity of employees (turning every workplace into business), which implies a high degree of employee competence and orientation Towards the participative style of management.

The process of democratisations, transitions, opening towards the EU, privatisations and arrival of foreign companies and praxis contributed considerably to transformation of approach to employee training and development within our organisations, from the *ad hoc* processes that originate from the goals and strategies, to a modern approach where human resources and their knowledge are gaining more and more significance.

IMPORTANCE OF TRAINING AND DEVELOPMENT

* Training and Development helps in optimising the utilisation of human resource that further helps the

employee to achieve the organisational goals as well as their individual goals.

* Training and Development helps to provide an opportunity and broad structure for the development of human resources' technical and Behavioural skills in an organisation. It also helps the employees in attaining personal growth.
* Training and Development helps in increasing the job knowledge and skills of employees at each level. It helps to expand the horizons of human intellect and an overall personality of the employees.
* Training and Development helps in increasing the productivity of the employees that helps the organisation further to achieve its long-term goal.
* Training and Development helps in inculcating the sense of team work, team spirit, and inter-team collaborations. It helps in inculcating the zeal to learn within the employees.
* Training and Development helps to develop and improve the organisational health culture and effectiveness. It helps in creating the learning culture within the organisation.
* Training and Development helps building the positive perception and feeling about the organisation. The employees get these feelings from leaders, subordinates, and peers.
* Training and Development helps in improving upon the quality of work and work-life.
* Training and Development helps in creating the healthy working environment. It helps to build good employee, relationship so that individual goals aligns with organisational goal.
* Training and Development helps in improving the health and safety of the organisation thus preventing obsolescence.
* Training and Development helps in improving the morale of the Workforce.

* Training and Development helps in creating a better corporate image.
* Training and Development leads to improved profitability and more positive attitudes towards profit orientation.
* Training and Development aids in organisational development, *i.e.*, Organisation gets more effective decision making and problem solving. It helps in understanding and carrying out organisational policies
* Training and Development helps in developing leadership skills, motivation, loyalty, better attitudes, and other aspects that successful workers and managers usually display.

IMPORTANCE OF TRAINING OBJECTIVES

Training objectives are one of the most important parts of training Programme. While some people think of training objective as a waste of valuable time. The counterargument here is that resources are always limited and the training objectives actually lead the design of training. It provides the clear guidelines and develops the training Programme in less time because objectives focus specifically on needs. It helps in adhering to a plan. Training objective tell the trainee that what is expected out of him at the end of the training Programme.

Training objectives are of great significance from a number of stakeholder perspectives:

* Trainer.
* Trainee.
* Designer.
* Evaluator.

Trainer

The training objective is also beneficial to trainer because it helps the trainer to measure the progress of trainees and make the required adjustments. Also, trainer comes in a position to establish a relationship between objectives and particular segments of training.

Trainee

The training objective is beneficial to the trainee because it helps in reducing the anxiety of the trainee up to some extent. Not knowing anything or going to a place which is unknown creates anxiety that can negatively affect learning. Therefore, it is important to keep the participants aware of the happenings, rather than keeping it surprise. Secondly, it helps in increase in concentration, which is the crucial factor to make the training successful. The objectives create an image of the training Programme in trainee's mind that actually helps in gaining attention. Thirdly, if the goal is set to be challenging and motivating, then the likelihood of achieving those goals is much higher than the situation in which no goal is set. Therefore, training objectives helps in increasing the probability that the participants will be successful in training.

Designer

The training objective is beneficial to the training designer because if the designer is aware what is to be achieved in the end then he'll buy the training package according to that only. The training designer would then look for the training methods, training equipments, and training content accordingly to achieve those objectives. Furthermore, planning always helps in dealing effectively in an unexpected situation. Consider an example; the objective of one training Programme is to deal effectively with customers to increase the sales. Since, the objective is known, the designer will design a training Programme that will include ways to improve the interpersonal skills, such as verbal and non- verbal language, dealing in unexpected situation, *i.e.*, when there is a defect in a product or when a customer is angry. Therefore, without any guidance, the training may not be designed appropriately.

Evaluator

It becomes easy for the training evaluator to measure the progress of the trainees because the objectives define the expected performance of trainees. Training objective is an important to tool to judge the performance of participants.

TRAINING AS CONSULTANCY

Training consultancy provides industry professional to work with an organisation in achieving its training and development objectives.

Estimation of Training Outsourcing

It has been estimated that 58 per cent of the emerging market in training outsourcing is in customer education, while only 42 percent of the market is in employee education. The training consultancies offer various benefits such as:

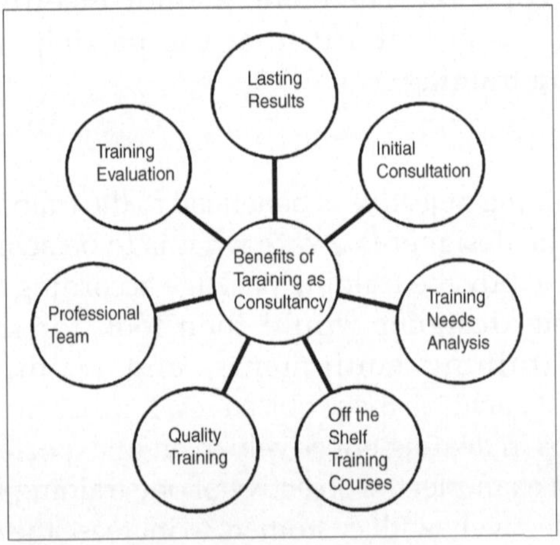

Training Courses that Consultancies Offer

* Business Training Courses:
  - Management Development:
    a. Conflict Management;
    b. Managing Diversity;
    c. Project Management;
    d. Stress Management;
    e. Time Management; and
    f. Senior Management Workshops.

- Sales:
  a. Negotiation Skills; and
  b. Sales Technique.
- Customer Care:
  a. Customer Care Training; and
  b. Managing Customers.
- Human Resource :
  a. HR Administration;
  b. Induction Training;
  c. Recruitment and Selection; and
  d. Successful Appraising.
- Personal Development Courses.
- Workshops on:
  a. Assertive Skills;
  b. Building Confidence;
  c. Coping with Change;
  d. Interview Techniques; and
  e. Maximise Potential.
- One to One Coaching:
  a. Focused entirely on personal objectives;
  b. Move forward at individual pace;
  c. Material used in tailor made to specific development Need; and
  d. A strict code of confidentiality.

Importance of Training Consultancies:

* It helps in enhancing company's image.
* It helps in strengthening the team spirit.
* It helps in applying knowledge, developing core competencies, and reducing work load.
* It helps in improving the work relations.
* It helps in developing focused and inspired staff.
* It leads to greater chances of success.

Consultants can provide help on following areas:

* Management Development.
* Team Building Leadership.
* Health and Safety Training.
* Interpersonal Skills.
* Sales Training.

TRAINING AND HUMAN RESOURCE MANAGEMENT

The HR functioning is changing with time and with this change, the relationship between the training function and other management activity is also changing. The training and development activities are now equally important with that of other HR functions. Gone are the days, when training was considered to be futile, waste of time, resources, and money. Now a days, training is an investment because the departments such as, marketing and sales, HR, production, finance, etc. depends on training for its survival. If training is not considered as a priority or not seen as a vital part in the organisation, then it is difficult to accept that such a company has effectively carried out HRM. Training actually provides the opportunity to raise the profile development activities in the organisation.

To increase the commitment level of employees and growth in quality movement (concepts of HRM), senior management team is now increasing the role of training. Such concepts of HRM require careful planning as well as greater emphasis on employee development and long term education. Training is now the important tool of Human Resource Management to control the attrition rate because it helps in motivating employees, achieving their professional and personal goals, increasing the level of job satisfaction, etc., As a result training is given on a variety of skill development and covers a multitude of courses.

Role of HRD Professionals in Training

This is the era of cut-throat competition and with this changing scenario of business; the role of HR professionals in training has been widened. HR role now is:

* Active involvement in employee education
* Rewards for improvement in performance
* Rewards to be associated with self esteem and self worth.
* Providing pre-employment market oriented skill development education and post employment support for advanced education and training.
* Flexible access, *i.e.*, anytime, anywhere training.

MODELS OF TRAINING

Training is a sub-system of the organisation because the departments such as, marketing and sales, HR, production, finance, etc depends on training for its survival. Training is a transforming process that requires some input and in turn it produces output in the form of knowledge, skills, and attitudes (KSAs).

THE TRAINING SYSTEM

A System is a combination of things or parts that must work together to perform a particular function. An organisation is a system and training is a sub system of the organisation.

The System Approach views training as a sub system of an organisation. System Approach can be used to examine broad issues like objectives, functions, and aim. It establishes a logical relationship between the sequential stages in the process of training need analysis (TNA), formulating, delivering, and evaluating.

There are four necessary inputs, *i.e.*, technology, man, material, time required in every system to produce products or services. And every system must have some output from these inputs in order to survive. The output can be tangible or intangible depending upon the organisation's requirement. A system approach to training is planned creation of training Programme.

This approach uses step-by-step procedures to solve the problems. Under systematic approach, training is undertaken on planned basis.

Out of this planned effort, one such basic model of five steps is system model that is explained below. Organisation are working in open environment, *i.e.*, there are some internal and external forces, that poses threats and opportunities, therefore, trainers need to be aware of these forces which may impact on the content, form, and conduct of the training efforts.

The internal forces are the various demands of the organisation for a better learning environment; need to be up to date with the latest technologies.

The three model of training are:

* System Model.
* Instructional System Development Model.
* Transitional model.

SYSTEMATIC MODEL TRAINING

The system model consists of five phases and should be repeated on a regular basis to make further improvements. The training should achieve the purpose of helping employee to perform their work to required standards.

* *Analyse and identify the training needs, i.e.,* to analyse the department, job, employees requirement, who needs training, what do they need to learn, estimating training cost, etc The next step is to develop a performance measure on the basis of which actual performance would be evaluated.
* *Design and provide training to meet identified needs.* This step requires developing objectives of training, identifying the learning steps, sequencing and structuring the contents.
* *Develop* - This phase requires listing the activities in the training Programme that will assist the participants to learn, selecting delivery method, examining the training material, validating information to be imparted to make sure it accomplishes all the goals and objectives
* *Implementing* is the hardest part of the system because one wrong step can lead to the failure of whole training Programme.
* *Evaluating* each phase so as to make sure it has achieved its aim in terms of subsequent work performance. Making necessary amendments to any of the previous stage in order to remedy or improve failure practices.

TRANSITIONAL MODEL

Transitional model focuses on the organisation as a whole. The outer loop describes the vision, mission and values of the organisation on the basis of which training model, *i.e.*, inner loop is executed.

* *Vision*—focuses on the milestones that the organisation would like to achieve after the defined point of time. A vision statement tells that where the organisation sees itself few years down the line. A vision may include setting a role mode, or bringing some internal transformation, or may be promising to meet some other deadlines.
* *Mission*—explain the reason of organisational existence. It identifies the position in the community. The reason of developing a mission statement is to motivate, inspire, and inform the employees regarding the organisation. The mission statement tells about the identity that how the organisation would like to be viewed by the customers, employees, and all other stakeholders.
* *Values*—is the translation of vision and mission into communicable ideals. It reflects the deeply held values of the organisation and is independent of current industry environment. For example, values may include social responsibility, excellent customer service, etc.

INSTRUCTIONAL SYSTEM DEVELOPMENT MODEL (ISD) MODEL

Instructional System Development model or ISD training model was made to answer the training problems. This model is widely used now-a-days in the organisation because it is concerned with the training need on the job performance. Training objectives are defined on the basis of job responsibilities and job description and on the basis of the defined objectives individual progress is measured. This model also helps in determining and developing the favourable strategies, sequencing the content, and delivering media for the types of training objectives to be achieved.

The Instructional System Development model comprises of five stages:

* This phase consist of training need assessment, job analysis, and target audience analysis.
* This phase consist of setting goal of the learning outcome, instructional objectives that measures Behaviour of a participant after the training, types of training material, media selection, methods of evaluating the trainee, trainer and the training Programme, strategies to impart knowledge, *i.e.*, selection of content, sequencing of content, etc.
* This phase translates design decisions into training material. It consists of developing course material for the trainer including handouts, workbooks, visual aids, demonstration props, etc, course material for the trainee including handouts of summary.
* This phase focuses on logistical arrangements, such as arranging speakers, equipments, benches, podium, food facilities, cooling, lighting, parking, and other training accessories.
* The purpose of this phase is to make sure that the training Programme has achieved its aim in terms of subsequent work performance. This phase consists of identifying strengths and weaknesses and making necessary amendments to any of the previous stage in order to remedy or improve failure practices.

The ISD model is a continuous process that lasts throughout the training Programme. It also highlights that feedback is an important phase throughout the entire training Programme. In this model, the output of one phase is an input to the next phase.

METHODS OF TRAINING

There are various methods of training, which can be divided in to cognitive and Behavioural methods. Trainers need to understand the pros and cons of each method, also its impact on trainees keeping their background and skills in mind before giving training. Cognitive methods are more of giving theoretical training to the trainees.

The various methods under Cognitive approach provide the rules for how to do something, written or verbal information, demonstrate relationships among concepts, etc., These methods are associated with changes in knowledge and attitude by stimulating learning.

The various methods that come under Cognitive approach are:

* Lectures.
* Demonstrations.
* Discussions.
* Computer based training (cbt).
  - Intellegent tutorial system(its).
  - Programmed instruction (pi).
  - Virtual reality.

Behavioural methods are more of giving practical training to the trainees. The various methods under Behavioural approach allow the trainee to Behaviour in a real fashion. These methods are best used for skill development.

The various methods that come under Behavioural approach are:

* Games and simulations.
  - Behaviour-modeling.
  - Business games.
  - Case studies.
  - Equipment stimulators.
  - In-basket technique.
  - Role plays.

Both the methods can be used effectively to change attitudes, but through different means.

Another Method is Management Development Method

* The more future oriented method and more concerned with education of the employees. To become a better performer by education implies that management development activities attempt to instill sound reasoning processes. Management development method is further divided into two parts:

* The development of a manager's abilities can take place on the job.

The four techniques for on the job development are:

1. Coaching.
2. Mentoring.
3. Job rotation.
4. Job instruction technique (jit).

OFF THE JOB TRAINING

There are many management development techniques that an employee can take in off the job.

The few popular methods are:

* Sensitivity training.
* Transactional analysis.
* Straight lectures/ lectures.
* Simulation exercises.

7

Librarianship

INTRODUCTION

To some people, librarianship may sound like an old-fashion term - something that smells of mothballs and is wrapped in parchment. The term librarian already evokes image of a certain type of staid personality and putting the suffix "ship" to it only adds lead to its weight. More than twenty years ago, when I started out in this field, I confess that I was not very keen to call myself a librarian too, preferring something with the word information or some other technically sounding clang in the job title. Somehow the transition from being an engineer to a librarian seemed a bit too drastic in those days.

However the words "librarian" and "librarianship" became more endearing to me as I grew older. At this point, I thought it aptly described what we do as a profession. Like many of you, I have a graduate degree in Library and Information Science, but what we do is not a science, not in the strictest sense of it.

The word librarianship is better for it encompasses humanistic elements that define our ethos and more importantly, puts the place of libraries as an institution squarely in the centre.

I know that some people will disagree with this and want to rip the library out of their information persona just as digital information now exists without being associated with any one media. Actually I am sympathetic to this view. Labels and their connotations can be devastating and create obstacles to the good things that we can do. However, I think there is much strength to be gained from libraries as an institution and it would be wise for librarians not to disassociate ourselves from it.

WHAT IS LIBRARIANSHIP ABOUT NOW

So what is librarianship? Particularly, what is it about now? We can take a very broad view, such as "the preservation and transfer of knowledge in all recorded forms across time and space for the benefit of humankind", which is part of the LAS Ethical Statement or we can draw on our practical day to day work and define librarianship as "being concerned with the principle and practice of selecting, acquiring, organising, disseminating and providing access to information in accordance with the specific needs of groups of people or an individual".

Both definitions are my own formulation, expressed in response to various demands in the course of my work. What we need is an empirical, up-to-date and aggregated view of what librarians today really think. So I turned to my colleagues at NTU Library for an answer. I asked each of the professional staff to give me a short spontaneous response on what they think librarianship is all about now. After going through all the responses, which ranged from one liner to 3 pages of passionate text, I manage to distill it into the chart. Basically I just tick the number of times a facet or its equivalent is mentioned – not very scientific but what I needed was just some indication.

Note that no questionnaire was used and the categories listed in the chart are created by me. Though the responses may be coloured by the nature of the work we do in NTU, I think it might be a fair representation of what most librarians in Singapore think. We have a very diverse group of staff representing many age groups, prior occupational backgrounds, fields of study and duration of library work experience.

A DEFINITION OF LIBRARIANSHIP

Many of the key elements of librarianship identified in the informal e-mail poll are what we would expect. What is interesting but not so surprising is that there is a strong emphasis on users and less on library collections and resources. This is probably one of the major but subtle changes in librarianship in the last 20 years. When I started out in librarianship there was much more focus on building and organising library collections. Even reference work was very dependent on good cataloging and organisation of library resources.

Though everything we did then was also aimed at helping the users, it was more implied than obvious. Today we seem to be more obsessed and anxious about our relationship with users, and for good reason as we shall discuss. Nonetheless, going by the e-mail poll, there seem to be some agreement on the shape and structure to the profession. There is a unique "aboutness" of the profession that can be articulated just as in the discipline of science, engineering, law, medicine, etc., Based on various sentiments expressed in the poll, I attempted to provide a collective view in the following definition of librarianship for the purpose of this presentation. "Librarianship is the discipline and profession that is concerned with helping individuals obtain reliable information to increase their knowledge in all spheres of their lives from the cumulated information store of mankind". This definition focuses on the intermediary or bridging role of libraries.

One of the respondents put it more colourfully as follows:

* "Librarianship is a bridge between two entities; people and information. Librarians consider who may need this bridge, when and where a bridge is needed, how it is to be built, how it can be best utilised. We are the planner, architect, builder, and marketer of bridges".

To play this role adequately, it is implied that libraries need to have a clear understanding of the needs of the user on one hand and the knowledge and availability of relevant information resources on the other. The definition also assigns an end purpose for our roles, *i.e.*, to help users obtain information that will increase their knowledge in all spheres of their lives. It makes a distinction between information and knowledge, as the latter is part of an individual's makeup and cannot be disassociated from it. We help people obtain useful and reliable information but it is up to the each individual to assimilate it and make knowledge their own. It is clear that most librarians in the survey look at librarianship as a predominantly intermediary function. The question is whether this is relevant today. Do users need or want us to help them obtain information? Are the information resources that libraries provide - the evidence base of knowledge cumulated in the past, highly desired by users anymore? Are people concerned enough about using reliable sources of information to make an effort to obtain it? There are many questions and exciting developments in library land today and it might not be possible to touch on all of them in this short presentation.

USERS

Librarianship has always been about serving the individual, whom we call by different names such as user, patron, customer, etc. Books or information resources are purchased for the individual because he or she needs them or we anticipate his or her needs. They are catalogued with great consideration of appropriate access points so that the individual may find them precisely. We lend out materials to individuals or provide databases for them to get the information to increase their knowledge and perform their work effectively or help in their personal development.

We have specialist reference librarians to answer questions from individuals and guide them in finding information. Librarians in public libraries run reading promotion Programmes to encourage the reading habits of individuals, from children to adults. What is more, individuals get these services mostly for free. Therefore all the work that librarians do leads to the satisfaction of the needs of individuals. However although we focus exclusively on the user, the user-library relationship has not always been equal. Generally users depends a lot more on librarians for access to information in the past than at present. The librarian had a strong intermediary function then as there were various kinds of obstacles to access.

These could be physical, administrative, system or skills related. For example, a researcher in the 1980s wishing to have a comprehensive literature search done would have to go through an expert online searcher in the Library to interrogate online systems such as DIALOG and BRS both for skills and cost reasons. Libraries then could therefore afford to treat their users with less alacrity. They either came to the Library or did not get the information they need. However that is not to say that libraries were not user-oriented. It is just that user-centred issues were not accorded high priority over other concerns.

The relationship changed drastically with the beginning of the end-user revolution. It started with bibliographic databases on cd-roms which enable users to use to their hearts' content without incurring expensive online charges or the librarian watching over their shoulders. Soon after that, purchased content became more convenient to use as they migrate to the web which gave users 24/7 access. The power of convenience cannot be underestimated. It is probably the single most important factor that determines the use of an information resource or system. In the last few years, the advent of Google, the proliferation of free content, the massive worldwide digitisation projects and the wide spread use of social networking tools have completed the end-user revolution.

Not only is it easier and more convenient to gain access to information but there is also an abundance of free information to be had. Today the perception among many people is that they can find decent amount of information on the Internet for their work or leisure without venturing into the Library or gaining access into its vault of online resources or print collection. Thus the alarming results from the 2005 OCLC study on college students that shows that 84 per cent of respondents use search engines to begin an information search and only one per cent start from a library web site. Thus it would appear that the relationship between libraries and their users have turned 180 degrees.

Today, there is much more thinking and activities among librarians on getting the attention of users and bringing them back to the fold of the library. This then is the first big change in librarianship today. Librarianship today demands much more thought and effort on connecting with users and maintaining their engagement. This emphasis did not appear overnight but has been gaining centre-stage gradually Since, the balance between libraries and end-users tipped towards the latter due to technological and societal changes. Users now have an attractive alternative to the Library.

The goals of librarianship, particularly its role in transmission of knowledge cannot be achieved without users occupying a huge chunk in the equation. Therefore there is an almost frantic rush to pamper to the whims and tech savvy habits of users, particularly those from the new generations who are more at ease with the QWERTY keyboard than with chalk and blackboard. This preoccupation has implications for how librarianship is and will be practiced. As suggested, see more librarians going to bed with users or being embedded in the working and social environment of users. This is a logical development as the Internet and its attraction will remain and grow and users will not divert from it to the Library unless librarians go out and lead them through our pathways, virtual or otherwise.

Furthermore, as users have less contact with libraries, there will be fewer opportunities for libraries to observe and study their real information needs to develop effective plans and services to achieve our mission. In a rapidly evolving environment it is critical to have this information and only by working closely with users can we achieve this. These imperatives require librarians to have the disposition and the interpersonal skills not traditionally associated with library work.

Librarianship is no longer centered in the backroom but in the frontline where the users are. Besides possessing knowledge and expertise in information content and users' information seeking Behaviour, librarians now need to be able to strive in the hustle and bustle of human-tohuman relationships and have strong advocacy and marketing skills. The key to making an impact on users is to raise their expectation of libraries and librarians. This can be done by librarians demonstrating our value directly in the work and interests of users.

Librarians could offer to participate as information architect and manager of specific research or study groups in a learning environment or workplace. For example, a librarian could set up highly specific information portals for individual research teams, linking them with resources from the library or elsewhere. He or she could be more involved in the informat on flow of the group by being their dedicated reference librarian.

Librarians could also host blogs for a course of study and contribute to discussion or provide pointers when matters relating to information sources and access surface. They can help individual users set up their own personal virtual libraries to aid them in their learning activities and studies. This type of approach goes one step beyond merely providing resources, tools and services for users to make use of on their own initiative or through the encouragement of the Library's outreach activities.

It creates and constructs a mini infrastructure that engages specific users with library expertise. It is highly targeted. Such close activities between librarians and users have advantages for both parties. The users will benefit from better information management and flow in their research or learning activities and the personal attention of expert librarians. They will also have a more heightened awareness of what libraries and librarians can offer. Librarians will have a more intimate knowledge of the real needs of users and the problems they face in information access and use by actually being involved in the users' workflow and processes.

This will lead to new initiatives in services and products that will solve real information problems and thus create greater value for libraries. Objections to such intense engagement with users would probably center on lack of resources and problems of sustainability. It could be argued that there is just not enough manpower resources in a typical library to sustain such schemes. However, not to find ways to do so would mean further disengagement with users and possible decline in the role of libraries.

INFORMATION RESOURCES

A key visible role of libraries in the past as well as the present is to provide access to information. If we go back to a few decades ago, information provided by libraries came exclusively from its print collection. A Library then was in total control of the information materials that it provided. It owned everything that it had. A typical user saw his library forming a huge part of his information diet. Today, a large percentage of what a library provides, particularly electronic resources is leased and can be taken away when subscriptions are not renewed. With the continued rise and supply of information in electronic format, libraries will own less and less of what is provided over time. If we look at the total universe of information available to a typical user today, the library owned resources, including leased resources form only a small proportion. Despite their pedigree and high potential value, library resources are hardly noticed in the sea of information. Much of the information diet of the ordinary person comes from the vast Internet.

Though most librarians complain about the quality of information available on the Internet, this is slowly changing. The massive book digitisation projects by Google, Microsoft, Open Content Alliance and others have put many hitherto inaccessible titles online. Many universities are putting up institutional repositories of their academic staff publications. There is an increasing number of open access journals. For example, more than 3,000 are listed in the Directory of Open Access Journals which is about 12 percent of total peer-reviewed journals. Scholars now have greater incentive to submit their publications to open access repositories due to increasing numbers of open access mandates by research funding bodies. Recently the US Congress passed a law that requires beneficiaries of National Institute of Health to submit publications arising from their funded research work to PUB-MED Central within one year of their publication. Similar mandates have been initiated by other major agencies in UK and Europe.

There is also an increasing number of educational resources from the *Open Educational Resources* (OER) Movement, which started in 2001 when MIT started to offer free access to a wide range of their courseware. Unlike the earlier days of the Internet, there is much more serious and quality information available for free on the Internet, though these are mixed with all the chips and chaff of web chatter. How will the explosion of free online content and their easy accessibility affect the way that librarianship is practiced? One of the key contributions of librarianship is the development of sophisticated methods of organising information or bibliographic control that allow information to be accessed efficiently. Put simply, given a large collection of information objects, the librarian can organise them to allow people to find an item or related groups of items with great precision and efficiency. Consider a library. Every item in the library has a corresponding record in the Library Catalog.

Everything is ordered, structured, controlled, accountable, retrievable and traceable even when there are millions of items. The Library Catalog is the heart of the Library – it symbolises the power of libraries. Its classification system, authority and vocabulary control, tracings, finding rules, even the dots and commas on catalog cards are marvels of organisation. Within seconds and without the aid of computers, one can collate comprehensively all books on the economy of Singapore or the treatment for depression. You can drill down on a record and identify the date the information first appeared, identify the person who produce the information and find his other works. In other words, catalogs or other index systems create a network of relationships between information items that allow users to draw conclusions, make inferences and act on them. Strangely with all the computing power of the Internet, Google cannot do this.

You can never be sure if the list you get is comprehensive. Most times, you cannot even establish the date the information was produced and who produced it.

Behind the power of the catalog lies the Labour and skills of librarians who painstakingly look through each book to create handles for users to find and collate it with other books. This is an example of the invisible intermediation role of librarians.

There is of course no such intermediation on the Internet. Is the first 10 items listed in a Google search result good enough or is deeper investigative and research work still valuable? Is the core competency of librarians in making sense of information through systematic organisation still relevant in the new information environment? The answer must surely be the yes. However the problem is the scale and perhaps the common sociological phenomena of diffusion of responsibility. The amount of information pages in the Internet is astronomical compared to a typical library collection. Even if we just take the good bits to catalog, it would still be daunting to even think about it. Also many of the digital files are updated and changed frequently and have many characteristics that are not amenable to traditional form of cataloging. As most web resources are not under the custody of libraries, there is also a question of who should do the cataloging which is where the diffusion of responsibility phenomena applies. The opening paragraph of the Report of the Library of Congress Working Group on the Future of Bibliographic Control summarises the state of thinking on the above in noting that,

> "The future of bibliographic control will be collaborative, decentralised, international in scope, and Web-based. Its realisation will occur in cooperation with the private sector, and with the active collaboration of library users. Data will be gathered from multiple sources; change will happen quickly; and bibliographic control will be dynamic, not static. The underlying technology that makes this future possible and necessary—the World Wide Web—is now almost two decades old. Libraries must continue the transition to this future without delay in order to retain their significance as information providers."

Without going into the current controversy over RDA (Resource Description and Access) development by the Joint Steering Committee for the revision of AACR2, it is clear that the library community is divided over the approach that future bibliographic control should take. I joined the library profession about 5 years after the publication of AACR2 and I remember having been tutored on the difference between AACR1 and AACR2 as a rookie librarian. The transition from AACR2 to RDA or its variants will be much more radical as it has to seriously take into account the new information environment which is much more global, user controlled, dynamic and complex. Changes in our approach in dealing with the organisation and access to information largely mediated by the web will have great impact on the theory and practice of librarianship. We have to watch this space.

INTERMEDIATION

In my interaction and work with librarians, including interviews with potential employees, I noted that one of the most common roles of librarian they cite is that of an intermediary between users and information. This implies that there is some kind of barrier or obstacle between users and the information out there which requires the mediation of a library or a librarian to connect the link. This is largely true in the pre-Internet era. However it would appear that this is no longer true in an era when everyone can have access to global information sources from the desktop of their homes or offices. The emergence of the global information network and its accompanying social upheavals has led many people to predict the death of the middle man and intermediaries not only in library work but in many other areas of commerce and society.

However the deluge of information and the convenience and ease of access to it also creates new problems and issues that are fertile grounds for librarians to explore and to establish their presence. Disintermediation in one area often cause shifts in others. In other words, life usually gets more complex, not simpler. Complex lives often require a greater variety of support systems and intervention. Though we often think of intermediation in terms of a librarian assisting a user in getting the information he or she wants, the intermediary role of librarianship can be expressed in many other forms. For example, the detailed bibliographic information that cataloguers provide to lead users to the appropriate text is a form of mediation. The classified arrangement of books on the shelves allowing users to browse related work is another. The librarian's negotiation for a right price with vendors in getting a database for users' access is yet another. Intermediation is therefore multi-dimensional. It happens and will be sustained when there is value in the intermediation act. We use an intermediary when he or she saves us time, does the work for us better, or does things that we have no expertise to do ourselves.

Therefore as long as librarians can add value and demonstrate it visibly in a middleman role between users and the information environment, intermediation will always occur. So, what are the possible intermediation roles for librarianship in a highly networked and content rich world? For an indication of this, it is instructive to read some of the recent literature on users' Behaviour on the Internet. One of the latest, from UK, was commissioned by the British Library and the U.K., Joint Information System Committee to investigate the searching and researching Behaviour of young people. The study found that despite early exposure to technology and regular use of digital resources, the information literacy skills of young people have not improved. It pointed out that "digital literacies and information literacies do not go hand in hand." Conclusions from logged files of user searches indicated that everyone exhibits a "bouncing/flicking behaviour, which sees them searching horizontally, rather than vertically".

They spend a lot more time navigating online than viewing and reading and are not able to develop effective search strategies. They have a poor understanding of their information needs and do not have a good grasp that the Internet is a collection of networked resources from different providers. Young people also have difficulties making relevant judgments about the pages they retrieve. It suggests that plagiarism is a serious issue for this "cut-and-paste" generation.

Are similar Behaviours prevalent among Singapore's Google generation and other Internet users? Only parallel studies can tell. However anecdotal information does suggest very similar characteristics. It is not surprising that people have problems using the Internet to seek information effectively. Behind the Google search box lie billions of documents that are not structured or organised systematically for retrieval by all manner of people and organisations with various agendas, motivation and interest in offering their content. Finding relevant and reliable information in an environment with abundant information is as problematic as in an environment with scarce information. When there are tremendous choices, the ability to pinpoint and select reliable, credible and useful information requires knowledge, expertise and experience. Interpreting the authenticity and reliability of what is found on the Internet with confidence would be difficult for most people due to the lack of context, explicit cues and metadata common in library and traditional information systems. Even before one starts typing on the keyboard, the ability to formulate the search question is a great hurdle. In short, information literacy or fluency skills is not a given.

It requires investment of time and effort to acquire. Given the common skimming and horizontal searching habits identified in the UCL study, it is unlikely that the majority of online users will acquire the necessary skills to get the most out of the information global house. They are going to need help. Although the librarian has the skills to help users mediate and maximise their use of global information environment, it does not necessary follow that the skills will be demanded by users. The convenience and ease of use and access to the Internet has lulled many Internet users into a sense of mastery over their information environment. In a survey of findings on end-user searching Behaviour, Markey concluded that "end users rarely use advanced system features and when they do, they are quite likely to use them incorrectly.

Although research findings demonstrate that end users are not conducting sophisticated online searches, the vast majority are satisfied with their searches. In fact, percentages of users who express satisfaction with the results of their searches reach into the high seventies and beyond". Libraries and librarians face two major obstacles in trying to play the intermediary role. Firstly, libraries are not on the radar screen of users as much as we would like. Secondly, even if libraries are, users will need to be convinced to make the effort to use libraries, whether online or offline. This brings us back to our first point of discussion on the importance of advocacy work. Like many things else, development of good habits of people during their formative years are crucial in influencing their Behaviour later. Good library Programmes in schools therefore play critical roles in influencing students to learn and develop good information literacy skills.

It is unfortunate that there is no concerted effort in this direction here in Singapore. As noted in the UCL report, "Emerging research findings from the US points to the fact that these skills need to be inculcated during the formative years of childhood: by university or college it is too late to reverse engineer deeply ingrained habits, notably an uncritical trust in branded search engines to deliver quick fixes". Libraries in tertiary institutions here can still play an important role. They will have the last opportunity to influence students in acquiring information literacy skills before they disperse into the working world with less opportunity, and lesser motivation and time to learn to get the most out of a complex information environment. Sometimes simple acts can go a long way. For example, one feedback we had from a teaching staff after our instructional classes for his students is that he noticed a remarkable change in their citation patterns. Instead of citing mainly Internet resources and Wikipedia articles, the students had changed to using scholarly materials in academic journals which they learned during the library classes.

This small change will have profound effect on their information seeking habits in the future. Active intermediary functions performed by libraries need also to take into account the Behavioural traits of users, particularly the young generation. Though there are many studies on user Behaviour in U.S., U.K., and other places, there is a paucity of such national data in Singapore. Availability of such studies will be important for libraries here to address users' needs effectively. At this moment we could only assume that the effect of globalisation has produced an internationally homogenised student profile that is applicable in our case as well. We know from various studies by Frand, Oblinger and others that users today learn by doing, using trial and error methods rather than systematic approaches, spent most of their time online, prefer to work in groups, are producers as well as consumer of information, etc.,

Libraries need to fit their intermediation approaches around these Behavioural characteristics. Traditional hard-core approaches in imparting knowledge will probably be less effective today. I would suggest that we take a "tourist guide" approach in our intermediation effort. A tourist can visit any place he wants in a country, but he will get a much better understanding and insight into the culture, history and social norms of the place and all the interesting nooks and corners if he is led by an expert tourist guide.

Similarly, anyone can wander around the global information environment, but experts such as librarians can provide tremendous added value by showing and leading users to unexpected resources, explaining their intricacies, pointing out trusted sources as well as "dangerous" areas. Such intermediation work is not only confined to librarians but libraries as institutions. Just as a country's tourism agencies build infrastructure, coordinate resources and provide support to the tourism trade, libraries can do similar things in the networked online environment to provide the facilities, tools and Programmes that will make learning in the virtual as well as the physical world a much more enriching place.

PUBLIC RELATIONS IN LIBRARIANSHIP

It is the relationship of your library with its borrowers, with the non-borrowers of your community, with your trustees or library committee, with dealers, collectors, salesmen of equipment; with scholars and contest solvers, with your staff and the administration for which you work. Public relations is with the public, and as true as in its Biblical context is the admonition, "Whatsoever you do unto the least of these . . ." "Curse or blessing," C. D. MacDougall calls public relations. Either is possible. For your public relations is what you make it. It cannot be shuddered at and wished away, but it can be welcomed and made to serve you well. It is with you every minute of every day. It is waiting at your library doors. It is observing the cleanliness of your hallways and public rooms. It is reacting to the service of all your staff, listening in on telephone conversations, reading your mail. It follows you home, into your personal life. It accompanies you on all your ventures into the life of your community. Public relations has been endowed with a kind of twentieth century magic by the corporations and their P.R. officers. Neither the corporations nor the P.R. men invented public relations. It has been with us Since, the beginning of trade. But the American business man has learned the foolishness caveat emptor of as a motto, has learned the dead end of selling wooden nutmegs.

He has made the good will of his public part and parcel of the assets of his business. Public relations is as much a part of the daily life of a library as it is of any business. Perhaps more so, for a library is not self-supporting and depends, even more than the usual business, primarily on the good opinion of its patrons. It is the day-to-day building of the atmosphere of good will in which a library can operate most widely and most effectively to give the best possible service to its public.

As R. L. Heilbronner wrote in Harper's Magazine for June 1957: "In a word, public relations covers a lot of acreage-blurring out into advertising, slopping over into selling, dipping down into publicity, and touching-or at least aspiring to-the 'making' of public opinion itself."

Edward W. Barrett, dean of Columbia University's School of Journalism, praises J. W. Hill, himself the ungowned dean of American P.R. men, for seeing "public relations as a broad management function - more precisely . . . as the management function of giving the same organised and careful attention to the asset of good will as is given to any other major asset of the business."

Public relations may well be the most important asset - "the priceless ingredient," to quote the phrase that one firm's advertising Programme has made famous - for bad public relations can cancel the good of every other asset. With a knowledge of the experiences of other libraries and other types of organisations, public relations becomes perforce a do-it-yourself Programme. Public relations is the asset, is the Programme, most expressive of the individuality, the personality, of each separate library. It may be patterned emulatively, but never imitatively. It must be done according to the needs of your library. It must express as attractively as possible your library to the public. First, public relations must be properly fitted into the administrative pattern of your library. Few libraries can afford the services of a special public relations officer. For those that can, fine. University and college libraries often can work through a campus public relations office.

In some cases, a city P.R. man is available to public libraries. Where a trained professional is available, it is an error both factual and tactical to direct public relations except through that individual. In other cases, public relations must be conducted as an auxiliary responsibility of the librarian or delegated to some other member of his staff. In both of these alternatives, however, it remains a function of management and the responsibility of the librarian. A library's policies in many fields must be worked out thoroughly and wisely by the librarian and his governing board.

Once worked out, policy must be implemented by actions which elucidate it in every function of the library and by every member of a library's staff. The right hand must know what to expect of the left hand. It is of basic importance for good public relations that all staff be kept as fully informed as possible, both of long-term library policy and immediate newsworthy developments which relate to that policy. If not with a single voice, the library must at least speak in a consistent accent.

The extent of a library's services and resources must be well enough known for any and every employee to respond with accurate answers or definite and proper referrals to patrons' questions. There is hardly a greater disservice that a library can do its public relations Programme than to permit an employee to answer an enquiry with a "that's-not-my-business" type of reply. It matters not how extensive a library's services are if the attainment of those services becomes a dismaying pursuit of referrals from one functionary to another. Good service is the handmaiden of good public relations. This does not mean that every library must provide every service. It does mean that whatever service a library provides must be done well.

A well considered "no" can be much more effective public relations than an ill considered "yes". Public relations is as important within your organisation as it is without. Staff relations are a part of public relations. Ability to work with a governing board is a part of public relations. And, once these relationships are satisfactorily established, each member of your staff, each member of your board becomes a part-time P.R. man for your library. But the more apparent aspects of public relations are those outside your management family. Public relations is with the public, but each library has several publics. There is its public which borrows books. There is a public made up of others in the same profession. There is a public, in some libraries at least, of scholars or professional users of materials. Relations with the general borrowing public are broadest, most demanding, and, yet, easiest. Here the field is reasonably well defined. Here publicity can be effective. Here patrons' response is quickest and most vocal; if you are taking the wrong tack, someone will tell you so.

Librarians generally have done good work with publicity, but it is too easy to forget that not all publicity is good publicity. Publicity begins at home, at least, in the library profession itself. Staff news sheets, exhibits, guides to exhibits are all part of a library publicity Programme. The incidence of library publicity material of this type pitched at a kindergarten level is more appalling than appealing. Is it necessary that adult human beings approach the problem of announcing a staff party as if they were writing for the amusement of low grade morons? The same approach pervades much of the material issued in the name of recruiting for librarianship.

If these things are done well, they make for good public relations. But there is no middle ground. It is better that they not be done at all than that they be done badly. Newspaper publicity must be controlled within the management function of public relations, but it is practicably possible to delegate responsibility in this area. It is helpful both to the library and to a paper that one person be responsible for newspaper publicity.

A minimum of experience can establish a satisfactory working relationship between a library and a reporter. He will know what he wants. It is your business to give him the facts. Handout journalism has been a corollary development of public relations as a profession. It is certainly not its healthiest aspect. Make information available to newspapers, but don't try to style it for them. Reporters are better reporters than are librarians. Notices and articles in the library press are another aspect of continuing public relations.

The unfortunate proliferation of library periodicals makes complete coverage impossible, cuts down the readership for any single journal, and lowers the average quality of writing on librarianship; but this is, nevertheless, a legitimate area for use in furthering public relations. Wide knowledge of one's own profession and of his colleagues in it is a prerequisite for general recognition of librarianship as a profession. Librarians are inclined to write too much solely for other librarians, talk too much to other librarians. Participation in national, regional, and local organisations of professional librarians is good public relations, particularly if such organisations reach other professions and the public in general. Individual participation by staff members is also good for a library. Individuals should be encouraged in membership in civic groups, professional organisations in specific subject fields, and in activity in communuity projects. As useful as professional exchange is, articles in the non-library press, speeches before Rotary, Kiwanis, and other civic or special interest groups are especially rewarding. Publicity and participation are merely vehicles of public relations. The public as a mass can be effectively reached through newspapers, radio, and television. The public as a special force in promoting the welfare of a library can be better and more directly reached through individual participation in the widest possible variety of activities.

Public relations as a continuing function is a more important and a slower process. It is axiomatic that repeated incidental mention of a celebrity is more important to his reputation than one large splurge of publicity about him. Every time the library is mentioned favourably, every time an individual connected with the library appears in the community in a favourable light, good public relations are being built. Every time a library is listed among the acknowledgments in a published book, every time an individual sees a creditable publication from the library, every time an organisation or an individual is helped by the library's services, the library increases in stature.

The cumulative effects are unlimited: better budgets, adequate staffing, more books, finer buildings, easier recruiting-in a word: better libraries. "Good will" is often listed in corporate assets as valued at $1.00 not because it is worth little but because it is an intangible beyond practical evaluation. Good will is priceless. It is public relations that build good will. Libraries are a public or institutional service, tangible examples of good public relations on the part of a municipality, a corporation, or an educational institution providing informational and recreational resources to its constituency.

Librarianship is a service profession. If librarians are to emphasise their work as a profession, interpreting as well as making available knowledge, this emphasis must be based on good service. It must be quality service at all levels of operations. Good service, conceived to support community and institutional goals, will automatically result in good public relations. Good public relations will create lasting good will.

ETHICS IN LIBRARIANSHIP: A MANAGEMENT MODEL

The study of ethics in the information professions is a subset of the study of ethics in general. Thus, a definition of ethics may be helpful in clarifying this concept. There is no agreement on the exact definition of the term ethics. Some use it to refer to the art of determining what is right or good.

It is also used in three different but related ways signifying:

* A general pattern or "way of life,"
* A set of rules of conduct or "moral code," and
* Enquiry about ways of life and rules of conduct.

As a concept, the purpose of ethics is to establish principles of Behaviour that help people make choices among alternative modes of action. Making such choices of ten involves ethical and lemmas, because these are marked by multiple and non-comparable dimensions. The dimensions are the results - both benefits and harms-that are going to affect the organisation, the society, and the individual as a result of a decision or action.

In essence, ethical behaviour is what is accepted as "good" and "right" as opposed to "bad" or "wrong" in the context of the governing moral code. The determination of what is right rather than what is wrong has been generally codified in the form of law, although not all situations have been, and can be, covered by any such codification. Laws are rationalised for the welfare of society; thus, any Behaviour considered ethical should also be legal in a just and fair society. This does mean, however, that simply because an action is not illegal it is necessarily ethical. In other words, just living up to the "letter of the law" is not sufficient to guarantee that one's actions can be or should be considered ethical. The following examples of ethical questions can be considered in this context:

* Is it ethical to take longer than necessary to do a task.
* Is it ethical to do personal business on the employer's time.
* Is it ethical to call in sick to take a day off to catch up on chores at home.
* Is it ethical to fail to report rule violations by a co-worker.

None of these examples is illegal. But many individuals would consider one or more of them to be unethical. The values held by an individual, group, or society are the basic components of an ethical system. Yet uncertainty is a fact of complex dynamic organisational life. The interests and values of another individual, group, or society and laws regarding both are unclear.

Ethical standards, therefore, are not universally accepted, but rather they are the end product of discretionary decision-making Behaviour affecting the lives and well-being of others. Ethics in the information professions is concerned with the application of moral standards to the conduct of librarians and other individuals involved in information dissemination. It is a type of applied ethics concerned with clarifying the obligations and dilemmas of librarians and other information professionals who make decisions regarding the acquisition, processing, and dissemination of information to individuals, groups, and society at large.

EVOLUTION IN/ OF ETHICALCONCERNS INFORMATION PROFESSIONS

Tracing the development of ethics as an area of concern for information professionals will help in identifying the factors that are responsible for and that influenced the evolution of ethical Behaviour. Although ethical issues in librarianship were of some concern prior to the 1960s, it was the rise of the social responsibility debate in the decade of the 1960s that caused ethical concerns to become of major importance to librarians and other information professionals.

The concept of social responsibility is fundamentally an ethical concept. It involves changing notions of how human needs should be met and emphasises a concern with the social dimensions of information service that has to do with improving the quality of life. Social responsibility provides a way for the information profession to concern itself with the social dimensions of service and be aware of the social impact of that service. Historically, librarians saw that their major responsibility was to the collection; caring for the materials within the library building was their primary concern. Many modern information professionals now acknowledge that they are responsible to any individual or group with an information need.

These stakeholders can be any constituency in the library's environment-users, non-users, employees, suppliers, government agencies, public interest groups, and host communities. Table illustrates a four-stage model of a social responsibility continuum. Stage one encompasses responsibility for the library collection. Stage two adds responsibility for employees. Stage three includes responsibility to library users-those individuals who have made a conscious decision to use the library's information resources. Stage four expands responsibility furthest by proposing that information professionals are responsible to society in general and includes users and non-users alike.

What information professionals do in terms of pursuing social goals depends on to what or to whom they believe they are responsible. A stage one information professional promotes collection development and maintenance. At stage two, information professionals accept responsibility for the employees in their organisation and focus on human resource concerns. Because they will want to get, keep, and motivate good employees, they are concerned with appropriate education and training, improved working conditions, expanded employee rights, increased job security, and the like. A stage three professional expands goals to include high quality service, an excellent collection, good relations with the public, and the like.

A stage four professional aligns with an active interpretation of social responsibility. At this stage, professionals see their responsibility to society as a whole. Their service is defined in terms of advancing the public good. The acceptance of such responsibility means that such information professionals actively promote social justice, support social and cultural goals, and take political positions even if such actions are perceived negatively by some. Each stage carries with it an increasing level of discretion. As professionals move to the right along the continuum, they have to make more decisions based upon situational variables not of their own making.

By the time professionals reach stage four, they are required to think about ethical dilemmas not necessarily solely within the context of their organisations but to decide what is right and what is wrong from a societal perspective. They may follow self-chosen ethical principles, upholding values and rights regardless of majority opinion. Obviously, not all professionals perceive reaching stage four as an appropriate goal. Some stay in stage one, which emphasises responsibility for collection maintenance and development, or stage two, which emphasises appropriate Behaviour for a librarian as a professional, or stage three, which emphasises fulfilling the duties and obligations of a professional librarian through high quality service to users. There never has been established any simple right-wrong dichotomy to help information professionals make decisions regarding their appropriate domain for ethically responsible action. The social responsibility movement of the 1960s did provide fuel for debate.

The concept of intellectual freedom, called the profession's "central ethic", was used to frame issues as diverse as civil rights, the war in Vietnam, women's rights, and the war on poverty. On one side, there were those who were in stage four on the social responsibility continuum, defining intellectual freedom as a series of value judgments supporting a radically pluralistic egalitarian society. On the other side were those who viewed social responsibility from stages one and two of the continuum, defending intellectual freedom from a position of collective and individual neutrality. As the debate waned in the 1970s, it was obvious to many proponents and opponents of the social responsibility movement that there were several key issues in the debate that had not been, and perhaps cannot yet be, settled.

One key issue concerns the operational definition of social responsibility. How shall a library's resources be allocated to help solve social problems? With what specific problems shall a given library concern itself? What priorities shall be established? What goals or standards of performance shall be established? What measures shall be employed to determine if a library is socially responsible or socially irresponsible? In the, past, the traditional library environment provided little or no information to the decision maker that was useful in answering the above questions. The concept of social responsibility itself provided no clear guidelines for ethical Behaviour. Given this lack of clarity, librarians who wanted to be socially responsible were left to follow their own devices or relied on some rather vague generalisations about social values and public expectations.

Another problem with the concept of social responsibility is that it has not always taken into account the environment in which the library functions. In the past, many advocates of social responsibility treated the library as an isolated entity that had the ability to engage in unilateral social action. Eventually, it came to be recognised that libraries are severely limited in their ability to respond adequately to social problems. There are physical, organisational, and attitudinal barriers that have to be overcome. The last issue that remains unresolved in the debate about social responsibility concerns the moral basis of the notion.

The term responsibility is fundamentally a moral one that implies an obligation to someone or something. It is clear to most people that librarians have professional responsibilities to acquire, process, and disseminate information products and services efficiently to users of libraries. These responsibilities constitute the reason for the existence of libraries. But why do librarians have social responsibilities and to whom? What are the moral foundations for a concern with the social impact of information services? The proponents of social responsibility, though well intentioned, have produced no clear and generally accepted moral principle that would impose on the information professions an obligation to work for social change. Various arguments have been made to try to link moral Behaviour of the profession to the performance of libraries.

Little has been accomplished, however, by way of developing a solid and acceptable moral argument for the notion of social responsibility. Thus, although those promoting social responsibility are wry moralistic in many of their statements, in debate with others, they do not articulate a philosophical basis for the social responsibilities discussed. The emotionally laden nature of the discussion on social responsibility presents the possibility that debate on the subject will continue indefinitely with little prospect of agreement being reached on the scope of the issues involved or their solution. Beginning in the late 1970s and continuing through the 1980s, a theoretical and conceptual reorientation has begun to take place regarding the information profession's obligations to its various constituencies. The new approach can be labeled "social responsiveness" and it has become clear that the shift from responsibility to responsiveness reflects a significant change of focus. This new focus has shifted the discussion from moral imperatives related to social responsibility to a more technical and neutral approach that includes social responsiveness.

The Public Library Association's guidelines for identifying roles for public libraries reflects this shift. The process described in the guidelines includes identification of both internal and external mechanisms, procedures, arrangements, and Behavioural patterns of the library's constituent groups taken collectively. It establishes mechanisms to judge the capability of libraries to fulfil certain roles. Attempts are made to identify key variables within the library that relate to its responsiveness and discover structural changes that will enable the library to respond adequately to social demands. The important questions are not moral, related to whether a library should respond to a social problem out of a sense of social responsibility, but more pragmatic and action oriented, dealing with the library's ability to respond and the changes necessary to enable it to respond more effectively. One of the advantages of this approach is its managerial orientation. The concept ignores the philosophical debate about responsibility and obligation and focuses on the problems and prospects of making libraries more socially responsive.

The process lends itself to analytical techniques in utilising specific methods, such as data collection and analysis and numerical interpretation of results. The utilisation of data through this process can help decision makers determine how best to institutionalise social policy throughout the library. Organisational structures can be evaluated; the roles of information professionals can be delineated; personnel policies can be structured to reward appropriate "socially responsive" Behaviour; and goal statements can be formulated that reflect the roles identified. Even though this approach seems to answer many of the questions faced by those concerned with the social responsibility debate, social responsiveness does not offer answers to all questions. The concept of social responsiveness does not provide guidance on how resources should be allocated to fulfill the various library roles. Libraries respond to the same problems in different ways and to varying degrees. And there is no clear data as to what pattern of responsiveness will be the most successful.

The philosophy of responsiveness does not help a library to decide what roles it should have or what priorities should be established. In the final analysis, social responsiveness provides no better guidance to management than does social responsibility on the best strategies or policies to be adopted for library service. It appears that library personnel, by determining the degree of social responsiveness and the pressures to which they will respond, decide the meaning of the concept and what services will be developed as a result. There is still a lack of moral principles or theory on which to base decisions. Societal pressures are assumed to exist, and libraries must respond to these in some manner.

Social responsiveness assumes a passive attitude to such pressures. The concept of responsiveness provides no moral basis for information professionals to respond to social problems. There is no explicit moral or ethical theory and no specific values for personnel to follow in making responses to societal demands. This position becomes quite evident when examining the statement of professional ethics developed by the American Library Association (ALA) in 1981. The 1981 statement makes neither mention of the Library Bill of Rights nor any other philosophical statement as a source of the foundational ethics of library service. Although a 1980 draft spoke of the need for "participation in professional associations [and] community activity in support of library Programmes and legislation", this point was left out of the adopted version.

Criticism of the draft document includes the assertion that, "it does not deal adequately with the ends and means of the library profession. Rather it is primarily a guide to attitudes Towards work, without examining the mission of that work". While the presence of an ethical code can stimulate debate and strengthen professional autonomy, these results can only take place if the effect of the code is one of clarification of the practice of librarianship rather than a clarification of the appropriate demeanor of the professional. In responding to such criticism, the question of managerial guidelines and principles becomes relevant. What criteria, other than self-interest, are relevant to guide information professionals in the development of socially responsible strategies? Shall these strategies be judged solely on their short term effectiveness, *i.e.*, in helping a library respond to a patron who wishes to remove a certain book from the shelves? Can libraries retain their neutral posture and still support those government leaders who support the interests of libraries and share traditional values of intellectual freedom and access? The nagging question of defining the social good or, in a public policy context, of defining the public interest, appears. And finally, the absence of a clear moral underpinning for whatever strategies are determined continues to present a problem.

If information professionals become proactive, does such Behaviour mean that they are attempting to minimise the impact of social change? Do not information professionals have a moral obligation that goes beyond their identified mandate to acquire and disseminate information? If information professionals do have social and political responsibilities as well as professional responsibilities, what is the moral basis for these responsibilities today?

ETHICAL DIMENSION OF DECISION-MAKING

In answering the preceding questions, the major premise is that management is basically an ethical task, and that many management decisions have an ethical dimension.

An ethical decision can be further defined as a decision where questions of justice and rights are serious and relevant moral considerations. These concepts are central ethical considerations in human affairs, and an ethical decision is one where a consideration of them is an important dimension of the decision. Can the decision be defended on grounds of justice? Is it fair and equitable in some sense to all the parties affected? Does the decision violate some basic human rights, such that it could be labeled an immoral decision? These are the kinds of questions that must be asked.

Bucholz has identified three levels of ethical issues which vary in scope and breadth-the individual level, the organisation level, and the system level. At the individual level, one makes day-to-day decisions that mostly involve the application of institutional policy to specific situations. When dilemmas arise, judgments must be made, some of which have ethical dimensions. At the organisational level, decisions are made for the organisation that will guide the Behaviour of employees.

These decisions may be broad in scope and involve consideration of social responsibility. At the system level, broad questions can be raised about the ethical foundations of information service; such questions are not tied to a particular organisation. The specific nature of the decisions involved at each of these levels can be seen if a concrete example is used. Information access issues are fraught with ethical dimensions and provide a useful vehicle to illustrate ethical dilemmas at each of these levels.

Let us assume that the basic organisational policy in regard to access is one of "free access to all library materials for all individuals." Ethics enters into access decisions at the individual level in borderline or exceptional cases that policy does not seem to cover. For example, does free access really mean that a ten year old can take out an "R" rated video? At the organisational level, the ethical dimensions of decision making come into play when selection decisions are made. Decision makers must make certain that the criteria and procedures that are established to make selection choices do not discriminate against certain writers nor points of view nor on the basis of irrelevant factors such as race, sex, or religious preference of either the author or selector.

Self-censorship of controversial materials is a constant problem that must be addressed. At the system level, ethical questions relate to information dissemination. Who has access to information and at what cost? How does information format affect access? Who is responsible for providing information for those who have limited skills to acquire it? These kinds of questions are settled through the public policy process and the eventual outcome is reflected in laws and regulations related to information access at local, state, and federal levels. These various levels of decision making and the ethical issues relevant to each level. Potential clashes exist at all levels. Institutional policy may require that a decision maker go agains this or her own ethical standards, producing significant internal conflict for one so involved. Institutional policy may not always reflect the ethical standards of the society at large, which may force society to develop laws and regulations to bring about change in institutional Behaviour.

Another example can be taken from the hiring process for librarians. Many libraries make an ALA-accredited degree an entry-level qualification for a professional librarian. Applicants for professional positions lacking this qualification are rejected. The ALA-accredited degree thus becomes a standard by which libraries hope to assure the recruitment of a high quality staff. Ethics enters into a decision to hire at the individual level in borderline or exceptional cases where applying the policy in a mechanical fashion does not seem just or equitable. For example, if an applicant does not have an ALA-accredited degree, should he or she be automatically rejected without looking at other information such as previous work experience or other academic credentials? Such a decision may not seem fair given the subjective nature of the hiring process in general.

Suppose a candidate with previous work experience, but without an ALA degree, is narrowly rejected for an academic library position and another candidate with an ALA-accredited degree, but no work experience, is accepted for a position. Is that fair considering that the work experience and academic credentials are not really comparable. And what about exceptional cases in which applicants may have other credentials, including doctorates? Should they be mechanically rejected without some special consideration? At the organisational level, ethical considerations come into play when one considers justice and rights in relation to the hiring policy itself. Does a hiring policy discriminate unjustly on the basis of race or sex, or can it be defended as fair and equitable? Are written employment tests biased in favour of white middle class applicants due to the concepts and language used in examinations: Is an applicant's right to equal treatment violated by the use of such examinations? And, given the fact that grades mean different things depending on the school one attended, is it fair that grades are used as a factor in making employment decisions? At the system level, questions can be asked about the justice of public service institutions such as libraries hiring only those who are citisens or legal residents of a given community. Do not all individuals have a right to apply for employment for which they feel qualified, regardless of their legal status or place of residence? These are serious ethical questions worthy of debate.

These examples serve to illustrate where ethical questions arise at different levels of decision making in libraries. The decisions made at all these levels benefit and burden individuals and groups differentially. Some individuals gain and others are affected adversely. Questions of justice and individual rights become relevant. The question for the manager to answer is, Whose rights should be respected and what concept of justice is appropriate?.

ETHICAL CONSIDERATIONS FOR MANAGERS IN LIBRARIANSHIP

Librarians as managers are constantly making ethical decisions whether they know it or not. They are constantly directing people. Towards or away from information resources that may directly impact their ability to enhance their lives or the life of their community. They are creating the future for their organisations, for their employees, for their users, for those who fund the service, and for society as a whole. Decisions about information access can affect human well being and social welfare, having ethical impacts that are significant for all those touched by the decisions. A recent article in the chronicle of higher education discussed "a revolution in the nature of resources that provide power". The suggestion is made that access to information resources must now be counted as a source of world power. As the ability to access information across the globe becomes possible through the use of technology, librarians will have more and more opportunity to influence decision making on a worldwide scale through appropriate information provision. This is an awesome responsibility and one that calls for ethical reflection of the highest order. Librarians must be encouraged to think more broadly and highly of their task. They must recognise that libraries are multiple purpose institutions that have many impacts besides cultural enrichment or recreation. Moral leadership of such institutions means recognising information agencies as part of an ethical system havingvarious values that are important to human welfare. The challenge to librarians is to incorporate these values into routine decision making and develop methods of analysis that are applicable to identifying appropriate goals for themselves and their organisations.

AN ACTION PLAN

The implementation of an ethical vision in librarianship requires action in several areas. An ethical perspective must be incorporated into the workplace as well as into the curriculum through which future librarians are being educated.

The following areas constitute what could be called an ethical agenda for librarians in both of these settings:

* In the educational setting, such a plan calls for a thorough integration of moral and ethical concerns into the library/ information science curriculum. Although separate courses in ethics may also be offered, integration of ethical concerns into basic courses such as Management or Reference is essential to make ethics more directly related to the roles and responsibilities of information professionals.
* Continuing education Programmes need to develop parallel efforts to maintain the work begun in the academic setting. Questions about ethics and moral aspects of librarianship must continue to be addressed as professionals move through their careers.
* Library boards of trustees and/or advisory boards must demonstrate a concern about ethics by raising ethical questions when appropriate. The moral implications of decisions and actions must
* Boards can acknowledge the significance of ethical issues by raising them in relation to goal setting and long-range planning.
* Information professionals at all levels must recognise the important role they play in institutionalising ethical responsibility throughout their organisations. Professional librarians have many channels open to

them to shape the library/information center, including the setting of objectives for units and individuals, developing and implementing the reward structure of staff, modifying organisational structure to accomplish goals, and developing and utilising appropriate measures of performance. Professional staff not only have responsibility for efficient and effective use of material and human resources but also must be willing to create a responsible institution that cares about and responds to the ethical and moral imperatives of its policies and actions.

* Information policy-making by various government bodies must be considered from an ethical point of view. Librarians have a role to play in the debate; they can make contributions to the discussion and provide insight into the formation of regulations regarding the dissemination of information. Librarians must be given the freedom to respond to information policy issues out of a sense of ethical responsibility; rules and regulations for the control of information flow must be evaluated as well as the inherent limitations of information dissemination systems.
* More research must be considered by both library school faculty and professional librarians into the ethical aspects of decision making by librarians. One of the themes of this article is that many in the profession of librarianship are ignorant of ethical issues, not having a good understanding of how such matters should be analysed and discussed. Research into ethical and moral issues can help overcome this ignorance. Scholars in the field need to apply their expertise to ethical questions and combine this with the work of those from other professional disciplines who have similar concerns.

This action plan suggests that a consideration of ethical issues must become a familiar comfortable part of librarians' thought processes. Ethical ambiguities are always present because no one can formulate policies that are going to be morally justified in all circumstances and in all places and times. It is important that those responsible for formulating, implementing, and evaluating policies should be made aware of these ambiguities and be ethically aware so as to act in a responsible and moral manner. Ambiguity, it should be noted, does not diminish the significance of ethical issues, which this discussion implies are pervasive in librarianship. In point of fact, the ethical dimension of librarianship represents a generalised concern for the improvement of quality of library service and professional conduct of librarians. A final caveat is in order.

Ethical Behaviour in librarianship does not mean that one should take no action, that is, avoid certain actions or books or ideas in an effort to keep out of trouble. On the contrary, the notion of ethics suggests that librarians take actions that are socially just. Only by actively pursuing social aims can librarians be ethically responsive. There is evidence to suggest that librarians choose not to choose, to "play it safe" with services and collections. Instead, librarians ought to exercise ethical judgement in their duties. Only by demonstrating the highest standards of ethical decision making will librarians inspire confidence and respect in the information arena.

THE EFFECTS OF LIBRARIANS' BEHAVIOURAL PERFORMANCE ON USER SATISFACTION IN CHAT REFERENCE SERVICES

As library users become more comfortable with using the Web for services and to search for information, librarians often have led the way in making reference services available to patrons online. Online real-time chat reference services have become increasingly prevalent in many types and sises of libraries, and, as with any other library service, it is important to evaluate the effectiveness of, and user satisfaction with, those services. This research reports the results and conclusions from a case study of a chat reference service intended to assess the usefulness of the 2004 revised "RUSA Guidelines for

Behavioural Performance of Reference and Information Services Providers". These were originally developed by the Reference and User Services Association (RUSA) in 1996 as Behavioural guidelines to support reference staff working at a physical reference desk.

The purpose of this study is to:

* Investigate, in a series of chat interviews, the extent to which librarians' Behaviours reflected those recommended in the revised guidelines;
* Assess the influence of those Behaviours on user satisfaction; and
* Examine the revised guidelines as a useful assessment tool in evaluating the efficacy of a chat reference service.

The results of this study will provide library professionals with a better understanding of the nature of chat reference interviews as well as test the usefulness of the revised guidelines in the context of chat reference services. The results of this study will better elucidate effective teaching methods and techniques for library educators within the area of virtual reference with respect to the reference question negotiation process.

BACKGROUND OF THE STUDY

The Original Guidelines and the Revised Guidelines

Perhaps one of the most important roles of professional associations is to establish benchmarking standards and develop useful guidelines to assist their members' practice. RUSA has been at the forefront in offering its members such support. Beginning in the 1980s, RUSA began developing reference interview guidelines intended to delineate those librarian Behaviours most likely to lead to an effective face-to-face reference interview. This effort resulted in the publication of the "RUSA Guidelines for Behavioural Performance of Reference and Information Services Providers" in 1996.

A handful of research studies conducted Since, that time have consistently indicated that use of the Behaviours prescribed in the original guidelines is positively associated with reference success. The original guidelines thus became widely recognised as the only Behavioural guidelines of its kind for reference staff. Besides the fact that the original guidelines were prepared by RUSA, a leading professional association among reference librarians, the continued use of the original guidelines in practice seems to suggest their usefulness as standards for reference staff training as well as performance evaluation. A revised and extended version of the original guidelines was published in June 2004.

This revision reflects the increasing need for Behavioural standards that can assist personnel who provide virtual reference services. Maintaining the five-component structure of the original guidelines, the revised guidelines subcategorised each of those five components into three settings: general, in-person, and remote.

The five-component structure is summarised as follows:

* First, approachability refers to Behaviours that ensure easy access to the reference staff by lowering barriers to personal assistance. Example Behaviours include making instructional and directional signs clear, making the presence of reference assistance visible, and establishing "word" contact with the patrons.
* Second, interest refers to Behaviours that exhibit librarians' interest in patron enquiries so that patrons can ask questions without hesitation. Example Behaviours include focusing attention on the patron, maintaining and re-establishing "word" contact, and clarifying the scope of the questions.
* Third, listening/enquiring refers to Behaviours that exhibit good listening and questioning skills so that librarians can identify patrons' real information needs, which sometimes are buried or poorly expressed. Example Behaviours are communicating in receptive and cordial ways, using proper written language, ensuring adequate probing, and rephrasing questions to ensure adequate understanding.

* Fourth, searching includes the application of effective search skills and related Behaviours that can enhance searching effectiveness and result in finding accurate answers. Example Behaviours include explaining search strategies, escorting patrons in the search process, and providing pointers and information sources.
* Finally, follow-up refers to the Behaviours involved in bringing proper closure to the reference transaction. Example Behaviours include asking patrons if their questions were completely answered, asking if they need additional information, referring them to alternative sources or agencies if their questions were not answered, and urging patrons to return if they need further assistance.

The revised guidelines have incorporated many Behaviours that pertain specifically to virtual reference. Yet, the core components and ideas remain the same as those set out in the original guidelines prepared for face-to-face reference service practice.

Librarians' Behavioural Performance during Chat Reference Service

The body of the reference service literature has consistently emphasised that the quality of the reference interview is an important factor in reference service effectiveness. In their seminal research, scholars demonstrated that reference librarians' verbal and non-verbal communication skills during the reference interview are crucial in delivering reference services successfully. This research has had a great affect on the research and the practice of reference services, and has brought attention to the need for pertinent staff training that can provide instruction in, and emphasise the importance of, verbal and non-verbal communication skills in the reference interview.

Saxton reported that reference effectiveness was most consistently predicted by the presence of verbal and non-verbal Behaviours prescribed in the original guidelines. Subsequent studies also reported similar findings, substantiating RUSA's initial intent to provide the original guidelines as a service assessment tool. Yet, many issues remain veiled regarding the interactions between librarians and patrons in virtual space in general, and reference interviews during chat sessions specifically.

Some of the important but unanswered questions are:

* How do reference librarians interact with their patrons in chat reference settings.
* Are the interactions in chat reference similar to, or considerably different from, those in traditional reference service.
* What staff Behaviours would be most conducive to user satisfaction with chat reference services.

Regarding these questions, some would argue that the interactions between patrons and librarians in chat settings should not be fundamentally different from those involved in the physical reference setting because both ultimately serve the same purpose—resolving information problems by answering questions. In essence, proponents of this position view chat reference as the same service delivered via a different medium, much like the telephone reference service that was new in the 1930s.

In contrast, others would contend that the particular mode of virtual communications is the very factor that makes chat reference different from the face-to-face or the telephone reference interview. After all, virtual communication lacks facial, aural, or environmental cues, which are crucial components in the physical reference setting, as well as the voice cues that are so crucial to phone reference. In the absence of clear understanding of the nature of chat reference interactions, identifying effective librarian Behaviours in the chat reference interview will be an important first step in helping librarians to achieve higher levels of service performance.

In this regard, specific Behaviours prescribed in the revised guidelines can be utilised as effective Behavioural standards to examine librarians' actual Behaviours while answering questions during chat sessions. Thus, the purpose of the present study was to investigate the extent to which the Behaviours prescribed in the revised guidelines are observed in chat reference sessions, and whether the presence of those Behaviours increases user satisfaction with chat reference.

For this purpose, three specific research questions were proposed for investigation:

* *Research question 1:* To what extent is each RUSA Behaviour observed in chat reference interviews.
* *Research question 2:* Is user satisfaction with chat reference higher when librarians perform the RUSA Behaviours during reference sessions than when they do not
* *Research question 3:* Which of the RUSA Behaviours performed during chat reference interviews could predict higher user satisfaction.

The findings of the present study will enable us to determine whether the RUSA Behaviours can lead to more effective reference services performance. Ultimately, the results of the study will help us to resolve the question of whether the revised guidelines can be effectively used as a pertinent training and service assessment tool for chat reference services.

METHODS

Setting and Participants

The present study examined chat reference services delivered through the Broward County public library system, the largest such system in Florida, with thirty-three regional and branch libraries. Since, August 2002, the system has used a chat reference service dubbed "24/7 Reference" delivered by the Metropolitan Cooperative Library System (MCLS), an association of libraries located in the greater Los Angeles area funded by a federal Library Services and Technology Act grant.

MCLS's 24/7 Reference was merged with Online Computer Library Center's (OCLC) QuestionPoint in August 2004. The data examined for the present study were online chat reference transactions initiated by patrons of the Broward Country library system, along with survey responses submitted by the patrons. While the patrons were mostly users of the Broward County system, the reference staff members who provided the service were from forty-nine library systems across the United States participating in the MCLS 24/7 Reference Programme. During the six-month duration of the research study, between January and June 2004, a total of 1,387completed or transferred transactions took place.

As the intention of this study was to analyse the influence of librarians' Behaviours on user satisfaction, only the transactions that had a corresponding completed self-report user satisfaction survey were selected for data analysis. Thus, the total number of transactions analysed for the present study was 422, comprising 30.4 percent of the total analysable transactions.

Coding RUSA Behaviours

RUSA Behaviours refer to the Behaviours prescribed in the revised guidelines. These Behaviours were coded through the analysis of 422 chat transcripts that show all patron-staff interactions as well as search activities, including co-browsing. Initially, librarians' Behaviours were coded against all fortynine items in the revised guidelines, which include all three modes of transactions. This decision was made because certain items listed under the in-person category also were applicable to the chat reference setting. Later, the initial forty-nine items were collapsed into ten types of Behaviours after merging similar items together and removing items that were either unobservable or irrelevant for chat reference.

For example, some items describe thought processes rather than actual observable Behaviours. Some Behaviours, such as providing information sources, were observed across multiple items. Finally, some items are applicable for physical setting transactions only.

Specific items in the five RUSA Behavioural areas were coded into ten Behavioural types in the present study. Approachability was observed by two Behavioural types:

welcoming and the use of patrons' name. First, welcoming was coded to be present either when an initial word contact was made or when a general welcoming atmosphere was observed from the librarians' written communications.

Other than these examples, the revised guidelines do not include many clear Behavioural indicators of approachability Thus, the second Behavioural type, the use of patrons' name, was adopted from the Guidelines for Chat Sessions within "IFLA Digital Reference Guidelines"; the assumption here is that the Behaviour could lower the patron's emotional barriers and thus enhance the librarian's approachability. Currently, there is no consensus about the effectiveness of using a patron's name during the chat session. Some think it is effective because it could make the reference interview more personable and approachable. Others think that it may intrude upon personal privacy. By observing its use, as suggested, be able to determine whether the use of patrons' names affects user satisfaction.

Interest was observed by using two items in the revised guidelines: focusing attention on the patron and maintaining word contact. The remaining items were excluded from coding because they were mostly applicable to the physical reference setting, e-mail, or pre-interview stage. Listening/enquiring was observed by two Behavioural types: receptive and cordial listening; and enquiring by rephrasing, clarifying, or asking questions. The rest of the items were excluded from coding because they were not easily observable or overlapped with other items. Searching was observed by two Behavioural types: searching for or with patrons, and offering pointers or information sources.

Some Behaviours, such as co-browsing, were coded as both when they involved searching and offering information sources. Four items were excluded from coding because they either pertain to listening/enquiring or follow-up, or indicate a cognitive process rather than an observable Behaviour. Finally, follow-up was observed by three Behavioural types: proper closing, offering alternatives or making referral, and asking to come back for further assistance.

RUSA Behaviours were coded by two independent coders for intercoder reliability in order to ensure the consistency. First, the primary researcher coded the entire 422 transactions. Then, the second coder, a reference librarian who received training for coding the RUSA Behaviours, coded every fifth transaction. This sample for intercoder reliability comprises 20 percent of the total transactions, which is the recommended percentage for social science research. Finally, the percentage agreement between the two coders was calculated for each Behaviour, which informs the level of agreement between two coders. The agreements were Welcoming, Use of patrons' name, Interest, Listening, Enquiring, Searching with or for patrons, Offering pointers and information sources, Asking if answered completely, Offering referrals, and Asking to come back for further assistance.

All these intercoder percentage agreements were either above or close to the generally acceptable threshold value of 80 percent. It should be noted that the use of the RUSA guidelines in the current study is differentiated from the approaches of the previous studies. While the earlier studies did not observe librarian Behaviours with respect to actual items in the guidelines or measured with a few items only, the present study used the entirety of the items in the revised guidelines as the coding scheme to analyse librarians' chat reference Behaviours.

RESULTS

User Satisfaction

User satisfaction has been one of the most frequently used outcome variables that measure reference service effectiveness. In the present study, user satisfaction was assessed through user responses to the following four questionnaire items: satisfaction with the answer, perceived staff quality, willingness to return to the service, and positivity of service experience.

First, satisfaction with the answer was assessed by asking the question, "Were you satisfied with the answer you received to your reference question?"

Among the 417 respondents who answered this question, 65.2 percent reported that they were satisfied with the answer received, and 21.1 percent of the respondents were not sure whether they were satisfied or not.

Finally, 12.6 percent of the respondents reported that they were not satisfied at all. Perceived staff qualitythe second indicator of user satisfaction, was assessed by the user response to the question, "The quality of the library staff service in answering this request was ________."

Among the 416 people who responded, 68.2 percent of the respondents answered that the librarians handling the reference questions were excellent. About 19.5 percent evaluated the librarians' performance as good, and 11.3 percent as poor. Willingness to use the service again, the third indicator of user satisfaction, was measured using the questionnaire item, "Will you use this service again?"

Among the 417 people who responded to this question, 77.2 percent answered that they were very likely to use the service again, 19.0 percent of the respondents answered maybe, and only 3.8 percent said they would never use the service again. Regarding positivity of service experience, among the total of 422 survey responses, 183 offered open-ended comments on the service.

Sixty-three percent of the respondents evaluated the experience positively, and 28.4 percent evaluated it negatively. About 10 percent of the respondents described it as either a mixed or neutral experience. Frequently mentioned expressions among the positive open-ended responses included "wonderful service," "quick," "helpful," "innovative," "cool," "good use of public money," and other comments indicating immediacy, convenience, and ease of use, including "human contact," "anytime 24/7," "likable," "interesting," and "time saver." Frequently mentioned expressions among those reporting a negative experience include "hard to use interface design," "didn't answer the question," "slow response time," "virtual librarians should access account," "virtual reference service coverage should be clearly indicated," technical problems, "waiting," "service delay," misunderstanding, hasty ending, listening skill lacking, and "poor service."

In addition to the patrons' negative and positive experiences expressed via the responses, mixed comments also were observed. An example of a mixed comment is "the idea of the virtual service is great but I didn't get much help." Comments that were categorised as neutral included suggestions for additional features, unawareness of the service's nationwide nature, additional information about the patrons' information needs or their background, or reports about problems experienced after the session ended. Finally, overall user satisfaction was computed by summing up the first three questionnaire items that measured different aspects of user satisfaction.

This computation was necessary because the user satisfaction items in the survey questionnaire were measured on a simple three- or four-point ordinal scale. These ordinal level measurements are not suitable for undertaking the inferential statistical tests that are crucial to answer the research questions of the present study. To resolve this problem, the three ordinal level variables were summed to create a composite variable, which increases the variability of the measure.

This data management procedure allowed the researchers to conduct necessary inferential statistical tests. Survey research literature indicates that a composite variable is generally more valid and reliable than a single question item because it increases variability of the measurement. The transformation of the existing three questionnaire items into a composite variable involved a series of conversions from a natural language answer choice to a numeric value. By carefully analysing the wording of the answer choices, a set of logical numeric values were assigned for answer choices of each of the three questionnaire items on the same five-point Likert scale.

First, for the satisfaction with the answer item, the numeric value assigned for "unsatisfied" was 1, 2 for "not sure," and 5 for "satisfied." For the perceived staff quality item, the value assigned for "poor" was 1, 3 for "average," 4 for "good," and 5 for "excellent."

For the willingness to return item, the numeric value assigned for "never" was 1, 3 for "maybe," and 5 for "very likely."

In order to determine the composite variable's reliability and validity, a classical theory alpha reliability and factor analysis were performed, respectively. First, the reliability test generated a score for the sample that had a Cronbach's alpha reliability coefficient of.845 for user satisfaction. This score is greater than the customary threshold value of .70, indicating that the composite variable is reliable. Second, the factor analysis result showed that the three questionnaire items were loaded on one-factor solution, with factor loading scores of .868, .916, and .876. All three items explained 78.64 percent of variance in the factor. This result indicates that the composite variable is measuring a single construct with a high score validity, suggesting that the composite variable is a valid measure of user satisfaction. The mean of the composite variable, user satisfaction, was 12.69, with a standard deviation of 3.44 in the range between a maximum value of 3 for "highly dissatisfied" and the minimum value of 15 for "highly satisfied."

The Presence of RUSA Behaviours in Chat Reference Interviews

Research question 1 of the present study asks to what extent reference staff members employ each of the ten RUSA Behaviours during their chat reference transactions.

The presence of the ten selected RUSA Behaviours ranged between 28.7 percent and 63.7 percent. The three most frequently observed Behaviours were comeback, interest, and welcoming. A complete comparison of this finding with those reported in the previous studies is not feasible because none has used the complete revised guidelines as a coding scheme. A couple of studies allow a partial comparison in the area of follow-up. Follow-up Behaviours were observed in approximately one-third of the total in-person reference transactions. Also in the physical library setting, Gatten and Radcliff reported that 29 percent of the proxy patrons were asked by the librarians if their questions were answered. In the present study, however, the three follow-up Behaviours appeared with greater frequency, ranging between 46.9 percent and 63.7 percent.

Their frequent appearance may reflect the use of the scripted words stored in the chat reference software Programme. It should be noted that not all RUSA Behaviours are expected to appear in a single reference session. For example, probing is not generally expected to occur in response to directional or circulation policy questions. Similarly, offering alternatives or making referrals are expected to occur mostly when reference staff is not able to provide a complete answer. Therefore, Behaviours with a low frequency in figure 7.6 do not necessarily indicate inadequate Behavioural performance on the part of reference staff. Rather, the information about the RUSA Behaviours should be more useful in its relationship with user satisfaction.

RUSA Behaviours and User Satisfaction

Research question 2 relates to whether chat reference users would be more satisfied with the service when librarians demonstrate a RUSA Behaviour than when they do not. Where the means of the user satisfaction are compared between when librarians showed the Behaviour and when librarians did not.

Across all but two Behaviours, user satisfaction was found to be higher when librarians performed the RUSA Behaviours than when they did not. A series of statistical analyses was conducted to determine the statistical significance of the difference in user satisfaction between when each RUSA Behaviour was present and absent. Both parametric statistics and non-parametric statistics were considered in our study to determine the most appropriate statistical technique for the tests. In general, parametric statistics are recommended when a test variable:

* Is measured on an interval or ratio level;
* Is measured on a sample size of sixty cases or more; or
* Is normally distributed.

When the data were examined with respect to these three criteria, the answer was not clear-cut. The test variable, user satisfaction, is an interval-level variable measured on the sample sise of 422, but is not normally distributed. Hence, the data were examined using both parametric and non-parametric statistical techniques, and the test results were compared. If the two statistical techniques generate identical results, parametric statistics are recommended to present the data, which is the case in the present study. When tested using SPSS 14.0, it was revealed that test results from both techniques were identical across all ten RUSA Behaviours. This result indicates that the Mann-Whitney U test results corroborated the results from the t-tests.

User satisfaction was statistically significantly different in six out of the ten RUSA Behaviours at the significance level of $\alpha < .05$.

Satisfaction was statistically significantly higher when reference staff showed the following six Behaviours than otherwise; that is to say, chat reference services were perceived to be more satisfying to the patrons when librarians:

* Used the patron's name during the reference interview;
* Communicated more receptively and listened more carefully;
* Searched with or for the patron;
* Provided pointers;
* Asked the patron whether the question was completely answered; and
* Asked the patron to come back if they needed further assistance.

This result is consistent with the findings of the previous studies conducted in face-to-face reference setting, which reported the positive influence of the original guidelines on reference success. Thus, the findings of the present study indicate that performance of RUSA Behaviours also are effective in the real-time chat reference setting.

CONCLUSION

By adopting the revised guidelines as a Behavioural performance assessment tool, the present study revealed that many Behaviours they prescribed are effective in enhancing user satisfaction with chat reference service. This study also attempted to explain why certain Behaviours in the revised guidelines were not related to satisfaction, as discussed in the findings. Combined, the results of the present study offer many implications for reference service practitioners, for the researchers investigating various phenomena in virtual reference services, and for the developers at RUSA working on future revisions of the revised guidelines.

First, the results of this study could be of significant assistance to staff training in the chat reference service practice. Consistent with the findings of the studies conducted in the physical reference setting, the results of this study also indicate that follow-up Behaviours should continue to be emphasised in staff training in the chat reference environment as a way to enhance both staff performance and user satisfaction. The present study also identifies places for future adjustments of the revised guidelinesAs pointed out earlier, some items in the Behavioural guidelines were not readily observed as an explicit Behaviour, while other items were not located in the proper category across the five areas. These items need further clarification if the revised guidelines are to be adopted by reference librarians as a practical Behavioural evaluation tool that can be used with few modifications.

In addition, inclusion of specific Behavioural examples for each item would be very useful, especially in the areas of interest and listening/enquiring. A future study could assess these areas utilising further development of the guidelines. Despite efforts to make this study as rigorous as possible, it is not without limitations and thus calls for further research. First, user satisfaction was examined as a way to investigate the effectiveness of chat reference services in the present study. Considering that user satisfaction is just one aspect of service effectiveness, researchers could employ other indicators of service effectiveness, such as answer accuracy or answer completeness. Another limitation is the fact that this study was conducted in a single public library system, although the observed librarians were from forty-nine library systems participating in a nationwide collaborative chat reference Programme.

It also should be noted that the current study observed only 30.4 percent of the total 1,387 analysable transactions. People who took the time to answer the online pop-up survey might not constitute an accurate representation of the entire user population of the chat reference service. Thus, our findings should be further confirmed by replicating this study in libraries of different types and sises and by enhancing the sampling technique. Finally, this study examined the usefulness of the revised guidelines by observing the use of chat reference only.

Nonetheless, the revised guidelines were developed to encompass various modes of virtual references, and thus similar studies should be conducted for other modes, such as e-mail and instant messenger, in order to develop further recommendations for the revised guidelines. The results of this study will encourage RUSA's further promotion and perhaps enhancement of the revised guidelines. This was the first empirical study that investigated the revised guidelines' value by assessing its actual items in the chat reference setting. By revealing the positive influences of the RUSA Behaviours on user satisfaction, the present study demonstrated that the revised guidelines are effective Behavioural standards for librarians' real-time chat reference interviews. Thus, by incorporating the recommendations of this study, RUSA could further promote the revised guidelines as a practical reference staff training and assessment tool.

Bibliography

Anderson, B.: *Journal of the American Society for Information Science,* Toronto: Thomson Nelson, 2008.

Anderson, B.: *The Basics of Librarianship,* Toronto: Thomson Nelson, 2008.

Banerjea, D.: *Library Organizations,* Kolkata: Allied Publishers, 2003.

Baruah, N.: *Public Libraries: An Introduction,* New Delhi: Long Life Publication, 2003.

Brenner, Diane, and Rowland, Marilyn: *Beyond Book Indexing,* NJ: Information Today, 2000.

Burge, E.: *Managing Multimedia Libraries,* London: Methuen Publication, 2000.

Byres,T. J.: *Information Processing and Management,* New York: Orgone Institute Press, 2004.

Clark: *How to Evaluate Integrated Library Automation Systems,* New York: Plenum Publication, 2003.

Collins, A.: *Managing library Cataloguing,* Chicago: The Hotel Monthly Press, 2006.

Gowri, R.A.: *Cataloging and Classification for Library Technicians,* New Delhi: Rawat Publications, 1999.

Gupta, R.: *Library Classification Facts and Analysis,* Rajesthan: Journal of the Association of Physicians of India, 2006.

Kapoor, S. L.: *Library Classification: Fundamentals & Procedure,* New Delhi: Sterling Publishers, 2003.

Lewis, W.A.: *Advanced Retrieval Methods for Online Catalogs,* US: University of Chicago Press, 2002.

Mayston, E. L.: *Cybrarians: The Information Professionals of the 21st-Century,* New Delhi: Oxford University Press, 2004.

McBride, K. B., & Dickstein, R.: *The Web Demands Critical Reading by Students: The Chronicle Of Higher Education,* London: Academic Press, 2004.

Nayar, Baldev Raj.: *The Film Preservation Guide: the Basics for Archives, Libraries, and Museums,* New York: Greenwood Press, 2000.

Parikh, K.S.: *Library Work,* New Delhi: Oxford Publication, 2007.

Punia, R.K.: *The Application of Expert Systems in Libraries and Information Centres,* New Delhi: Northern Book Centre, 2006.

Raj, M.: *Library Administration,* New York: Institute of Modern Studies. 2006.

Rao, M.: *Staff Training and Handling: A Guide for Libraries and Archives,* Cambridge: Cambridge University Press, 2006.

Sareen H.K.: *Makers of Modern Strategy for Library Administration,* New Delhi: Sterling Publishers Private Ltd, 2000.

Sarin, V. I. K.: *Leadership in the Library,* Mumbai: Manaktalas, 2003.

Index